TRYING CASES TO WIN

Direct Examination

HERBERT J. STERN

Wiley Law Publications
JOHN WILEY & SONS, INC.
New York · Chichester · Brisbane · Toronto · Singapore

In recognition of the importance of preserving what has been written, it is a policy of John Wiley & Sons, Inc., to have books of enduring value published in the United States printed on acid-free paper, and we exert our best efforts to that end.

This publication is designed to provide accurate and authoritative information in regard to the subject matter covered. It is sold with the understanding that the publisher is not engaged in rendering legal, accounting, or other professional services. If legal advice or other expert assistance is required, the services of a competent professional person should be sought. *From a Declaration of Principles jointly adopted by a Committee of the American Bar Association and a Committee of Publishers.*

This book is sold with the understanding that the publisher is not engaged in rendering legal, accounting, or other professional services.

Library of Congress Cataloging-in-Publication Data

ISBN 0-471-57128-8

Printed in the United States of America

10 9 8 7 6 5 4 3 2 1

Printed and bound by Courier Companies, Inc.

Author

Herbert J. Stern is nationally known as a skilled trial lawyer and recognized as one of the nation's finest teachers of trial techniques and strategies. A partner in the Roseland, New Jersey, law firm of Stern & Greenberg, Mr. Stern is a former United States district judge for the District of New Jersey.

After graduating from the University of Chicago Law School, Mr. Stern began his career by serving as an assistant district attorney for New York County in the Homicide Bureau. During that time he conducted the grand jury investigation into the death of Malcolm X.

Mr. Stern established his reputation as an advocate while serving with the Organized Crime and Racketeering Section of the United States Department of Justice after trying several significant cases against such notable adversaries as Edward Bennett Williams and Simon H. Rifkind. While serving as United States attorney for the District of New Jersey, Mr. Stern won a national reputation for unprecedented convictions of public officials, including the mayors of Jersey City, Newark, and Atlantic City.

Mr. Stern holds five honorary degrees and has taught at the University of Chicago, Harvard, Yale, and Columbia law schools and lectured nationwide for state bar and CLE programs. He has served as co-director of the University of Virginia Law School Trial Advocacy Institute since 1980.

In addition to *Trying Cases to Win*, Mr. Stern has authored *Judgment in Berlin*, an account his experience as a United States judge for Berlin presiding over the trial of two fugitives from East Berlin who were accused of hijacking a Polish plane to West Berlin. A biography of Mr Stern titled *Tiger in the Court* was published in 1973 by Playboy Press.

Dedication

This volume is dedicated to the memory of the great trial lawyers of yesterday: to Emory Buckner, to John W. Davis, to Isidor J. Kresel, to Martin W. Littleton, and to Max D. Steuer. It is my hope that these recollections of past masters will help to build a tradition of trial lawyering in both study and practice.

This volume is also dedicated to the men and women who have served, who now serve, and who will serve as assistant United States attorneys for the District of New Jersey. It is my hope that the efforts of those who began the great enterprise under Frederick B. Lacey in 1969, and who have maintained it in these past many years, will continue to build a tradition of excellence in the service of the public.

Table of Contents

Preface

As noted in the preface to Volume I, this multi-volume work called *Trying Cases to Win* began many, many years ago when as United States attorney for the District of New Jersey I first gave impromptu lectures on trial lawyering in the evenings to the lawyers in the office.

Trying Cases to Win is by no means finished. In truth, it may never be, for our knowledge of advocacy grows and changes over the years and the generations of trial lawyering. I have no doubt that once I have completed all the volumes of this work—for the third volume will deal with cross-examination, and the fourth volume with summation, expert witnesses, and related topics—additional critical insight from others as well as myself will compel revisits to topics already covered.

This, the second volume of *Trying Cases to Win*, deals exclusively with direct examination. Since the content and organization of this volume, like that of the first, embody my ideas about both advocacy and how to teach it, I have continued in the three crucial areas mentioned in the first volume: theory, tradition, and transcript.

Trying cases is not just a matter of doing what comes naturally; that is really just trial and error—which for the client may mean trial *by* error. Nor is trying cases as simple as performing a series of mechanical steps. And so I attempt to do more than merely discuss and demonstrate how to craft questions and to introduce evidence during direct examination. We will turn to theory, studying direct examination as an argument, a tool of advocacy, as well as studying the craft needed to apply that theory.

We will advance our study by returning to the the rich tradition left to us by past advocates, learning from both their successes and their failures. Thus I have again dealt with advocates such as and Emory Buckner and Max Steuer. And I have again turned to the greatest advocate of our time, Edward Bennett Williams.

Since transcript is one of the testing grounds of theory, our study of advocacy would not be complete unless we again closely examined actual trial transcript. Though the study of transcript is demanding, it is also rewarding.

As in the first volume, I have quoted numerous other writers on the subject of advocacy. Though I often disagree with their advice, I still recommend that you read their works.

As with the first volume, it is my hope that this second volume of *Trying Cases to Win* will offer inspiration, entertainment, and practical how-to-do-it advice to students of advocacy at all levels. The argument begun in the first volume continues here—and will continue in subsequent volumes—because I believe it is important to our profession that we engage in critical examination of what we do in our courtrooms. We owe this to more than just ourselves and our clients—we are also obligated to those who will come after us.

Acknowledgments

This second volume of *Trying Cases to Win* represents the work of many years and many people.

The first acknowledgments must be made to Rick Olson and Mark Helland, my original publishers. Their patience and faith in this concept are what made the launching of this work possible. Perhaps their greatest contribution was in giving me a splendid editor, David Johnson, whose tireless dedication helped to transform often episodic observations into a cohesive presentation. The fact that he consented to stay with the project has made this second volume possible.

Now that John Wiley & Sons has become the publisher of this work, Kathy Osborn has taken charge and given enormous insight, encouragement, and guidance.

Many other people have contributed observations, suggestions, and corrections to this work in its draft stages, particularly Judah Best, William Braniff, Douglas F. Broder, George G. Campion, Thomas F. Campion, Harry Downs, Steven M. Duncan, Otto F. Feil, III, Ralph Adam Fine, Barry I. Fredericks, Arthur J. Greenbaum, Jessica Justice, Vincent P. Maressa, Jr., Steve Nelson, June C. Platt, William S. Rosen, Stephen A. Saltzburg, David Simpson, Vicky H. Speck, James D. St. Clair, David S. Stone, Mike Tigar, and Robert L. Weinberg. They all have my deepest thanks. I am also indebted to Jean Kent McNutt for her typing.

Finally, I wish to acknowledge with thanks permission to quote from the following works:

S. Goldberg, *The First Trial* 225, 226 (1982). Reprinted with permission of the West Publishing Company.

I. Goldstein, *Trial Technique, 1st Edition*, 251, 253, 254, 260–262 (1935). Reprinted with permission. Published by Callaghan and Co., 155 Pfingsten Rd., Deerfield, Illinois 60015. Call toll-free 1-800-323-1336.

S. Hamlin, *What Makes Juries Listen* 202–204 (1985). Copyright © 1985 by Sonya Hamlin. Reprinted with permission of the author. Published by Prentice Hall Law & Business.

E. Imwinkelreid, *Evidentiary Foundations* 82, 85, 123. Copyright © 1980 the Michie Company. Reprinted with special permission from the Michie Company, Charlottesville, Virginia.

T. Mauet, *Fundamentals of Trial Techniques* 12, 14, 88, 94 (1980). Reproduced by permission of Little, Brown and Company.

Editor's Note

Although we have sometimes used the masculine pronoun for simplicity and clarity, we intend that pronoun to refer to both genders.

Chapter One

Introduction

From the very first, the writers and the practitioners recognized the importance—and the difficulty—of direct examination in the trial of cases. Or at least they said they did. In 1910, Francis L. Wellman wrote:

> The impression prevails quite generally in the profession that the direct examination of witnesses requires far less skill than the cross-examination.
>
> I am inclined not to agree with that view, and it is a matter of regret that so little attention is paid to the examination-in-chief, while many arts are exercised to produce effects in cross-examination.[1]

But even as the earliest writers and doers of trial work *mouthed* deference to direct examination and openings, they extolled cross-examination and summation as the highest and best and most difficult and important work in the courtroom.

Thus, after arguing for equality between direct and cross-examination in his chapter on direct, Wellman, in the same work, opens his chapter on cross-examination with these words:[2]

> *By far* the *most* fascinating part of the advocate's work is the cross-examination of witnesses. . . .
>
> Cross-examination is generally considered to be the *most difficult* branch of the multifarious duties of the advocate. Success in the art, as someone has said, comes most often to the happy possessor of a *genius* for it . . . this *all-important* prerequisite of a competent advocate.[3] (Emphasis added.)

Why did most early observers and the doers of trial work *mouth* deference to direct examination and openings while they extolled cross-examination and summations? Because they did not regard either opening or direct as an *argument*. In their view, the lawyer was not to advocate until cross and summation.

Opening statement (not opening argument) was viewed as anything but an opportunity to argue and persuade. Indeed, it was the antithesis of argument, as prohibitions against persuasive speech and objections to "argumentativeness" crept into the lore and then the practice of law. And so the advocate was taught not to advocate at the outset of the case. We have already examined the consequences of this view of opening on the organization and delivery of openings.

Direct examination was similarly viewed. The advocate was taught *not* to advocate while examining his own witnesses. Indeed, he was to avoid any role of prominence in the examination. The witness was to "tell his own story," and to tell it in chronological order—a narration by the witness, preferably with a minimum of intrusion by the examiner. Advice like "Let the witness sell himself" abounded.

Here is Irving Goldstein, the leading authority of his era, in 1935:

> To present the witness to the greatest advantage, it becomes of utmost importance that the trial attorney remain in the background as much as possible and permit the witnesses to "sell themselves" to the jury, rather than attempt to convince the jury of the attorney's great ability as a trial lawyer by putting himself in the foreground. . . .[4]

Now, of course, no one suggests that an attorney should *ever* try to inflate himself before the jury. But that is really not Goldstein's point here. What he is saying is that an attorney conducting a direct examination should behave differently from when he is advocating. Thus, quoting from a 19th century authority, he advises:

> "Now the best thing the advocate can do under these circumstances is to remember that the witness has something to tell, and that but for him, the

> advocate, would probably tell it very well 'in his own way.' *The fewer interruptions therefore the better*; and the fewer questions the less questions will be needed. *Watching should be the chief work*; especially to see that the story be not confused with extraneous and irrelevant matter. . . ."[5] (Emphasis added.)

For the advocate, the practical consequence of this view of direct examination was to minimize his participation and maximize advocacy by his witness. One last quote from Wellman, in 1910:[6]

> As soon as the witness gets thoroughly at ease and started, *the fewer interruptions the better. He should be permitted to tell his own story as far as possible*,[7] but the advocate should always register in his own mind the important facts and see that they are all clearly brought out. (Emphasis added.)

As we will shortly see, this remains the prevailing view today. Unfortunately, the consequences of this view of direct examination are lethal to advocacy by the advocate on direct examination, just as the consequences of the view that an opening statement is not an argument are lethal to advocacy by the advocate during opening.

One final question before we begin. Why was it alluring then—and still alluring now—to believe that an attorney should not only refrain from advocacy on direct examination, but should do all possible to minimize his role as he examines?

I firmly believe it is because we trial lawyers have never thought through and developed the techniques of examination that would enable us to overcome the prohibitions against "leading" on direct examination and thus would permit us to communicate with the jurors even as we examine our witnesses. If we lawyers do not see how we can speak to our jurors while we conduct direct examinations, we cannot even imagine how such an examination could be a platform for our advocacy.

And so, the tradition grew that the purpose of a direct examination was simply to present the witness—who would present the facts—and not simultaneously to persuade the tribunal what those witnesses and their testimony *proves*. But that, I believe, was and is wrong.

Well, then, what is the purpose of direct examination?

ENDNOTES

1. F. Wellman, Day in Court 142 (1910).
2. *Id.* at 179, 180.
3. But, of course, by 1910 Wellman had already produced the first edition of his classic, *The Art of Cross-Examination*. This work, first offered in 1903, was entirely devoted to cross-examination and is the most enduring work in all the literature on trial work.
4. I. Goldstein, Trial Techniques 251 (1935).
5. *Id.* at 261, quoting from Harris, Hints on Advocacy.
6. F. Wellman, Day in Court 153 (1910).
7. Note that the words "the fewer interruptions the better" are similar to those used by Harris.

Chapter Two

The Purpose of Direct Examination: To Argue Your Case

If the purpose of opening is to "argue your case to the jury," and the purpose of voir dire is to "argue your case to the jury," then what is the purpose of direct examination? Why, to "argue your case to the jury," of course—and to achieve the Wimbledon Effect as you *argue* your case right through your witness.[1]

By Wimbledon Effect I mean that the jurors' heads should be swinging back and forth between the attorney and his witness, as though the two figures were at each end of the well of the court—and the jurors were positioned between them much like spectators and, hopefully, fans in the viewer benches. As every experienced trial lawyer knows, if a lawyer on direct is standing at the end of a jury box (which is where he should position himself if the judge allows), with the jurors' heads swinging between him and his witness (their heads never stuck in one direction for longer than a minute or so), then this lawyer is making hay with that jury.

What techniques can we employ to achieve this Wimbledon Effect, and what do we do that gets in the way of it?

To sum it up: the fear of asking questions is the enemy of the Wimbledon Effect because it leads to the inability to question and thereby to the inability to argue on direct.

NARRATIVE ANSWERS

The fear of asking questions drives us to use narratives. When we use the narrative form of direct examination, we transfer the responsibility for arguing our case to our witnesses. This makes it easier for us to examine. Why? Because our role is diminished. And as our need to question diminishes, the witness is forced to provide more of the dialogue and to carry the presentation. He begins to argue the case for the lawyer. Our witness then becomes the rower of the boat and we become passengers or coxswains, at the most, prompters throwing out cues and setting the tempo by occasional questions.

In truth, witnesses are often trained to respond in long narrative answers because *we lawyers* fear that *we* will fail to have the magical words needed to develop their testimony. So we encourage these outpourings from our witness out of fear that the evidence might not otherwise be heard. But when we use these long witness narrations, the jurors' heads get stuck in one place. There is no swinging back and forth. There is an unremitting stream from one side of the well of the court. It is a one-sided argument presented by the witness, who assumes the face of interested party, not a neutral from whom information is plucked rather than offered.

WRITTEN DOWN QUESTIONS

The fear of asking questions also drives us to the written down question. This, too, is the enemy of the Wimbledon Effect and our ability to use the direct examination to argue. When lawyers question from a prepared script of questions, they produce what I call the Charlie Chaplin Effect.

In the earliest Charlie Chaplin silent films, you see a herky-jerky Chaplin who bounds across the screen in choppy steps. He is not even in view the entire time. The ancient camera, unable to move the film quickly enough, does not capture or play back all of Chaplin's steps as he moves across the scene. And this transforms his undoubtedly smooth gait, in real life, into fragmented and disconnected steps; the missing motion disconcerts the viewer.

The viewer of the courtroom scene is similarly disconcerted by questioning from a script. Why? Because no examiner can even hope to write down the quantity of questions necessary to script all of the verbal steps needed to make the back and forth of the testimony into a smooth, flowing presentation, rather than a herky-jerky, episodic implantation of points into the record. No written script, certainly not one of less than hundreds of questions, could possibly achieve that filling of gaps and interstices necessary to flowing, connected, and even comprehensible presentation.

By the same token, training witnesses to give long narrative answers, rather than short responsive ones to specific questions, leads to what I like to think of as The Buster Keaton Effect. In Keaton's films we see him take every step. But he takes them so quickly that we cannot comprehend them. He moves so rapidly that he is gone before we truly know that he has been there. When Keaton and the train he is chasing leave the station, they both leave together, and in so great a rush that we who are left behind gasp in our effort to comprehend what we have just witnessed.[2]

THE USE OF QUESTIONS

The skillful advocate controls the examination. He is not the presenter of his pad of questions. He does not hold a pen or a pencil, checking off as he "covers" his questions or makes his points. Nor is he the passenger sitting in the rear of a toboggan hurling along under the hand of his witness. The advocate uses questions to control the pace of the examination, varying the amount of information coming from the witness to avoid ennui. To be sure, sometimes the answers will be longer, sometimes shorter—but always at the election of the advocate.

The advocate uses questions to break important pieces of testimony into small digestible pieces, so that the tribunal does not choke on huge chunks of information. And the advocate uses questions to dwell on areas he wishes to dwell on, to obtain the repetition of significant portions of testimony, (frequency), often using illustrative aids (vividness and frequency), and, when the subject has been fully mined and refined, the advocate uses his questions to "transition" away—moving through time and over space with the greatest of ease, even though it may indeed be years and even whole continents that he is transitioning away.

Before this concept can be fully grasped, others must be disputed. We must learn that the purpose of a direct examination is *not* simply to put evidence into the record whether or not the significance of that evidence is understood at the time. The purpose of direct is *not* to prepare for the argument that will come later, at summation. We must also learn that it is essential for the tribunal to understand what we do *when we do it*, for there is little hope that we will be able to redeem memory and understanding days, much less weeks, later. The Summer of direct examination is far, far more than the storing up of nuts for use in the Winter of our summation. What is not understood will not be remembered. And what is not remembered later is useless later. Most important, the witnesses to the testimony sitting in the jury box are not reserving judgment until later. They are deciding as they listen, if they have not already made up their minds—in which event they are selecting out confirming information and doing their best not to answer, or not to understand or even not to hear, the remainder.

We must also realize that our listeners do not understand that our intent is to be anything less than perfectly clear in the moment. Our jurors do not believe that we do not intend to give them a present message but are merely storing up nuggets for later use. Indeed, throughout the direct, the jurors are asking themselves, "What is the lawyer trying to tell me through the witness?" And they are also asking themselves, "How does this testimony help the lawyer's case?"

MAXIM: No matter how lawyers regard direct examination, jurors see it as a message from the lawyer who called the witness.

In sum, the jurors regard the examination of witnesses as an argument by the lawyer—whether or not the lawyer does.

THE FOUR TASKS OF THE DIRECT EXAMINATION

We must never lose sight of the fact that a direct examination is an argument to the tribunal through the witness. Nevertheless, it may be helpful to view the direct examination as having four tasks.[3] Each task must be successfully discharged for the examination to be fully successful:

1. The testimony must be *clear*. If it is not clear, if the jury does not understand it, then it is worthless.
2. The testimony must be *memorable*. If it is clear, but its significance does not remain with the jury, it is worthless.
3. The testimony must be *credible*. Clarity and memorability without believability is worthless.
4. The testimony must be *invulnerable* to cross-examination. If the testimony is clear, memorable, and believable, but is then destroyed on cross-examination, it is less than worthless. It will destroy your case and, particularly, you as an advocate.

HOW TO ACHIEVE CLARITY AND MEMORABILITY

The only way to achieve *clarity* and *memorability* is to ask lots of questions.

Written scripts, as noted, destroy clarity and memorability by the Charlie Chaplin Effect, even as they are lethal to *credibility*: what truth talker or truth giver needs a script?

Narrative answers destroy *credibility* by turning the witness into an advocate, a kind of co-counsel intent on rowing your boat, rather than an unaligned repository from which you take information piece by piece, even as narratives suffocate *clarity* and *memorability* under a blanket of information. And both the written script and the narrative responses make the witness vulnerable to cross-examination.

There will be no script available when the adversary cross-examines. Then the witness will be on his own. And the long narratives of the direct will, at a minimum, have provided the cross-examiner an opportunity to show the witness' bias. Worse, the narratives may also provide fertile areas for cross-examination, since in the process of long narrative answers most witnesses will stumble here and there, either by occasionally saying too much, or too little, or both. In the last analysis, there is no such thing as a "good" witness or a "bad" witness. There are only effective or ineffective examiners, and preparers of witnesses.

Written Questions Must Be Avoided

Every trial lawyer has written questions for direct examination at some time in his life. We *all* at least begin that way. Unfortunately, some of us never stop.

Nothing is more amusing than the typical sight of a direct examiner with a pen or a pencil in his hand. He is not making notes as his witness speaks. What is he doing? *Checking Off!* As each question is asked, the examiner checks it off a written list. Covered![4]

Such examinations can never be an argument through the witness. They do not even try to be. The goal of the examiner is instead to simply get the information into the record. If the jury understands it in the moment, well and good. If not, it does not matter to the lawyer who intends to explain it later in summation.

"I know they don't understand it now," the lawyer nods as he returns to his table, "but I will tie it up later." This is a commonplace saying around the courthouse in every county in the United States. In my view, this saying is nothing but a confession of failure. The job of the advocate is to make himself understood in the moment. The chances of bringing anyone—much less the six or 12 in the jury box—back to a subject days or weeks later is at best a long, long shot.

Some writers suggest that it is sometimes useful not to be too clear or precise: leave something for the jurors to figure out themselves, say these thinkers, for what the jurors think they have discovered on their own will be more potent than what they believe they learned from you.

Well and good, *if* you can be sure that the jurors will indeed discover the point for themselves. But how can we be sure that they will? If there is anything for certain about trial work, it is that even when we are at our clearest and at our best as advocates, we cannot be certain that the jurors have even understood the point, much less appreciated its significance to the case.

If we doubt this, just recall again the times you have spoken to your jurors after a verdict in one of your cases. Have you ever failed to be amazed at how much they seem to have missed and how much they seem to have created out of whole cloth? As noted earlier, much of this apparent weirdness is no doubt explainable on the basis that no people, jurors included, give the real reasons for what they do, or how they vote, which in truth lie in the deep-seated emotional recesses of their thought processes. When this is coupled with the fact that jurors will exercise denial in an effort to erase material opposed to their positions, and will exercise rationalization to put material into the case to buttress their own positions (*see* Volume I, pages 130, 131) we can well understand the seemingly warped picture that the jurors play back for us after the trial.

We simply cannot afford the luxury of leaving anything unsaid or undone in the hope that the jurors will fill the gaps with their own discoveries. No one opts for opaqueness in the courtroom, not if he can have clarity. It is simply too chancy.

Why then are we advised that it is sometimes best to leave a space for the jurors to fill in? Because we want to believe that it is. And why do we want to believe it? Because all of us sometimes simply fail to be clear, and we ease the pain of our failures by narcotizing ourselves into the belief that our unclarities are better than the explicitness of others. But it is not so. Not on the odds. The winds that blow in the courts are far too uncertain for us to abandon the tiller to vagaries of unpredictable conclusions that we hope the jurors will come to by their own unguided devices.

But we have left our direct examiner with his list of questions. He is reading them out, checking them off as he goes. His head bobs up and down as his eyes go up from the writing on his pages to the witness and back down again as he intones the next question. Soon he has a veritable Niagara of yellow cascading down over his podium as he turns page after page of his yellow pad, while sounding as though mouthing a catechism.[5]

If he does not have a pencil to check off the covered questions, then he is likely doing a mental checking off. Each answer of the witness is followed by this lawyer's mumbled "okay" or "thank you" as each question on the list is successfully intoned and then answered. Recall the young lawyers questioning the jurors on voir dire during the Seattle case in Chapter Fifteen of Volume I. Remember how they kept saying "okay" after each answer and before putting the next question? It was more than a quirk of speech peculiar to just these two youngsters. It is the symbol of an entire approach to and execution of the presentation of testimony.

This mental checking off is just as much the enemy of a smooth, flowing *argument* on direct as is the physical checking off of written questions with a pen or pencil. What the lawyer is saying is, "Covered," "It's in the record," "Thank God the job is done."

How to Avoid Writing Questions for Direct Examination

To free ourselves from written questions, we must understand *why* we write them down. And to do that we have to stop kidding ourselves.

When asked, most of us will say that we write down questions in order to remember what we want to elicit from the witness. But that is patently untrue. If we wanted to remember what we want to bring *out* of the witness, we would not write down questions; *we would write down answers*.

Thus, if we seek to remember to establish that it was eight o'clock, we would not write down "What time was it?" We would write "It was eight o'clock," or better yet, simply "8:00 a.m." And that little note is all that we need to remember what to bring forth from the witness. The truth is that we do not write questions to remind us what the *witness* is to say; we write our questions out of fear that we will not have the words of art needed to *elicit* the information from the witness.

LESSON: The entire secret of asking questions on direct is: never focus on the words you will use in the question. Never try to form the words on paper or in your mind. Hear instead the words of the witness, as you want him to say them. If you do that, the words of the question will automatically come to you. If instead you focus on the words you will use, you will freeze your ability to speak and drive yourself to either the use of a script so you can speak or a witness narration so you will not have to.

As frightening as this may sound to the uninitiated, a moment of practice will empirically prove its validity. As you read the answers, see if it is true that the question automatically comes to you:

I arose at 8 a.m. yesterday morning.

Hearing that answer, your question automatically became, "What time did you get up yesterday?"

I felt sick when I got out of bed.

Your responsive question to that next answer in your head was undoubtedly "How did you feel when you got out of bed?" And so it goes. Each prospective answer begets its own question, not vice versa![6]

What Notes Should You Have for Direct Examination?

It should be plain that your notes should focus on the answers, on what you want to hear from the witness, not on what you will say to elicit the answer. What then should your notes look like?

Your notes should be fragmentary passages—never full sentences. The function of the particular note is to remind you of the next portion of the witness' story, not the exact words he will use to translate the portion of the story into the next piece of testimony. How do you achieve this?

Your notes should be the product of the same process you used in formulating your notes for opening. That is, you can write the full story of the witness out—if you have the time and the energy—and write it out in the first person, as though it were the witness mouthing the words. When you have it written out, you have his testimony as you would most like to hear it. Your job is to get the witness to say it in a nonherky-jerky presentation on the one hand, and without having the witness rattle it off in a long narration. But in your effort to achieve the result, *you must not show the narrative statement to the witness.*

The witness must not see the statement you have crafted in his absence because that might well turn your work product into something discoverable as either the witness' adoptive statement or something used by the witness in preparing his testimony. Even were these dangers absent, I would advise against showing the writing to the witness because, for reasons which follow, I believe that such exposure to scripts in any form is counterproductive.

Indeed, I suggest that the initial writing not survive, that its life end immediately as you reduce the fully written out narration into a fragmentary outline, whose function is to remind you of the next point to make through the witness by your next series of questions. When I take the time to block out a direct examination fully, this is what I do, just as I do with an opening (*see* Volume I, pages 229, 230). When I do not have the time, then, as with an opening statement, I skip the first step and do not write it all out. Instead, I go immediately to step two, and start out with the fragmentary outline. The more experienced you become in the trial of cases, the less you feel the need to write out the full opening or the full story on direct—and, to be sure, the less you actually *need* to do it to be able to do a passable job. And yet, when I do find the time to do both steps rather than telescoping them, the opening and directs that I do are better, even though the end product fragmentary notes may look pretty much the same whether or not there has been a fuller writing first.

HOW TO ACHIEVE SMOOTH, CONNECTED DIRECT TESTIMONY

As you stand at your podium with your fragmentary notes—and for this purpose I recommend three-holed notebooks with pages you can turn—[7] your task is to get the witness to tell the story as it looked when it was all written out, and to tell it in the form of a Q & A that replicates the smoothness of the original tale, without recourse to the use of long narrative from the witness chair.

Not all writers agree that this is the proper goal for the presentation of testimony. Indeed, most do not. The majority of writers today, like writers in the first half of this century, advise to use witness narrations. In their view, the jury wants to hear the witness, not the examiner—and they fear that the constant Q & A needlessly breaks up the testimony and is distracting to the tribunal.

We have seen quotations to this effect from both the vintage works and the modern authorities. But, for reasons already given, and more to come, I do not agree. Testimony, to be *clear, memorable*, and *credible*, *must* be delivered in digestible bites without advocacy from the witness.

Those who prefer to believe that it is best to let the witness tell his own story, I think, prefer to believe this simply because it *seems* to be far easier to present witnesses in that way than by using the methods I am about to demonstrate.

Looping

To transform the otherwise episodic, choppy, and rough Q & A into the smooth, connected story of the initial writing, the examiner strives to hear the next answer that will connect into the preceding one, tongue and groove. This technique is called "looping" by some experienced examiners. It is achieved by fitting each answer into the last, sometimes with the aid of questions that form the link by repetition of the earlier answer or through the use of *transitions*. Let us return to our modest example.

> Q: What time did you get up yesterday?
>
> A: It was about 8 a.m.
>
> Q: How did you feel at 8 a.m.?
>
> A: Well, when I got up I felt sick.
>
> Q: Did you seek any medical attention, as soon as you felt sick?
>
> A: No, not immediately.
>
> Q: Why didn't you call for help as soon as you felt ill?

And so it goes, each question tying into the last answer so that the tongue and groove or "looping" effect is achieved. And for those purists who believe that any of the questions were leading, we will have an answer and a remedy in just a moment.

Transition Questions

Transition questions are not questions. Because they are not questions, they are not and cannot be leading. These are instead statements by examining lawyers designed to avoid jarring the jury and to achieve "tongue and groove" and "looping" when the subject is to be changed. For example:

> Q: Mr. Jones, I would now like to leave the subject of how you felt yesterday morning and direct your attention to the afternoon, okay?
>
> A: Yes.
>
> Q: Where were you yesterday afternoon at approximately 2 p.m.?
>
> A: I was in the hospital.

Experienced lawyers use transition questions to help transform the Q & A from episodic fragments and into a connected tale given without the Charlie Chaplin Effect or recourse to the Buster Keaton Effect. As noted above, because transition questions are not questions, they cannot be leading. They can and should be used generously, and without fear. They can and do move the tribunal backward and forward through time, even decades ("I would like to direct your attention 10 years later, if I can, Mr. Jones."), or over whole continents of geography ("I would like to leave the subject of your experience in Nebraska, and to direct your attention to La Spazia, Italy, for a moment."). Transitions are the hallmark of experienced lawyers. We rarely hear the novice use them. But they are essential tools in smoothing out and bridging testimony, thus enabling the jury to follow what is being presented without falling into the void between otherwise unconnected thoughts and points.

Leading Without Leading

Even with proper notes, and even with spontaneous formulating of answers and not questions, and even with all of this used in combination with looping and transition questions, the examiner will not be able to argue his case through the witness to the jury and achieve the Wimbledon Effect—unless the examiner also knows how to control the witness, the flow and the pace of the examination, by leading without leading.

We must recognize at the outset that although both the definition of leading and the prohibition against it are universal, both are illusory.

The universal definition of leading is, of course: "a leading question is one that suggests the answer." This seemingly objective definition is in reality entirely subjective. What one person finds suggestive, another may not. Let us examine some of the common jargon in our courts.

Q: What happened next?

Is that question leading? What does it suggest? Is it suggestive because it implies that something happened next? So what if it does? The question does not suggest *what* happened next.

Q: What, if anything, happened next?

Is this question less leading because it is less suggestive that something happened next? Is it any less or any more revealing about what happened?

Thus, because we want to sound natural and normal, we should say, "What happened next?" rather than, "What, if anything, happened next?"

The simple fact is that the seemingly *objective* definition of leading is in truth *subjective*. What may be suggestive to one judge may not be to another. It is a matter of taste and judgment. To be sure, when we are at the margins, most would agree that the questioning was leading, or that it was not leading. But when we draw closer to the center, most of us would disagree. Watch.

1. Weren't you in Chicago on May 11th?

2. Were you in Chicago on May 11th?
3. Do you recall whether or not you were in Chicago on May 11th?

Most of us would agree that the first question was leading. Many would say the second question is not leading, particularly if it is heard after the first and will therefore subjectively sound less marginal. And almost none would say that third question is leading. Why? Because it appears to offer a choice.

LESSON: In the subjective world of what is or is not leading, you can make any question sound not leading by appearing to give a choice, and you can make any question actually not leading by, in fact, giving a choice.

The mere addition of the words "do you recall whether or not" beguiles the listener into believing that a choice is offered, and thus makes the question appear to be nonleading, or at the least less so. The operational words here, of course, are "whether or not," which seem to remove the curse from an otherwise direction-pointing and hence leading question. This technique only appears to offer a choice.

The offering of real choice, however, provides a truly nonleading setting for the control of witnesses and the testimony without directing any particular answer: "Was it a weekday or a weekend?" "Was it before noon or after noon?" Let us test this lesson. A witness has just testified that the defendant punched her:

1. Did he hit you with his right hand? [Sounds leading.]
2. Do you recall whether or not he hit you with his right hand? [Sounds not leading.]
3. Did he hit you with his right hand or his left hand? [In actuality, not leading.]

This technique of guiding the witness through his testimony, or at least portions of it, by controlling the examination through "leading without leading" enables the examiner to take control of the examination away from the witness. On the other hand, the use of open-ended questions turns the examination over to the witness, who will then make the decision as to how much information to give in response.

Open Questions and Closed Questions

Thus, although we should ask,"What happened next?", not, "What, if anything, happened next?"[8] if we desire to open the questioning and therefore the subject and the length of the witness's response, we must be aware that these are "open questions" as opposed to "closed questions" that control and guide the witness's answers.

Questions that turn the examination over to the witness are called "open questions" because the witness can pour out as much or as little as he wishes. "What happened next?" is such an open question. It invites a narration.

On the other hand, questions that call for very specific answers—such as, "What color was the light?"—are called "closed questions" because they narrow and limit the ability of the witness to answer. When we lead without leading by giving choices, we almost invariably use closed alternatives and hold the witness on a tight leash. "Was the light red or yellow or green?" The question is not leading, because it suggests no particular answer, and yet it controls the witness by forcing him to speak about the subject we want, while confining the answer to a narrow area of that subject.

It must be emphasized that I am *not* suggesting that all or even 90 percent of your questions should closely confine the witness, forcing him to answer exclusively in narrow responses. That would indeed be foolish advice. The wise lawyer varies the pace of the interrogation by controlling the flow of and varying the amount of information that the witness gives. But no examiner can achieve pace unless he knows how to regulate the amount of information flowing from the witness. The hand of the examiner must rest with vigilance upon the spigot. And the control spigots to testimony are the techniques of leading without leading to monitor the subject matter, closed and open questions to regulate the amount of information released on the subject, and transition questions to glide smoothly from one subject into another when the examiner determines that the time has arrived.

HOW TO ACHIEVE AS MUCH REPETITION AS YOU WISH

In Chapter Five of Volume I, I discussed the law of frequency. It is essential that your jury, or for that matter your judge, hear your important material more than once. Every seasoned trial lawyer knows not only that once is not enough but that even twice may be insufficient.

To make testimony memorable, indeed to be confident that it is even clear, the examiner must achieve a certain amount of repetition. Events happen rapidly in a courtroom. A line of testimony can be missed, drowned by a cough or suffocated in a mumble. An important point can be totally lost in a momentary distraction. The able attorney must learn how to have testimony repeated.

And yet the tradition and the practice in court conspire together against clear communication on direct examination, through their condemnations of leading, and their prohibitions against repetition. The objection "asked and answered" rings in all the courts of the land. I sometimes translate that objection, "He hurt me once, your Honor; please don't let him do it again."

No one ever objects to the repetition of helpful testimony, and all of us object to the repetition of hurtful testimony. To overcome the objection to repetition, the examiner must learn how to repetitively elicit favorable testimony from a witness, *at will*, by mastering at least some and probably all of the following techniques.

Repeating the Last Answer in the Form of the Next Question

At the simplest level, the interrogator achieves repetition by becoming an echo of the witness.

Q: What happened next?

A: I saw the defendant shoot the deceased.

Q: What happened after you saw the defendant shoot the deceased?

A: I saw him run away.

Q: What happened after you saw the defendant run away?

And so it goes. Our examiner becomes a Greek chorus, echoing the words of the witness' last answer in the form of the examiner's next question. In this way repetition is easily achieved. While this is not a bad technique, it is not the highest form of the art. But it is certainly far, far superior to pretending deafness in order to achieve repetition, and some lawyers do indeed pretend not to have heard in order to achieve repetition. Watch.

Q: What happened next?

A: I saw the defendant shoot the deceased.

Q: What was that? I didn't quite catch that.

As ludicrous as it sounds, this technique is still common today, even as it was a hundred years ago. Indeed, if queried, many attorneys would opine that it is a good technique. But no advocate who cares about his *ethos* would dream of doing such a thing. It is a ploy. Worse, it is an obvious ploy. And if a juror should smile upon hearing it, that smile would be a disaster for the advocate. For that smile would signal that the juror understood that the advocate before him has just told a lie. And at some level, that juror will also understand that if the lawyer would tell a lie in court just to get a good answer repeated, what lie is beyond such a lawyer if it would win the case? Feigning deafness, then, to get a good answer repeated is the kind of technique we should put aside as both unethical and imprudent.

Why is the mere repetition of the last answer in the next question not the highest form of the art? What are the drawbacks of the technique of repeating the last answer in the form of the next question? There are three.

First, this technique achieves only one repetition of the critical testimony. In the work of the courtroom, where even "twice is not enough," twice is all you get if you confine yourself to simply repeating the last answer in the form of your next question.

Second, if you keep using this chorusing as your only or even your main technique, sooner or later your adversary will discern what you are doing and will object to your repetition of the testimony. What will he say? "I object, your Honor. Mr. Jones is continually repeating the last answer in the form of the next question." He may, to be sure, lose the objection. But, if you keep doing it and if he keeps objecting, sooner or later the judge will also see what you are about and will stop you.

Third, and perhaps most important, this technique relies on open questions, which turn the control of the examination over to the witness ("What happened after . . . ?"). In that moment, the examiner's hand is off the spigot and the witness is free to spout off on his own. In short, this technique uses questions that will call for long narrative portions of testimony and opens the examiner and the examination to the unrestrained judgment of the witness.

That is not to say that this chorusing is a bad technique, or that it should never be used; only that it must be used sparingly. For if it is the main tool of repetition, it runs the risk of being stopped, and, when constantly used, it constantly passes the baton to the witness, who may run away with it.

Achieving Repetition by Using Closed Questions That Call for Narrow Detail

Seasoned trial lawyers achieve repetition by asking for the details of an event through narrowly constructed questions. These questions *appear* to call for corroborative detail, which the examiner *seems* to be interested in. What he really wants, however, is to keep the entire scene before the tribunal.

> Q: What happened next?
>
> A: I saw the defendant shoot the deceased.

Q: Could you see the gun in the defendant's hand when he fired?

A: Yes.

Q: Which hand did the defendant use to fire the gun?

A: His right hand.

Q: Are you able to demonstrate to the jury how the defendant held the gun in his right hand, and how far his hand was from his body, at the time he shot the deceased?

A: I believe that I can.

Q: With your Honor's permission, may the witness rise and show the jury—

And so it goes. One shot has become many. The entire scene—the defendant shooting the deceased—has remained before the jury for an extensive period of time. And even when the discharging of the pistol was not directly alluded to by either the examiner or the witness, the jurors continue to see the entire scene in their minds, including the shooting itself. This use of many closed questions, apparently aimed at the corroborative detail of the event, even when not directly focused, keeps the entire event before the jury. The jury, and for that matter the judge, will continue to see the shooting even when it is not directly mentioned.

But our examiner is not nearly finished, unless it pleases him to be. Indeed, if it please him, he can go on and on and on. How far apart were the two men at the time of the shooting? Their positions are explored and developed. The victim falls to the floor. The examiner can become interested in the position of the body. As the defendant makes his hasty exit, he drops the gun to the floor. The examiner becomes interested in the position of the gun, its distance from the body, how long it took before the defendant fled the scene, and so forth. Even the positioning of the furniture in the room can receive our attention.

Again, I am *not* suggesting that short answers are the *only* mode, or that there are no limits to any of these techniques. You *must* vary the pace. Longer answers must be evoked to flavor the examination. But it is done at the election of the examiner, not at the whim of the witness, and it is done because the lawyer *decides* to do it out of a desire to change pace, and not out of the felt necessity to transfer control to the witness in order to be able to produce the information.

And there are, of course, limits to the technique of getting repetition by closed questions that call for details. Too much can ruin any good thing. Nonetheless, this technique of achieving repetition is particularly effective in a courtroom setting where lawyers and judges by tradition expect examiners to call for corroborative details of an event. And this technique is particularly effective as a tool when it follows an occasional long narrative answer—for it serves to break the testimony into digestible pieces even as it revisits it:

> Q: Where did you go on May 11th?
>
> A: Well, first I visited my mother in Detroit and then I went on to see my aunt in Chicago.
>
> Q: I would like to direct your attention, first, to your visit with your aunt in Chicago. [Transition.]
>
> A: Yes.
>
> Q: Did you go alone or were you accompanied on your trip to Chicago? [Leading without leading—because it gives a choice.]

The trip can be explored, if meaningful to the case. The visit can be extensively inquired into, if it pleases the advocate. And when it is time to leave for Detroit, the examiner tells us that it is now time to go.

> Q: I would now like to direct your attention to the events of the latter part of the day, to your trip to see your aunt that you mentioned earlier. . . .

In this way, transitions become more than orientation points designed to smooth the flow of the questioning; they become tools of repetition as well.

Achieving Repetition by Means of Illustrative Aids, Demonstrations, and Physical Evidence

At the end of an earlier hypothetical Q & A, after the examiner had used detailed questions to have the jury re-see the defendant shooting the deceased, the examiner asked the witness to physically demonstrate the way he observed the defendant holding the gun at the time of the shooting. This is yet another technique to cause repetition and thereby achieve frequency.

After you have had all of the questioning and the answering you want, you employ the tools of the easel, the blackboard, and even rough physical demonstrations to play the scene—or some of it—through again. And now you are engaging the tribunal's eyes and ears, thus invoking the law of *vividness* as well as *frequency*. (*See* Volume I, pages 120–123.)

It is essential that the sketching and the acting out be done *after* the testimony has been fully explored, because if the illustrative aids are used too early, they will appear to eliminate the need for the additional detailed testimony.

LESSON: As a general rule, the advocate takes the oral details first, and goes on to invoke the illustrative aids later.

By definition, *illustrative aids* are not evidence. They have no *independent* evidentiary worth. Their only function is to make clear, to illuminate or to illustrate the testimony or other matters that *are* in evidence. Illustrative aids are merely marked for identification. They are not marked into evidence. In most jurisdictions, they will not go to the jury at the end of the case. If, for some reason, the particular illustrative aid is marked into evidence, it will cease to be called an illustrative aid marked for identification, called Exhibit ___ *for identification,* and will thereafter be referred to as Exhibit ___ *in evidence*.

Because illustrative aids are not evidence or in evidence, they do not have to be foundated. And because they do not have to be foundated, they can be used with greater ease, flexibility, and maneuverability than the exhibits you intend to place into evidence. They need not be to scale, or particularly accurate. They may be rough and ready drawings hastily constructed before the jury itself.

By way of illustration: your witness has just described the scene of an accident. You have elicited all of the detail that you wished during oral testimony, using some or all of the techniques that we have identified. You then ask the judge for permission for the witness to go to the blackboard or to the easel. You will likely use a blackboard if—on the odds—you do not wish the drawing to survive. You will instead use a piece of easel paper if you believe you might need a more permanent medium, one that you will use again—either with another witness or even during summation.

Why might you wish a less ephemeral and vulnerable record than a blackboard? Because an illustrative aid can be used for more than one witness. Indeed, one witness can add to a sketch drawn by another, building the illustrative aid—and, as we shall see, a possible future evidentiary exhibit—witness by witness. When the exhibit has been the work of more than one witness, it is customary for subsequent additions to bear the initials of the witnesses who added to the exhibit at the places of their contributions. And so it goes. A diagram or sketch that is at first used merely for vividness and for frequency can begin to take on a life of its own. Ultimately, you may even wish to offer it into evidence. And if it has been properly foundated, you will be able to. Even if you do not ultimately place it into evidence, you may still use it at the end of the case during summation. But there it stops. For if it has not been formally received into evidence, it will not usually be sent into the jury room at the end of the case. How does one use an illustrative aid, and how are exhibits marked for identification?

> Q: If I recall correctly, Mr. Jones, you have told us that the defendant shot the deceased in your apartment in your presence?

A: Yes.

Q: Would you be able to diagram for us the positions of the defendant and the deceased in the room when the defendant fired his gun?

A: Yes.

Q: With your Honor's permission, may the witness descend from the stand and approach the easel?

Assuming the judge gives permission, and judges usually do—particularly when asked in the above jargon—the witness leaves his seat to stand by the easel, and off you go. As the diagramming goes on, names can be placed upon the paper to correspond with the X's and Y's used to designate the positions of the parties—if the witness knows the names. At the end of the exercise, you might even be able to move the exhibit into evidence. But the introducing of evidence and the laying of foundations is for later. Enough for now to study how to use *vividness* and *frequency* in the context of illustrative aids to testimony.

At the end of the sketching, you will ask for the exhibit to be marked for identification. You should do this because anything that is physically handled by or shown to the witness should be given an identification number for purposes of the record. Without that marking, later references to the exhibit will be obscure in the record.

In most jurisdictions, no permission need be sought to mark things for identification. The process goes like this:

Ms. Jones: I would now like to mark this sketch as plaintiff's exhibit 12 for identification.

A plaintiff's sticker is affixed, and thereafter the sketch will be known as "plaintiff's 12 for identification" unless and until it becomes plaintiff's 12 in evidence; or until, at the end of the case, it is given back to the attorney to add to his memorabilia.

"For the Record"

Another method of achieving repetition is to summarize or recapitulate testimony by providing descriptions "for the record."

A witness testifies that he saw the defendant shoot the deceased. "How far was the defendant from the deceased when he shot him?" you inquire. "Oh, from about that table to the jury box," the witness responds. All in the courtroom know the distance the witness is indicating, for they can see. But the record is silent. And no one reviewing it—certainly not an appellate court—can have any idea of the distance that the witness perfectly described to those in attendance at the trial.

From this fact has come the traditional advice to younger lawyers to describe in inches, feet, pounds, or whatever objective measurement the witness has thus indicated in visual terms to the jury, *so that the record will be clear*.

That advice is laughable. In the overwhelming majority of instances, no reviewing court cares about these trifling factual matters by the time the case reaches it. Few if any appellate judges read the record, and fewer still with that sort of attention to detail. And there is usually no reason that they should. In the main, they sit to review legal issues that have nothing to do with the close measurements that can be life and death in the trial court.

It is therefore foolish for lawyers to routinely invoke measurements and thereby invite disputes and interruptions from adversaries in the midst of their directs by attempting to "clarify" the record for the benefit of an appellate court that likely could not care less.

But, *occasionally*, such measurements provide an opportunity for an attorney to summarize testimony and create a lethal repetition of testimony. Watch:

> Q: Now, Mr. Jones, if I heard you correctly, I think you indicated that this defendant was the distance from the jury box to the table from the deceased when he fired his gun?

> A: Yes.
>
> Q: Counsel, can we agree that Mr. Jones here is indicating that it is his testimony that there was a distance of 20 feet between the two men at the time he saw the shooting?

In this way statements "for the record" can be used to make things clearer for the jury, which probably does care, rather than for the appellate court, which probably does not.

And, provided that the witness has already testified to seeing the defendant shoot the deceased, the attorney can even say:

> Q: Counsel, can we agree that Mr. Jones here is indicating that it is his testimony that the defendant was 20 feet away from the deceased when the defendant shot the deceased?

HOW TO MAKE A WITNESS CREDIBLE

It is not enough for the jurors to understand and to remember the testimony of your witnesses. The jurors must also believe them—else what is the point of the exercise?

Some of the techniques that diminish or bolster clarity and memorability also diminish or bolster credibility. Scripted and/or narrative answers, for example, tend not to be the most credible, even as they are not clear or memorable. But some techniques focus primarily on the credibility of the witness, and the bolstering of it.

The Proper Introduction of Witnesses

Witnesses must be properly introduced to the jury—or to the judge if it is a trial to the court. Many of us fail to do this. Why? Because as lawyers we become enmeshed in the details of our case and its component pieces of exhibits and testimony and we overlook the things that are most important to the tribunal: *who* is this witness? Is she a steady, reliable person—or is she a flake? Does the witness have a motive to lie, or is he unaligned? These matters are more likely to drive the jury in its quest for the truth than whether or not the witness wears glasses and whether the street light was near or far at the time the witness claims to have made the observations.

Do Not Ask Witnesses Their Pedigree "for the Record"

When you call your witness, do so with a sense of solemnity and importance. None of this head down, mumbling "The plaintiff calls," or "The prosecution calls." It should be, "The people of the state of _____ call," or "Mary Brown calls _____." The summoning of your witness is an event of significance. Do not depreciate it. Do not make the moment vanish into nothing. And do not vanish yourself; that is, try not to leave the room to get the witness.

There is something more than a little odd about a lawyer abandoning a full courtroom to fetch the next witness. Use a junior if you have one, or the court bailiff if there is one, or even ask the departing witness to ask the one outside to step in, if the witnesses have been excluded from court. If necessary, ask for a very brief recess. But, if you can avoid it, do not simply turn your back on all within the room and exit, to reappear with the next witness in tow.

After the witness has been called to the stand with a degree of decorum, and indeed formality, you must introduce your witness properly. Think in terms of "authenticating" the witness—even as you would authenticate an exhibit.

The name of the witness is not insignificant. Do not make it so by telling the court that you are asking for the name and pedigree only "for the record," e.g.:

Q: Will you state your name for the record?

When lawyers say that they speak "for the record," they signal that they do not speak of important matters to the present tribunal. It is only a matter of form. When lawyers tell a judge that they are making such and such an argument "for the record," they signal that they expect *that* judge to find against them, and are speaking to the court that sits in review.[9] In sum, the phrase "for the record" is counterproductive—except, as we have seen, to create repetition through speech by counsel.

The jury wants to know if your witness works and, if so, what he does. Ask him. The jury wants to get the flavor of *who* the witness is. Attempt to elicit it. The jury wants to know if your witness is partial or neutral. Tell the jurors that the witness is unaligned, if he is, and by all means tell them if the witness is friendly to your side if that is so. You certainly do not want to sit on that information on direct if you are going to hear it from your adversary on cross.

Let us take a famous short problem used by one of the advocacy course books. It goes something like this:

> A woman who has been working late steps off her bus after 9 p.m. It is dark. We are entitled to assume that she is tired. As she walks from her bus, a man grabs at her handbag. She resists. He hits her. She releases the bag and he flees. The encounter has been brief. Her view of him has been fleeting.
>
> The next day, the defendant mugs a police officer and is arrested. The victim of the previous evening is brought to the police station. She is shown only one person—the defendant—and on the basis of the one-person lineup identifies him as her assailant.

The authors of the problem instruct the advocate in training to conduct a direct examination of her. Although this problem is often assigned to younger advocates in training, it is a far more difficult direct examination than appears at the first. The brief view of her assailant at night in a highly charged moment, coupled with her identification of the suspect in a highly suggestive setting, makes this a difficult case and therefore a difficult examination for the direct examiner. And if the advocate concentrates on the lighting, the phase of the moon, the quality of her vision, and the like, he will be making an error. The jury knows that this woman is about to identify the defendant as her assailant. What they want to know is whether they should *believe* her. And for that they want to know *who* she is.

> Q: Miss Fitzgerald, will you tell the judge and the jury your full name?
>
> A: My name is Gail Fitzgerald.
>
> Q: Are you employed?
>
> A: Yes.
>
> Q: By whom are you employed?
>
> A: I work for Dr. George Brown, a dentist.
>
> Q: How long have you worked for Dr. Brown?
>
> A: Twelve years.
>
> Q: Has that been 12 consecutive years, or was it interrupted? [The examiner is in control—leading without leading.]
>
> A: No, it was 12 straight years.
>
> Q: Are you the only employee of Dr. Brown?
>
> A: No, we have three other assistants and staff.
>
> Q: Well, as to the four of you, does one of them supervise you, or do you supervise the other three? [Again leading by alternatives.]
>
> A: I am the supervisor in Dr. Brown's office.

The last answer could have been achieved by merely asking, "Who is the supervisor among the four of you?", but we are practicing our skills and making muscles, although in the courtroom we would surely not exercise the same degree of control as we do over the witness in our hypothetical.

> Q: Now, Miss Fitzgerald, in addition to being a full time employee and a supervisor of three others in Dr. Brown's office [looping and transitioning], do you attend any educational courses?
>
> A: Yes. I am taking a master's degree at night.

And so it goes. The witness is being introduced to the jury as a steady, sound, reliable person—one who would not likely point the finger at another lightly, and not the sort to easily take suggestions from a policeman in the station house or, for that matter, from the lawyer in his office. And if this kind of examination keeps on going, then the defendant will be half way to prison even before the prosecutor reaches the issues of the initial assault and the later identification.

But the examination will likely not continue in that vein, for the defense attorney will soon be on his feet, objecting. And what will his objection be? *Irrelevant.* He will object to continuing this part of the examination on the grounds that the witness's background, in such detail, is irrelevant to the charges before the court.

The amusing aspect of this is that lawyers never object to true irrelevancies. They only object when they are getting hurt. And in our little hypothetical, the defense attorney had better object, because if the witness continues to give these "irrelevancies" the defendant will more likely be convicted than if he can stop her.

Does that mean that the judge will overrule the objection? Absolutely *not*! While all judges will let some pedigree in, all judges will pull the curtain at some point. At what point will that be? That depends entirely on the judge. But just about all judges will become uneasy when they sense that this buttressing of the witness's credibility has reached the point where it has become outcome determinative. When that point is revealed, or, with some judges, well before that, the judge will sustain the objection on the ground that the testimony is "irrelevant."

And what will the impact of that adverse ruling to you be upon your jurors? It is not likely to be adverse. On the whole, lawyers worry too much about losing objections. While no one wants to be seen as an incompetent, or an obstructionist or just plain wrong in the eyes of his jury, everyone who tries a lot of cases is going to lose a lot of objections. And while you should neither make nor stimulate objections frivolously, you simply have to face the fact that you will lose—and win—many thousands of such petty skirmishes in your career as a trial lawyer.

Even when you object and win you may be a loser in the eyes of a jury, which may see you as an impediment to vital information. In this instance, for example, where the judge has sustained the objection to your questions on the pedigree of your witness as irrelevant, you may be the winner, as the jury may feel that the inquiry is not irrelevant as far as they are concerned. No matter what anyone says—including the judge—those jurors know what they need to know.

Let us take the typical civil case. Our Gail Fitzgerald has not been mugged. She has instead witnessed an automobile accident. It is still late at night. She is still tired. Now the plaintiff's lawyer has called her to the stand to testify that the light was red when the defendant entered the intersection. But the jury is still more interested in *who* she is than in the condition of her eyesight.

> Q: What is your name please?
>
> A: Gail Fitzgerald.
>
> Q: Miss Fitzgerald, I would like to ask you some questions about yourself . . .

Plaintiff's counsel now goes through the same pedigree that the prosecutor elicited in the criminal case. And then, when he is finished or has been halted by a successful objection, he goes on with his *argument*.[10]

> Q: Miss Fitzgerald, before asking you any questions concerning what you saw, I would like to ask you, do you know the plaintiff in this case?
>
> A: No.
>
> Q: Do you know the defendant in this case?
>
> A: No.
>
> Q: Miss Fitzgerald, do you have any financial interest in the outcome of this case?

A: No.

Q: Well then, I would like to direct your attention to the evening of May 11th of last year. Can you tell us where you were about 9 p.m. that evening?

And so it goes. The witness begins the substantive portion of her testimony only after she has been properly called, introduced, and authenticated.

Notice: the attorney is not merely eliciting information. He is arguing his case. And so we return to her testimony, this time in the criminal case. She has testified that as she stood on the street after alighting from the bus, a man took hold of her pocketbook, she resisted, and in the struggle the assailant struck her. Let us watch as our advocate develops the testimony. In places we shall assume a successful objection, although many judges would not sustain one, and demonstrate how it makes no difference if the objection is sustained or overruled.

Q: Do you or do you not have a picture in your mind of the face of the man who struck you? [Is this leading? Many would say "no," for it does not suggest any certain answer.]

Objection sustained. [Assuming the objection and the rulings, we are not deterred.]

Q: Do you remember what the man who hit you looked like?

A: Yes.

After the first question—the objection to which we assumed was sustained—the second question may not even be objected to. If it is, the objection is likely to be overruled. In any event, the jury, having heard the first question, is likely to hear it again as rephrased.

Q: Do you see the man who assaulted you in the courtroom?

A: Yes.

Q: With his Honor's permission, will you kindly descend from the stand and point him out to the jury? [Witness leaves the witness chair and walks over to the defense table, where she points with outstretched arm to the defendant.]

Q: Now, if I heard you correctly, you said that defendant grabbed your pocketbook? [You can now and forever after refer to the defendant as the actor because she identified him as such in court.]

A: Yes.

Q: With which hand did he seize it?

A: It was his left hand.

Q: What did you do when he put his hand on your bag?

A: I tried to pull it back.

Q: As you and the defendant struggled over your handbag, did he do anything with his right hand?

In light of her last answer, the examiner's use of the word "struggled" is not suggestive. It merely recasts the testimony, "loops" back, and argues forward.

A: Yes.

Q: What did he do?

A: He hit me.

Q: Did he hit you with an open hand or with a closed fist?

A: No, it was with his fist.

Q: Where on your face did the defendant's blow land?

A: My eye.

Q: Did he punch your left eye or your right eye? [We can now call it a punch because of the prior testimony.]

And so it goes. Using the technique of leading without leading through alternatives, of repetition through questions that repeat answers and through questions that call for details in order to keep the event before the mind's eye of the jury, one blow has become many. And when we have achieved all the repetition we care to by these techniques, followed by demonstrations—if sensible—and/or diagrams, if we care to use them, we will transition away.

> Q: I would now like to leave the subject of the assault and ask you whether or not you required any medical attention, ok?
>
> A: Yes.
>
> Q: Did you in fact need medical assistance?
>
> or
>
> Q: I would like to leave the night of May 11th for a moment, Miss Fitzgerald, and ask whether or not you saw the defendant again, after he assaulted you, and before today.

The attorney can now take it as given that the defendant assaulted the witness and move on to the issue of identification. And while the attorney is on the issue of identification he may, if it pleases him, argue to the jury that the witness has a special reason to be able to remember the face of her assailant.

> Q: Now, Miss Fitzgerald, where were you looking as you struggled with the defendant? [As we have noted, you may say "defendant" if she has already identified him in court; if not, you must say something like "your assailant."]
>
> A: I was staring into his face.
>
> Q: Did you have a reason to want to stare into the face of the man you were struggling with?
>
> A: Yes.

Objection sustained. [We assume that it is, although many judges would not sustain an objection.]

Q: Did you or did you not have a reason for staring into the defendant's face?

Objection sustained. [Again we assume a contrary ruling.]

Q: Why were you staring into the defendant's face?

A: I was desperately trying to read his intentions. To see what he was going to do to me. I was trying to read his eyes. [By this time the jury has the point. The objections have not hurt the examiner. They have helped him. Experienced lawyers do not fear objections. They use them as opportunities.]

It must be emphasized that these examples may well be overdone. But they are offered to illustrate techniques that really do work in the courtroom setting—techniques you will use with reason and judgment in the individual situation you find yourself in. With these techniques, you really can argue your case through the witness to the jury, and you can achieve clarity, memorability, and credibility for the witness with the jury. You simply cannot be as effective if you use a pad of written out questions or if you simply turn the examination of the witness over to the witness and "let the witness tell his own story."

As one who has taught as well as done trial advocacy for many years, I have found it useful to teach the method of direct examination by asking the examiner to define a single point he wishes to argue to the jury through the witness—and then to do it through his questions and the witness's answers. Once the point is entered, nothing must be allowed to intrude until it is closed. And through these *techniques* of examination, which are really *tools of advocacy*, a point of the argument can be made.[11]

ENDNOTES

1. The strategic notion of examination as "argument" will be developed after we have established the tactical techniques that make argument possible on direct.
2. See contrary advice in T. Mauet, Fundamentals of Trial Techniques 94 (1980):

   > Use open-ended questions. Effective direct examinations are best achieved by using open-ended questions which elicit descriptive responses. This serves two functions. First, such questions let the witness *tell the story* and reveal the important evidence himself. Second, they minimize the presence of the lawyer. Remember that during direct examinations the witness should be the center of attention. Your questions should *merely guide* the witness from one area to another as he testifies, and *break up* the testimony into digestible capsules. (Emphasis added.)

   But how can open-ended questions break up anything? In my view they cannot, because control is transferred from the examiner to the witness. Moreover, as we shall see, this notion of direct examination as story telling is as fallacious on direct examination as it was on opening argument.
3. This concept of the direct examination as an argument cannot be fully presented or grasped until the tools—the craft of direct—are identified and mastered. But once that is done, we will return to this concept.
4. See contrary advice in T. Mauet, Fundamentals of Trial Techniques 14 (1980):

   > How should you prepare direct examinations for inclusion in your trial notebook? Two methods are in general use: a. The Q & A method. Under this method, every

question you intend to ask and the witness' anticipated answer are written out. This method is usually employed by inexperienced lawyers during their first few trials. Its advantage is that you can draft your questions in proper form in advance. However, make sure you do not show the actual written questions and answers to the witness, since opposing counsel may ask him if he prepared or saw any outlines of his examination. The disadvantages are that, unless you are a great actor, your questions will sound as if they are being read from a script, creating the impression to the jury that the whole direct examination has been created and choreographed in advance. It also weds you to the script and hinders flexibility. b. The witness narrative method. Under this method you write out in outline form what the witness will say and do on direct. You then simply follow the narrative, posing questions that will elicit the desired answers. The advantages are that your questions will sound fresh and spontaneous and you retain flexibility during the direct examination.

Note all exhibits to be qualified at the top of the page, so you can pull them from your files in advance of the examination. The testimony narrative splits the page in three columns: dates and times, witness narrative, and exhibits to be identified. This makes it visually simple to know where you are and what you should do next at any time during the examination. As the testimony progresses, you simply *check off* what has been testified to and what exhibits have been identified and offered. (Emphasis added.)

5. Some authors counsel that the written down question is the best way to prepare and that an examination from such a script is the very best way to present testimony.

> Sometimes lawyers feel embarrassed about bringing their written questions to court. I have often heard them say that it doesn't look good for counsel to read questions from a paper or a set of cards in front of a jury. It might seem as if he hadn't fully mastered all the details of the case. In fact, the contrary is true. Written questions are a sure sign of preparation, and the better the questions and the more effectively organized they are, the more obviously thorough the preliminary work of the lawyer has been. Ideally, of course, he should have such a compete grasp of the facts that he does not appear to be reading his questions word for word, even though this practice is not, in my opinion, to be feared or condemned. If a lawyer has gone over his questions often enough in advance, as an actor does his script, he will find, after a while, that he needs to consult them only occasionally to prompt himself; he will be referring to them as a guide rather than leaning upon them as a crutch. I believe that when a trial lawyer comes to court with prepared questions for conducting his examination of his own witness and, for that matter, even questions anticipated for cross-examination, he is fulfilling to a very high degree his solemn obligation to his client to be ready for trial in every aspect.

[L. Heller, Do You Solemnly Swear, 67, 68 (1968).]

Obviously, I believe the very opposite is the case. Prepared scripts instill insecurity, not security. They force the focus onto the "words" rather than on the thoughts. Suffice it to say that while my views are obviously not universal, I have never seen a truly clear advocate come to court with written-out questions.

6. As the cited quotation indicates, that Mauet does offer an alternative to the Q & A method of interrogating in direct. He calls it the witness narrative method.

> b. The witness narrative method. Under this method you write out in outline form what the witness will say and do on direct. You then simply follow the narrative, posing questions that will elicit the desired answers. The advantages are that your questions will sound fresh and spontaneous and you retain flexibility during the direct examination.

[T. Mauet, Fundamentals of Trial Techniques 14 (1980).]

Unfortunately, Professor Mauet neither condemns the Q & A method nor shows the neophyte how to use what I believe he unfortunately terms the witness narrative method.

7. There is a special reason for this, which we will come to when we deal with integrating exhibits into notes.

8. These stilted phrases that lawyers think they use to avoid leading are useless anachronisms that only throw off a cloud of jargon and remind the jurors that you are a lawyer. Here is Irving Goldstein's advice nearly 60 years ago:

> Connectives. One of the greatest boons of the trial attorney in properly presenting testimony upon direct examination is through the use of *connectives*. Connectives are those few words generally utilized to inconspicuously prompt and guide the witness in telling his story. It assists the witness and enables the

> trial attorney to make his proof much more simply. It helps to lead the witness over troublesome situations without being subject to objection and at the same time helps put the witness at ease. It also eliminates "jerky spots" as well as embarrassing pauses and gaps in the continuity of the witness' story. It helps to keep the interest alive in a more natural telling of the story. These connectives should be used whenever possible and necessary. The following are some of the connectives most commonly utilized:
>
> 1. "What happened then, if anything?"
> 2. "What did you then do, if anything?"
> 3. "What did he then do, if anything?"
> 4. "What occurred then, if anything?"
> 5. "What followed then, if anything?"
>
> The use of the words "if anything" in conjunction with these connectives, eliminates the possible objection that the examining lawyer is assuming that something further happened or that something further was done. The words "if anything" should therefore *always* be added.

[I. Goldstein, Trial Technique 253, 254 (1935).]

9. Indeed, as a U.S. district judge, I always knew that when a lawyer told me that he was making a motion "for the record," that he expected to lose it . . . and I acted accordingly.

10. Even as we focus our study—for this moment—on the techniques needed to be able to argue on direct examination, we must never lose sight of our goal, which is to argue on direct.

11. I recognize, of course, that we have not yet identified how to organize the direct into an argument by the lawyer. But we have to start someplace. And if we do

not first learn how to speak to the jury through the witness, we cannot hope to even imagine what to argue to the jury through the witness.

Chapter Three

Edward Bennett Williams Introduces His Witnesses

THE *CONNALLY* CASE

For a practical example of how a master introduces his witness to the jury on direct examination, let us return to the trial of John B. Connally, and to his lawyer, Edward Bennett Williams. We have already observed how the master opened to the jury (*see* Volume I, pages 256–271). Now let us see how he introduced and presented Connally to that jury.

Even more than the jurors want to know who any witness is, they want to know who the defendant is. Williams does this with care. We are given a lot of information, but not too much. Williams keeps in tight control. Connally must not be permitted to go on and on by himself. A narrative here might seem too much like boasting. The pace is varied, of course, but it is always Edward Bennett Williams whose hand is firmly on the spigot, deciding how much to let out of Connally.

By Mr. Williams:

Q: Would you state your full name, please?

A: My name is John Bowden Connally, Jr.

Q: Where do you live, sir?

A: I live in Houston, Texas.

Q: How long have you lived there?

A: I have lived in Houston since January 1969.

Q: Where were you born?

A: I was born in Florisville, Texas, a small town near San Antonio, February 17, 1917.

Q: Where did you go to school?

A: I went through fifth grade at Florisville, Texas, and then my father, who was a bus driver, moved the family to San Antonio, and I went through the tenth grade—from the sixth through the tenth grades in the public schools at Harlandale, on the south side of San Antonio, until 1932, when my mother and father moved the family back to Florisville, and I graduated through the eleventh grade at Florisville High School in June of 1933.

Q: And where did you go after that, sir?

A: In September of 1933 I entered the University of Texas at Austin.

Q: And what course did you take there?

A: In those days you could take a pre-law course of two years, and I entered pre-law at the University of Texas in 1933, then followed that by three years in law school.

Q: All in all it was a five-year telescoped course; is that right?

A: Yes, it was.

Q: When did you graduate from law school?

A: I actually got my degree in 1941, but I left the University to come to Washington in the fall of 1939. I came up to see Secretary, then Congressman, Lyndon Johnson.

Q: How long did you remain in Washington on that occasion?

A: I was here and back and forth with him until the spring, early spring of 1941, when I went back to Austin shortly before he entered the race for the United States Senate, which he did on the death of Senator Morris Shepherd, 1941.

Q: Did you manage that campaign?

A: I wouldn't say that I had the title, necessarily, but I did, yes.

Q: And he lost in that election?

A: Yes, he did, by 1311 votes.

Q: Now, during 1941, after being admitted to the Bar, did you practice law or did you sever your connection with law for a period of years?

At this point Williams loops three or four answers back ("I actually got my degree in 1941, . . .") and then changes topics by leading without leading through the giving of alternatives ("Did you practice law or did you . . . ?")

A: No, I didn't practice law. In 1940 I had joined the Naval Reserve. I got a reserve commission as ensign in 1940, and in September 1941 I was called to active duty with the Navy.

Q: And did you—

A: I stayed. I was retired from the Navy, not retired but got out of the service on January 3rd, 1946.

Q: Did you serve a portion of that time in Washington?

A: Yes, I did.

For approximately a year I was attached to the Office of the Undersecretary of the Navy, who at that time was Mr. James Forrestal.

Q: And thereafter?

A: Thereafter I went and spent almost a year in North Africa on the staff of General Eisenhower.

I came back in the fall of 1943 and went through a fighter-director school for 90 days.

I went to the Pacific and served the rest of 1944 and until after the war with the Fast Carrier Task Forces commanded by Admiral Spriggs and Admiral

Spruance in the Third and Fifth Fleets, until the war was over.

Q: And that was until the date of severance?

A: Well, I was actually relieved, I believe, in October. My terminal leave expired January 3rd, 1946.

Q: Were you married in 1940?

Notice, Williams wants to change subjects. So he does so. He simply drops back some six years and leads the witness on to the changed topic. Suppose there had been an objection. It would not have mattered. Williams would simply have reworded the question to "When were you married?"

A: Yes, sir. My wife and I were married in 1940, December the 21st.

Q: And you presently have three children?

A: Yes, we do.

Q: They are all grown?

A: Yes, they are.

Q: And you have grandchildren?

A: We have four grandchildren.

Q: Where do your children live?

A: All of our children live in Texas. Our son and daughter-in-law and grandson live in Houston, our daughter and her husband, our son-in-law, have three children, three of our grandchildren, and they live in Austin, and our youngest son and his wife live at the ranch at Florisville.

Notice the detail on the family life of the witness. Williams knows what is important to jurors. But he does not overdwell on these things. He does it just enough. And to be the correct amount it must be *he*—the examiner—that must do it by maintaining control. Notice how Williams has brought him suddenly up to the present with a discussion of grown children and grandchildren. We will have much to say later about the organization of the examination into an argument. But none of it is possible unless the examiner is in control.

Now Williams returns Connally to the past.

> Q: Did there come a time when you returned to reside in Washington, D.C.?
>
> A: Yes, sir.
>
> I had assisted Congressman Johnson in each of his campaigns, beginning in 1937 when he first ran for Congress in a special election, and I again managed his campaign for re-election in 1946, right after I got out of the service, and then in 1948 he ran for the United States Senate again, and I managed his campaign. He was successful during that election.
>
> I came to Washington again with him, Nellie and I did, and the children, in January, 1949, and stayed here approximately a year with him helping him organize and set up his office in 1949.
>
> Q: And after a period of service with him, '49 to '50, what did you do?
>
> A: I returned to Texas to re-enter the private practice of law, in which I remained for the next decade.
>
> Q: Was there still another occasion when you came back to Washington in the early sixties?
>
> A: Yes, sir. I came back in 1961, in December—I forget—in late December.
>
> Mr. McNamara had called me, asked me to come to Washington, which I did. He interviewed me, and he later asked me to become Secretary of the Navy. And we came back and I served in that capacity, Secretary of the Navy, during substantially all of the year 1961.

Q: And after your period as Secretary of the Navy, what did you do?

A: I resigned as Secretary of the Navy to go back to Texas to seek the office of Governor of Texas, and was so engaged in the campaign all of the year 1962.

Fortunately I was successful, and I was inaugurated in January, 1963, and served that term and two following terms.

I served three terms as Governor of Texas, going out of office, retiring from office in January, about January 20th, 1969.

Q: Did you run for a fourth term?

A: No, sir, I didn't.

No man has ever been elected four times as Governor of Texas. I didn't seek the office the fourth term.

Q: What did you do after your service as Governor?

A: I then went to Houston in January 1969 to re-enter the private practice of law. That's when I moved to Houston.

Q: And with what firm did you become associated?

A: I joined the firm then of Vinson, Elkins, Searles, Connally and Smith.

Q: And that is in Houston?

A: Yes, sir.

Q: Is that the law firm with which you presently practice?

A: Yes, it is.

Q: Was there a period during which you were absent from that law firm?

A: Yes, sir.

In December 1970 I was in Washington. The President of the United States asked me to come over to see him, totally without any forewarning whatever. He asked me to come to Washington to be his Secretary of the Treasury.

I demurred, I begged off, asked for time to think about it. I asked for a month. I got a week.

He called me the following week, asked me to come back, and we again had a long talk about it. And about the middle of December 1940—I mean 1970—I agreed to come back to Washington as Secretary of the Treasury.

Q: When were you actually sworn in as Secretary?

A: I was sworn in February the 11th, 1971.

Q: And you moved back to Washington, of course?

A: Yes, sir.

Q: For that period?

A: Yes, sir.

Q: And the ensuing year and a half?

A: Yes, sir.

Q: Will you please tell the court and jury with what problems you were basically occupied in February and March of 1971, during the initial weeks in which you served as Secretary of the Treasury?

And with that, Williams glides Connally into the subject matter of the case.

No doubt the question arises as to whether a witness in a nonjury case should be as carefully introduced to the judge as Connally was introduced to his jury. The answer is yes. For as we have repeatedly noted, judges—all their protestations notwithstanding—function on the same emotional level as jurors. The judge wants to know the same information that the jurors want to know.

THE *JONES* CASE

To demonstrate the point, let us skip back a few years, before Connally was on trial before a jury, to the trial of Walter Jones before Judge Whipple without a jury (*see* Volume I, pages 278–283). We want to see whether Williams introduces Jones to the judge any differently than he introduced Connally to the jury. We also want to see whether Jones tells his own story or whether Williams does it with—and sometimes for—him. Williams calls Jones to the stand. The examination begins:

By Mr. Williams:

Q: Where do you reside, Mr. Jones?

A: 234 Tappan Road, Norwood, New Jersey.

Q: Norwood, New Jersey, you said?

A: Yes, I did.

Q: How long have you lived there, Mr. Jones?

A: Some 35 years.

Q: How long have you lived in the state of New Jersey, all your life?

A: No, sir, since approximately 1924.

Q: What is your occupation?

A: I am a lawyer.

Q: How long have you been a lawyer?

A: Since 1937.

Q: Of what bars are you a member?

A: Member of the New Jersey Bar, member of the bar of this district and I am a member of the United States Supreme Court.

Q: Where did you get your law training?

A: I got my law training in what was called then New Jersey Law School, which is now known as Rutgers University.

Q: Where did you get your pre-law training?

A: At a school called—then the University of Newark, which is now known as Rutgers University.

Q: Did you go to the public schools here in New Jersey?

A: I went to the grade schools in Teaneck, New Jersey. I went to the high school in Bogota, New Jersey.

Q: Did you do postgraduate work in law?

A: I did postgraduate work in law looking toward a doctor of jurisprudence degree. I did meet that work except for the writing of the thesis, and received in its place instead a master of law degree from New York University.

We notice how the two examinations, Connally and Jones, begin much the same way. The deep background of each man—from elementary school on forward—is mined, and some of the nuggets are brought forth into the courtroom. Judge or jury, it obviously made no difference to Williams. And now, just as with Connally, Williams brings out the details of Jones' family.

Q: Are you married, Mr. Jones?

A: Yes, I am.

Q: How long have you been married?

A: Thirty-four years.

Q: Do you have children?

A: I do have children, yes.

Q: How many?

A: Four.

Q: Are they grown or are they in school?

Williams is knee deep in the examination. He leads with alternatives to take the precise information that he desires to elicit. Jones is not sailing on his own. It is Williams who has the hand on the tiller.

> A: My children are all adult. My first child is Walter Henry Jones, the III. My second child is Graham Oscar Jones. My third child is Susan Hensaw Jones. My fourth child is Deborah Rachel Jones.
>
> Q: Your boys are members of the bar here in New Jersey?
>
> A: Both my boys are admitted to practice in New Jersey.

Now, of course, this kind of an examination cannot be done for every witness called to the stand. That would be inappropriate, and the judge is not likely to permit it to go so far. But these men were defendants in a criminal case, on trial for their professional lives. Greater latitude is of course permitted. But the point is that in *all* cases, *all* witnesses of importance should be authenticated with some degree of care. And *all* witnesses in *all* cases are to be treated as witnesses, not as co-advocates. But Williams—even in this nonjury case—is not finished.

> Q: In addition to practicing law have you engaged in any public service?
>
> A: Yes, I have engaged in public service.
>
> Q: Would you tell his Honor just in a brief way what, if any, public service functions you have performed?

A: Well, my first and very earliest was to serve as a justice of the peace under the old Constitution. Thereafter I became a member of the Assembly of New Jersey. Thereafter I became a member of the Senate of New Jersey. During the course of my stay in those houses I was a majority leader in the Assembly. I was a speaker in the House of the Assembly.

I served as acting governor for a short period of time.

I was majority leader in the Senate.

That is my service in the legislative sense in New Jersey, Mr. Williams.

Q: Are you a member of any public body now?

A: Yes, I am a member of the Port of New York Authority, Port Authority of New York and New Jersey.

Now Williams is finished with pedigree. It is time to bring Jones around to his business activities and introduce his role in the formation and the activities of the Midland Bank, which is the centerpiece of the trial. Let us watch how smoothly Williams accomplishes this, and ask ourselves if such an examination is a possibility either with written out questions or a witness programmed to give testimony in the form of long narratives.

Q: In addition to practicing law, and in addition to performing the specific public service functions that you have described for his Honor, have you been affiliated with any commercial enterprise?

A: Yes, I have.

Q: And with what enterprise have you been associated?

A: Mr. Williams, I have been associated with a few enterprises. I wish to be responsive. Are you speaking in the sense of owning stock?

Q: Yes.

A: And being associated in a commercial sense, as well?

Q: Yes.

A: Well, then, the answer to that is I have been associated with a corporation called Hoke, Inc.

Q: Hoke, H-o-k-e?

A: Yes, it is, sir.

Q: And tell his Honor what Hoke, Inc., is and where it is located, where its principal place of business is.

A: Hoke's principal place of business, which is a manufacturing plant, is in Creskill, New Jersey. It manufactures fittings and valves and it is a firm that does a highly specialized and technical work in fluid controls.

Q: Approximately how long have you been associated with this company?

A: The '40s, Mr. Williams.

Q: And do you have—

A: I would say middle-ish '40s.

Q: Middle '40s?

A: Middle-ish, yes.

Q: Do you have other persons who are associated with you in this venture as co-owners?

A: That is to be divided into two portions. When I first became associated there were two other co-owners. One was Donald B. Salmon and the other was Dr. Wilbur O. Teeters.

Q: Are they the same gentlemen whose names have been mentioned during the course of these proceedings as directors of the Midland Bank?

A: Yes, they are, sir.

Q: Is Mr. Salmon now deceased?

A: Yes, he is.

Q: Mr. Teeters, Dr. Teeters, is still alive?

A: Very much so.

Q: And still associated with you in Hoke?

A: Quite.

Q: Hoke is engaged in the space program, is it not?

A: It is engaged in space and atomic energy programs, among other things.

We see how Williams not only loops the testimony together into a smooth, connected story, but also achieves a conversational tone with the witness, minimizing the strictness of an interrogation mode and facilitating spontaneity. Now Williams is ready to frontally address the charges in the indictment. Watch him completely change topics by transitioning.

Q: Now, Mr. Jones, directing your attention specifically to the year 1958, did you have any part in the formation, creation, of the bank about which there has been so much testimony in this trial, the Midland Bank in Paramus, New Jersey?

A: I did have an association, yes.

Q: Would you tell his Honor what that was?

A: Well, I will reply directly to the question. It was as counsel.

Q: When was that bank formed?

A: In 1958.

Q: And who, as best you can remember at this point, were the persons who joined together to form that bank, to apply for the charter and to create it?

A: Dr. Grant, Dr. Ralph Shaw, Mr. Joseph McBride, Teeters, Dr. Teeters whom I have mentioned, Donald B. Salmon, Peter Moraites. I think there are one or two others that just escape me.

Q: You have to keep your voice up.

A: I think that there are one or two others that escape me just at this moment.

Jones was simply not the witness that Connally was. So Williams had to do a little more for him. Watch the examiner pick up the thread by leading without leading through alternatives.

Q: Were these gentlemen acquaintances, friends, or clients of yours?

A: All three. Not necessarily all three, but they were one of three, as the case may be, as applied to each individual.

Q: They were either acquaintances, friends, or clients, is that correct?

A: Correct.

Q: Did you serve on the original board of directors of this bank?

A: No, I did not.

Q: Did you serve in any capacity other than as counsel to the bank?

A: I served as counsel to the bank.

Q: Did you, Walter Jones, own yourself any stock in this bank at its inception?

A: No, I did not.

And so it went—a steady stream of dialogue, given in a supple, back-and-forth manner, with the object clearly to influence the listener in the moment, and not simply to put information into the record to be "tied up later."

We have identified how the lawyer prepares himself to be able to elicit this kind of testimony. The question then remains, "How do you prepare witnesses to be able to give testimony in this conversational manner?"

Chapter Four

Witness Preparation and Delivery of the Testimony

SCRIPTED TESTIMONY

It is common in the literature of trial advocacy to find advice like that offered by Professor Mauet:

> Prepare the direct examination of the witness and review it with the witness—*repeatedly* . . . go over the *actual questions* in light of evidentiary requirements. . . . If possible, review the testimony in an empty courtroom. Preparation should continue until the witness is *thoroughly familiar* with your questions and answers them in the clearest, most accurate way. (Emphasis added.)[1]

In spite of the abundance of such advice, I believe that the *worst* way to prepare the witness to testify is to practice the questions and answers with him, over and over, attempting to achieve crafted and memorized word-for-word answers by the witness to memorized word-for-word questions by the direct examiner.

Neither party can hope to remember all that stuff—and only one of them will be allowed to have the script before him during the testimony.

Lawyers who use scripts to prepare witnesses will craft and recraft the questions and the answers until they are word perfect, then reduce the script to writing and keep a copy of the script before them while questioning in court (for fear that they will forget the magical words), but they will not allow the witness a copy on the stand (quite correctly fearing that the adversary would then have the absolute right to discover and receive a copy of the dialogue). Witnesses are thus burdened by the impossible duty of remembering all the words while the examining attorney is relieved of that responsibility by his copy of the written script. I have even observed attorneys who keep before them both portions of the script as they enquire—that is, both the written out questions and the written out responses of the witness. What they can do with that dialogue in open court is truly beyond me.

Nothing is more destructive of credibility than the woodenness of testimony from prepared scripts. The reading of the questions alone is lethal to the credibility of the answers. The jurors will surely understand that there is, or has been, more than one half of a script and that the rest of the dialogue was also prepared word for word.

Even when none of the words are actually written down by either the interrogator or the witness, a focusing on the *exact* words of either the questions or the answers destroys spontaneity and therefore credibility. Such memorized performances are largely impossibilities in a courtroom setting, where no one but the judge speaks for very long without intrusion.

There are too many interruptions and unpredictabilities for such performances at a trial. Objections, whether or not sustained, will surely derail an interrogation that has been so finely preplanned. And when those interruptions come, neither the witness nor the examiner will have the flexibility or the self-confidence to deal with the unexpected if both parties depend on a rehearsed script that focused on the exact words to be used.

That is not to say that a *particular* answer on a critical point that will arise either on direct or on cross should not receive focused attention. And if some particular words are required by the law, for example, those words should not be neglected. But that sort of particularized need is a far cry from the routine programming of witnesses to make exact answers to precise questions, which only serves to burden both the lawyer and the witness. Edward Bennett Williams could not have produced the transcripts of Jones and Connally using such pretrial techniques—and neither can any of us.

Even "dress rehearsals" of the testimony, wherein the attorney and the witness practice the entire performance from beginning to end, should be avoided. They do not help—and, as we shall see, they can hurt.

VIDEOTAPING TO PREPARE WITNESSES

Today we have the ability to rehearse witnesses by videotaping their trial runs before trial and then critique their performance to improve it. And many writers recommend videotaping to prepare witnesses.

While no one can deny that such techniques can be effective in smoothing out unconscious mannerisms that abrade or annoy, the practicing before a video camera swings the focus of the witness away from the *substance* of the testimony and onto the *form* of its delivery. The witness begins to perceive himself as a performer. There is at least the danger that naturalness and spontaneity will be lost when the witness is put before the tribunal and is then busy trying to remember and to act out his acting lessons in addition to the substance of his information.

This might well be a risk worth taking—particularly if you can spend sufficient pretrial hours before the video camera so that the witness's *habits* of speech are altered. But there is one factor that overrides this possible advantage, and it should make every attorney unwilling to prepare witnesses on camera. Suppose your adversary learns that there have been such videotaped sessions. What will you do when he demands the out-takes? How will you explain why they no longer exist? How will you explain why the videotaping was necessary to begin with? And why were two or three or more such sessions necessary? And just what is going on here, anyway?

The clear implication of the revelation that videotaping was employed to prepare the witness is that it was used to make changes in either his testimony or the way he gave it. If the jurors come to believe either, it is lethal to the witness . . . and to the lawyer.

On a cost-benefit analysis, then, I believe such videotaping has the potential for more harm than good.

PREPARING WITNESSES IN EMPTY COURTROOMS

Some writers suggest practicing with witnesses in an empty courtroom to give them the feel of the place and to remove the pretrial mystery and therefore the pretrial anxiety. We have seen Professor Mauet give just such advice.

Such visits to empty courtrooms do help some—but, again, at what cost? Suppose your adversary should discover that you have done such a thing to prepare your witness. Would the revelation to the jury of such practice sessions be worth their benefits? Your personal answer should determine your own pretrial conduct.

SELF-CONFIDENCE PREPARES WITNESSES

The best prepared witnesses are the ones who are most confident in their mastery of the facts and who understand the *significance* of those facts to the case they are testifying in support of. In sum, they should know their story,[2] why it is significant to the case, and how to defend it. They should *not* be made to worry about the precise words they will use to tell that story when on the witness stand. If they try to focus on the precise words to use, *they* will inhibit their speech when testifying, just as *we* would inhibit our speech if we focused on the precise words when opening or questioning. (*See* Volume I, page 229.)

Yet it is the natural inclination of *all* people to worry about just this wrong concern: the words to be used. The task of the trial lawyer is to minimize this natural—but wrong—focus of the witness, rather than to maximize it by harping on precise words during pretrial preparation. How do we relax witnesses about their language on the stand? By telling them not to be concerned about it, for one thing.

HOW TO PREPARE WITNESSES TO TESTIFY

We can help train our witnesses for their testimony even as we conduct our initial interviews. We should use some of the same techniques of courtroom questioning in our pretrial interviewing, not in an overt effort to teach how to answer, but in a subliminal exposing of the witness to the cadence and the form of the questioning.

After a while, the witness should be told that this is the very way the questioning will be done in the courtroom; that there is no magic to the forms of questions or to the forms of answers; that it is the job of both of you—witness and lawyer—to get the truth out and that either one may stumble, from time to time; and that when one stumbles, it is the other one's job to help get the truth out in an intelligible way.

A witness who *knows* his facts, who *understands* their significance to your case, who is testifying in *themes* rather than phrases, who is aware of the order in which you will present those themes, and, finally, who feels that he can defend the positions he will be taking in his testimony—such a witness is not only very well prepared; he is a working partner on the witness stand. He can confidently follow your lead and moves, much like a dance partner. But unlike dance partners, since your routines will *not* have been memorized, you and your witness *will* be able to change cadence as the unanticipated vicissitudes of the courtroom intrude on your performance.

Preparation for testimony, as pointed out above, should be done in *themes*—that is, the witness should concentrate on the points to be made, not on the words that will be used to make them. True preparation of the witness, then, does not focus on going through the direct like running through a performance. Rather, the witness is prepared on the cluster of material—sometimes out of chronological order—necessary to make the point. That is what is meant by preparation in *themes*. Sometimes all the themes can be covered in one session, sometimes in several different sessions. But the emphasis is on mastering each individual theme, not on putting them together. That putting together will occur naturally enough once the individual themes are mastered.

Of course, not every witness has the motivation or even the intellectual ability to cooperate with this sort of preparation or presentation. But, then, such witnesses will not be inclined or intellectually able to memorize scripts for you, either. If a witness does not want to help you, any kind of preparation is academic. And if a witness lacks the intellectual ability to be fully prepared in this way, he is not likely to be better prepared by a prepared script.

It should be emphasized that this discussion of witness "preparation" deals with preparation for the presentation of information that has already been obtained from the witness. The topic of how to obtain the data in the first place is reserved for a later work. It may seem odd to say, but it is not possible to fully describe the techniques of obtaining the most favorable information from one's own witness until the subject of cross-examination is explored.

Let me illustrate the points discussed above, and others, not by a direct examination, but by a cross-examination. We return to the *Colonial Pipeline* trial. Fred Stewart has testified for the government. He has already been cross-examined by several defense attorneys, including former Judge Simon H. Rifkind. Now he must face the one to be feared the most, Edward Bennett Williams. This cross by Williams will be the most important task he will face in defending Zirpolo. For only Stewart has any direct testimony against Williams' client. Later, when we deal with the subject of cross-examination, we will examine more of this testimony. But, for now, the following excerpt suffices to make the discussion clear.

It was important—for reasons we will examine another time—for Williams to make the point (if he could) that Fred Stewart's testimony against Zirpolo had been embellished beyond his initial grand jury testimony during pretrial preparation by the prosecutor—in this instance, me.

> Q: Now, on June 29 of 1968 here in this building, Mr. Stern for the first time undertook to question you about the events which were germane to the case which we are trying here, is that so?
>
> A: Mr. Stern and Mr. Goldstein.
>
> Q: He was an associate of Mr. Stern's, is that correct?
>
> A: Yes.

Q: And on June 29 you spent most of the day discussing the facts, as you recalled them, of this case?

A: I did.

Q: Is that correct?

A: Yes, sir. A good part of the day. I don't remember just how many hours.

Q: And did you the next day, June 30, do the same thing?

A: I don't believe so. I believe that—

Q You had that day off, June 30?

A: Perhaps.

Very nice, that "You had that day *off*" business. The suggestion, of course, is that Stewart was hitched to a plow, going over the same field again and again, particularly since he had been questioned by the Colonial lawyers for three days before they had brought him down to me.

Nonetheless, Stewart had testified that he had made mistakes in his earlier statements, even in the grand jury, and that his memory was better at trial and more accurate than his earlier statements. Because Stewart's trial testimony was more lethal to Williams' client than the earlier statements, Williams *had* to go after the claim of better recollection.

Q: But it was the very next day, was it not, Mr. Stewart, July 1, when you appeared before the grand jury?

A: That's correct.

Q: Do you remember the day of the week?

A: It was toward the end of the week. I am not sure.

Q: That was on Friday, was it not?

A: It could be. I am not sure.

Q: And it was then on July 1 that you gave your testimony before the grand jury in this case?

A: Yes.

Q: And you completed it on that day?

A: Yes.

Q: Now, yesterday under examination you testified, did you not, that your recollection is more vivid today than it was when you testified before the grand jury?

A: That is true.

Q: And is that true today, it is more vivid now than it was on July 1, 1966?

A: It is.

Q: After having had the interrogations of June 1, June 26, June 27, June 28 and June 29, today your recollection is better?

A: Yes, sir.

So far, Williams is well ahead. But Stewart is comfortable. He *knows* that he has a reason to have better recollection at this time than earlier. And he sits there ready to pounce. Then, Williams steps into it. He asks a question that deals with Stewart's reasons for having a better recollection, calling for Stewart's state of mind. It is the kind of "question" that should rarely be asked.

Q: Now, is that because, Mr. Stewart, that you have had further interrogations by Mr. Stern since the grand jury returned the indictment in this case?

A: No, that isn't the reason. The reason is because I had had the opportunity to see numerous documents, letters, memorandums, my old files when I was with Colonial. It has all jelled in my mind from referring to these memoranda.

Williams lowered his guard and Stewart hit him with the "reason." It was the last sort of thing—or theme—that Williams wanted to hear. And he had to increase the tempo of his own ripostes.

> Q: Excuse me, have you in fact been interrogated a number of times by Mr. Stern?
>
> A: Yes, sir.
>
> Q: I believe you said in response to Judge Rifkind's question that it was more than five, is that correct?
>
> A: I expect so.
>
> Q: How many would you estimate for us?
>
> A: I don't know.
>
> Q: Give us an estimate. Was it as many as 25?
>
> A: I don't think I'd go that far, because there were times when I would call Mr. Stern and ask him if I could come over and look at certain documents.
>
> Q: Now, did you—
>
> A: And we would talk when I would come over.

Stewart lunged right under Williams' riposte. And this hurts even more because it is not the adversary coaching the witness—it is the witness reaching out himself. Now Williams reaches for one of the old tried and true lines of cross-examination—questions about pretrial preparation by the adversary, with the suggestion that the witness has been scripted, or at least rehearsed to the point of perfection. He intends to delve into my pretrial preparation of the witness.

> Q: Have you gone over your questions and answers with Mr. Stern since you have been here in Newark this time?
>
> A: I have been shown the grand jury testimony.

Q: And then did Mr. Stern put questions to you and did you make answers?

A: I did.

Q: How many times have you done that?

A: I couldn't say, Mr. Williams.

Q: Have you done it since you came here on November 13?

A: Yes. He's asked me questions.

Q: Have you read Mr. Giles' testimony?

A: I have not.

Q: Now, when you went over your questions and answers, did you go over them in the same form as they were put to you here in examination when Mr. Stern called you as a witness yesterday?

A: I couldn't say that, because when you are talking in a general conversation he is not confined to the limit that the court puts on addressing a question.

Williams is not having any obfuscating by Stewart. He wants to know if there has been a rehearsal. So he asks him.

Q: Mr. Stewart, did you not in fact go through a rehearsal of your direct examination since this trial began?

A: I wouldn't call it a rehearsal, no, sir.

I was happy that even back then I knew enough not to script or practice roles with witnesses. But Williams did not like that answer at all. And so he made the error of again opening the testimony to Stewart's subjective thought processes.

Q: What would you call it?

> A: Well, he wanted—he would naturally want to know my answer to certain questions.
>
> Q: Well, he had the grand jury testimony, didn't he?
>
> A: He did.

This time Williams escaped the fire. In fact, he scored. But then he opened up of the matter of "reasons" again, and this time Stewart really nailed him.

> Q: So was the only reason that he went over this, as far as you know, so that he would know the answer to your questions? Or was it so that you would answer the questions confidently and after having repeated your answers many times?
>
> A: No. The only assurance Mr. Stern has ever given me, he just wanted me to tell the truth and that's all.

Every experienced cross-examiner knows that, sooner or later, if he keeps pushing into this area he will hear that, or something like that.

But Williams had gone too far to quit. More than that, I think Williams really did not believe that I had neither scripted nor rehearsed Stewart. And so he went right back at it, trying to demonstrate that Stewart had been taught or at least learned his lines before testifying, the way Max Steuer demonstrated it in the *Triangle Shirtwaist Fire* case.[3]

> Q: But, in fact, you have gone over your answers several times with him since this trial began?
>
> A: He has asked me questions and I would give him an answer the best I could remember or understand.
>
> Q: Did you not go through your direct examination with him beginning with your name and ending with the last questions on the meeting in March 1964?

A: You mean the grand jury testimony?

Q: No, did you not go through with Mr. Stern a direct examination out of court wherein he began by asking you your name and then taking you through all of your testimony until you concluded at the end of the 1964 events about which you have testified?

A: You mean did he at any time put me through that? Not completely. We would dwell on different phases of the case, different transactions at different times. But as far as a dress rehearsal is concerned, we never had a dress rehearsal.

Williams was struck. And he did what I and most others do when we get hurt during our own cross-examinations—we repeat the last answer. That may be a good technique for direct, but it is usually the sign of a lawyer in trouble in cross. Watch.

Q: Never had a dress rehearsal?

A: No, sir.

Q: Just had questions and answers in segment form?

A: He never brought me in and sat me on the witness stand and said, "Now, this is it," no.

Q: Never put you on the witness stand?

A: Of course not.

Q: He interrogated you in his office, did he not?

A: Sir?

Q: He interrogated you in his office, did he not?

A: Yes, but not in a sense of a dress rehearsal.

The segments that Williams referred to, back then in 1968, are the *themes* or the *lines* of direct examination that we referred to in advising how to prepare a witness to testify. Stewart was in fact telling the truth. He was prepared to testify then, some 25 years ago, in just the manner this work now advises.

Well, Williams knew he had to give up on that scripted witness business. But he decided on one last strike. He would make an effort to get my notes of the preparation sessions with Stewart. But first he had to see if there were notes.

> Q: Well, at the time that he interrogated you in his office, did anyone take down your answers?
>
> A: No, not that I know of.
>
> Q: Did anybody make notes?
>
> A: He occasionally made a note on the blackboard.
>
> Q: On the blackboard?
>
> A: On the blackboard.
>
> Q: But not on any paper?
>
> A: No.
>
> Q: What was the purpose of making notes on the blackboard?
>
> A: You'll have to ask Mr. Stern that. I'm sure I don't know.

Well so much for that. The rest of the commentary must be reserved for the subject of cross-examination.

But this segment of testimony does illustrate the dire straits I would have found myself in if I had listened to those who advised the use of scripts and rehearsals in empty courtrooms or used videotaped productions on Stewart. If I had done such things, or any one of them, Edward Bennett Williams would have had me for lunch.

OPENING STATEMENTS PREPARE WITNESSES

As noted in the chapter on openings, your opening, and for that matter the opening of your adversary, can help to prepare your witnesses to testify (*see* Volume I, pages 167–170).

Openings help to give witnesses an overview of the case, a picture of the entire mosaic of which their testimony may be only parts—and disconnected parts at that. Thus, if the jurisdiction permits it, the trial lawyer should at least consider having key witnesses hear the openings.

The openings also provide the advocate with an opportunity to physically introduce witnesses to the jury, should he care to do so.

WITNESSES TEND TO GET BETTER AS THEY TESTIFY

The experience of testifying itself conditions witnesses. Most witnesses get more comfortable in the role, and therefore better at testifying, after the initial discomfort has worn off and the proceedings and procedures become more familiar.

One way I have found to relax witnesses, and therefore to stimulate more conversational and flowing testimony, is to begin on material the witness is very comfortable with. Most often that will be the witness's background and pedigree.[4] If the witness is a *very* important one, and if he is particularly nervous on the stand, I have sometimes found it useful to proceed only 10 or 15 minutes into the testimony, and then to try to obtain a brief recess—and *not* to touch on any critical matter before the recess.

I have found that when the witness resumes the stand he feels more like a veteran. The initial shock has worn off, and the testifying goes easier.

EYE CONTACT WITH JURORS

By the Witness

A witness should not avoid eye contact with the jurors while testifying. But neither should he go to extraordinary lengths to seek it. So often one sees a witness—particularly an expert witness—constantly addressing the jurors directly, smiling at them, almost wooing them. I believe this to be an error.

A witness does best by not appearing too partisan, by not becoming an open and declared sales person for the side that called him to the stand. Testimony should be taken, not offered.

Of course, there is nothing wrong with an occasional glance over to the jurors, in a natural sweep of the witness's attention amongst all who sit in the well of the court. But for me, the witness should sit in a composed position, answering the questions as they come and directing the answers to the person who posed the questions. More than that smacks of acting.

For me, there is a critical moment when the jurors leave the box for a recess. Very often the judge keeps the witness on the stand while the jurors file past him and out into the corridor through a door behind the witness box. If that is the setup, and the jurors do file past the witness, the witness should be instructed to keep his head up and not be busy collecting his papers, or half in and half out of his seat, or twisting around. The witness should sit still—or stand still, if that is the court etiquette—facing straight ahead, ready and willing to meet the eye of any juror walking past the witness chair.

Jurors sit like stone while under scrutiny—particularly at the outset of the trial. Later, they begin to give subliminal clues as to their thoughts. But even then they are rarely totally responsive while in open court. But as they occasionally meet the witness's eyes during testimony, and particularly as they make eye contact as they file in and out of court, they are more expressive. This is so because, in some part, they cannot help showing something and because, in major part, in the comings and the goings they do not feel they are closely observed.

Witnesses, particularly those who are in the stand for days rather than hours, can be instructed to look for those little signs and can often give the examiner valuable intelligence as to the identities of friends and enemies on the jury. And witnesses can even identify moments of strength and weakness in their own testimony, on occasion.

By the Lawyer

If the examiner stands at the end of the jury box (assuming the typical courtroom with judge, witness, jury) during the examination—as he should—he can command the entire well of the court between his direct and his peripheral vision. He can see the judge and the witness directly before him. If he is *slightly* behind the shoulder of jurors six and 12, he can see the jurors and likely even his adversary in his peripheral vision.

Placed at this spot, the attorney *knows* that if he can hear the witness so too can each and every juror. And placed in that spot, and if he remains in place except when approaching the witness with an exhibit, and if then he neither uses a written script nor elicits long narrative answers, he can achieve the Wimbledon Effect from the jurors in the box who sit between him and the witness he is *interrogating*.

Again, neither the trial lawyers nor all those who comment on them and advise them agree with this advice. For example, here is what Sonya Hamlin advises:

> Where you stand during the examination can affect both the witness' delivery and the way the jury responds to the testimony.
>
> Very often lawyers tell me they like to stand to the side of the jury box during their examination. They feel this causes the questions to sound as if they came from the jury. It also causes the witness to look at the jury and gives the lawyer a chance to discover whether the witness is speaking loud enough for the jury to hear him. All of this is true, and it is sometimes useful, but there are some other points to consider when you plan to do this.
>
> Jurors can also be distracted because they cannot see the lawyer or the interaction between the lawyer and the witness. Then, too, it is very difficult to ask the jury to focus totally on one person, someone who may not be very eloquent or charismatic. It is more interesting to watch a dialogue between two people than to see only one person and hear an amorphous other voice. Also, if you stand at the far side or at the back of or behind the jury box, you may make the witness feel abandoned, as he sees you becoming part of the jury, drawing away from him. You might factor these thoughts into your decision about where to stand. It is more interesting to

give the jury an opportunity to look at two people: to see you, to get the lift of your energy and your commitment, and then to see the witness answer.

Therefore I suggest you control yourself and how you ask in order to make your witness star. If you ask open-ended questions, a springboard for a full witness answer, you will not detract from the witness if you are visible. You will not take over center stage if you ask short questions that get him to talk. You will be a participant, not a competitor.

Moving closer or backing away should also be done in relationship to the subject matter. Your measurement here is to think of how you would have this conversation in a room. When would your instinct tell you to get closer? What part would you want to hear coolly, objectively, from a more removed place? When are you part of the dialogue and when should the witness show how he handles it alone?

There is one other area to consider. Where you stand should also be measured against the physical placement of the jury box. How far away is it? What does it make the witness and the jury do? Where is the sun? Will it make the witness strain to see and hear you? What other statements are you making by choosing to distance yourself from the witness if you move around? Are you denying your connection? Are you comfortable with what is being said? Spatial relationship is a powerful hidden persuader.

The rigidity and formality of the lectern mitigates against the warmth you'd like to convey as you examine. But, many jurisdictions require using it. Use it as an instrument (though it hums but one sound); choose when to come out from behind it and step forward (softer, more intimate, a closer look at an issue) and when to let the issue ring out from behind the lectern or step back and make the witness look like he needs no help.[5]

I think that most of Hamlin's advice is wrong. A lawyer shuffling back and forth is distracting. His back must often be to the judge or to the jurors. Of course, you must approach when offering an exhibit or, perhaps, when closely examining one. But perching next to a seated witness, peering down on him, is usually just plain rude. Indeed, it is a pose often assumed by cross-examiners to make witnesses feel uncomfortable. And as for showing friendship to the witness in the presence of the jury, that is exactly the wrong thing to do.

An advocate's job is to be intimate with no one who comes to court. An advocate does best when he is perceived to be correct. Do not strive to be witty, or to be charming, or to be loving, or even to be loved. Just be thought to be right! If you achieve that, the rest will invariably take care of itself.

ENDNOTES

1. T. Mauet, Fundamentals of Trial Techniques 12 (1980). Mauet concludes this advice with the following observation: "However, preparation should not continue to the point where testimony sounds memorized or rehearsed." But this prescription is contrary to the earlier advice, which is to first craft the "*actual* questions" (which means the lawyer must write them down), and then go over it "*repeatedly*." In my view, this is exactly the wrong approach and will, if exactly followed, inexorably lead to a witness and a lawyer who sound as though they are going through a catechism. The final suggestion, then, to be sure to present spontaneity, merely covers all the bases of advice without showing us how to achieve that suggested spontaneity in the face of a prepared script that has been repeatedly practiced.
2. The term "story" here does not mean a chronological tale. It is rather the position of the witness as to the facts of the case.
3. We will study this very famous cross-examination when we reach that subject.
4. As we shall see, this is but an incidental benefit of beginning with who the witness is and not the primary reason to begin the examination at that point.
5. S. Hamlin, What Makes Juries Listen 202–204 (1985).

Chapter Five

Applications of the Principles to Cases

Let us revisit the Calley problem we employed in the chapters on opening.[1] But now the openings are concluded. It is time to call a witness to the stand. And the one that has been called is Dennis Conti himself—the main government witness upon whose credibility everything will hinge or hang.

Consider for yourself how you would conduct that direct. You must make the testimony clear and memorable and persuasive, to be sure. But you must also not neglect that fourth task—to make the testimony as invulnerable to cross-examination as you can. And so we must employ our techniques of leading without leading, of using repetition to dwell on topics until we are sure we have made our points, and then transitioning away once we have made them. And above all, we must not forget that we are making an *argument* to the jury through the witness. Indeed, it is to achieve that—the ability to *argue* your case through the witness—that we have been studying these *techniques* of the examiner in control.

And so we must now also worry about the organization of the direct because, as with any argument, the organization of what you say is as persuasive as what you have to say. We have fully explored the critical reasons why organization of any argument is key (*see* Volume I, pages 199–209). We must now apply these principles to the organization of the argument in the form of the direct examination if that argument is to be persuasive. And so we must introduce the witness properly and organize the presentation so that clarity, memorability, and credibility are all established, without making the witness unduly vulnerable to cross-examination.

The reader may wish to construct a direct of Conti with this all in mind, or even to try one out with a colleague. Whether you have chosen to do so or not, let us take a look at what an experienced and enormously gifted trial lawyer did with the same problem.

DIRECT EXAMINATION—MIKE TIGAR

Michael Tigar is one of the nation's leading trial lawyers and professors of trial advocacy. A former partner of Edward Bennett Williams, indeed Williams' "second chair" at the Connally trial, Tigar is a former chairman of the Litigation Section of the American Bar Association, and at this writing the Joe Jamail professor of trial advocacy at the University of Texas School of Law.

At the University of Virginia Law School's Annual Advocacy Institute, Tigar was given nothing but the problem about one hour before he was asked to perform, and was requested to demonstrate the *techniques* of a direct examination before video cameras.[2]

Let us then examine Tigar's presentation. Does he attempt to authenticate the witness by introducing him? Yes. Are his questions written out or prepared? No. Is he making an argument? Yes. Does he achieve clarity, memorability, and credibility? Yes. But does he achieve the fourth goal—has he made his witness less or more vulnerable to cross-examination?

MR. TIGAR: We call Dennis Conti. Mr. Conti, you've already been sworn.

THE WITNESS: Yes, sir.

DIRECT EXAMINATION

BY MR. TIGAR:

Q: Will you state your full name, please, and spell out your last name for the reporter?

A: Dennis James Conti. C-o-n-t-i.

Q: Mr. Conti, I'm going to ask you, if you would, sir, to keep your voice up as we're talking so that all of the people within this room can hear you, sir.

A: Yes, sir.

Q: How old are you, Mr. Conti?

A: Twenty-eight.

Q: What is your business or occupation, sir?

A: I'm a truck driver.

Q: Where do you drive a truck?

A: For the Bishop Shipping Company in Providence, Rhode Island.

Q: Is that a delivery truck or an over-the-road truck, or what kind?

A: Over the road.

Q: Did you serve in the Armed Forces of the United States of America, sir?

A: Yes, sir. I did.

Q: And were you honorably discharged?

A: Yes, sir. I was.

Q: Directing your attention, sir, to March the 16th, 1972. Were you serving with the Armed Forces of the United States in Vietnam?

A: Yes.

Q: Let me ask you, sir. Where did you take your basic training?

A: Fort Dix, New Jersey.

Q: Did you enlist in the Army or were you drafted?

A: Enlisted.

Q: When were you assigned to Vietnam?

A: It was about late November, 1970.

Q: All right. Coming back to March of 1972. Did you have occasion, sir, to be in the village of My Lai?

A: Yes, I did.

Q: When did you arrive in the village of My Lai?

A: It was early in the morning of the 16th.

Q: How did you get there?

A: By helicopter. There were about six helicopters that were sent out to My Lai.

Q: And did there come a time on that day, sir, when you saw Lieutenant William Calley?

A: Yes.

Q: And do you see Lieutenant William Calley in this courtroom, sir?

A: Yes, I do.

Q: Will you point him out, please, for his Honor and the members of the jury?

A: Right there.

MR. TIGAR: May the record reflect that the witness has identified the defendant, Lieutenant William Calley.

Q: Where did you run into Lieutenant Calley on that day, sir?

A: Now—

Q: The first time?

A: Shortly after I got into My Lai, itself. It was on a—along a trail that ran east-west through the hamlet.

Q: Did he say anything to you, sir?

A: Yeah. Right after I saw him he said, "Round up the people." And I went back into the village and did that.

Q: Who did you round up in response to Lieutenant Calley's order to you, sir?

A: About four or five Vietnamese. I found them in the village of—women and kids.

Q: Were they all women and children, or were there any men?

A: Well, when we got back to the trail, and I went down the trail a little bit and found Lieutenant Calley, there were about 30 or 40 Vietnamese there. I remember one old man. The rest were all women and children.

Q: Who was standing there in addition to Lieutenant Calley and yourself? I mean military people, if anybody.

A: Corporal Meadlo.

Q: What happened then?

A: Well, Lieutenant Calley told us to push the people into a rice paddy, to try to keep them under guard. So Meadlo and I took them down the trail a little bit. Took them off the trail and put them in the rice paddy and made them squat down and bunch up together so that they wouldn't run away.

Q: Did Lieutenant Calley give you another order thereafter?

A: Eventually, yes, sir.

Q: About how long after all these people were sitting there bunched up so they couldn't run away did Lieutenant Calley give you another order

A: Probably a half hour.

Q: And what did he tell you to do?

A: Well, he—he told us to take care of those people. And we said, "Fine."

And he left and he came back a little while later, maybe 10 minutes, maybe 15 minutes later, and said, "I thought I told you to take care of those people."

We said, "We are."

He said, "I mean kill 'em."

Q: After Lieutenant Calley said "kill them," sir, did he say anything else?

A: Well, he said, "Come on around here to the side and we'll get in—get in a line and fire into 'em."

Q: Did you obey that order?

A: No, sir.

Q: Did Corporal Meadlo obey that order?

A: Yes, sir.

Q: Did he kill some of those people?

A: He was—he, along with Lieutenant Calley, was firing into 'em. Yes, sir.

Q: Could you see them firing and the people?

A: I was standing right behind Lieutenant Calley and Meadlo—yes, sir.

Q: Will you tell his Honor, please, and the members of the jury what you saw?

A: Well, they, they began firing into this group of people, which sounded like both automatic and semi-automatic fire to me, and there was screaming and yelling and people trying to get up and it lasted about two minutes.

Q: Did there come a time, sir, when Corporal Meadlo stopped firing?

A: Yes. After about two minutes—he started to cry. Then he said, "I can't do it any more. I can't kill any more people." And he handed me his weapon.

And I said, "Oh, no. If they're going to be killed, let Lieutenant Calley do it. I'm not going to do it."

Q: Did Lieutenant Calley kill any more of the people there?

A: Well, shortly after that, yes, sir.

Q: Please, as best you can, sir, describe to his Honor and the members of the jury what you saw Lieutenant Calley do?

A: Well, right after I handed Meadlo's weapon back to him, I saw there were a few kids left. I don't know, three or four kids still alive and Lieutenant Calley killed them one at a time.

Q: Did there come a time later that day, sir, when you encountered Lieutenant Calley again?

A: Yes, sir.

Q: About how long after he shot these children did you encounter him?

A: About a half hour.

Q: Where was he?

A: Well, it was on the—on the other side of the village. I had gone over there because I had heard some rifle fire. And I looked up and saw two men standing on top of the dike. It was Lieutenant Calley and Sergeant Mitchell. And they were firing down on the other side of that dike.

So I—I moved to the left where I could see behind the dike to see what was there. And there were people there. And they were firing directly down into the people.

Q: Were these people Vietnamese, so far as you could see, or were they Americans, or what?

A: All the ones I could see were Vietnamese.

Q: Continue. What sex were they? Could you tell?

A: Looked to be—it was hard to tell with the children. But the older people looked to be women.

Q: And there were some children down there?

A: Yes.

Q: Will you tell the jury exactly what you saw there as you walked up by where Lieutenant Calley was standing on the dike looking down at these people?

A: Lieutenant Calley and Sergeant Mitchell had their weapons up on their shoulders and they were firing down into the dike again with their automatic and semi-automatic fire. And there were people screaming and yelling and trying to get up and they kept firing. And, finally, I remember an older woman got up and Lieutenant Calley shot her and hit her in the head and blew it off.

MR. TIGAR: Pass the witness.

This little direct examination was delivered in less than 10 minutes by a lawyer who had no notes, much less written-out questions or any kind of a script. All Tigar had before him was the problem (*see* Volume I, pages 287–292). And the video camera records that he often consulted the problem. But what that means is that when Mike Tigar looked down at the problem before putting the next question, he was looking at the witness's statements in framing the question. In other words, *he was reading and forming the answer in his head and then allowing the question to come to him*!

As we go on to dissect the examination we must in fairness keep in mind that all Tigar was asked to do was to provide a *brief* demonstration of a direct examination. He had therefore to concentrate on technique. We must also remember that all the facts he had to work with were confined within the little problem. In real life, of course, the examiner would have had much, much more material and the examination would have gone on for a much, much longer period of time. Nonetheless, let us now proceed to dissect the examination against both the principles of advocacy and the techniques of examination we have identified.

> MR. TIGAR: We call Dennis Conti. Mr. Conti, you've already been sworn.
>
> THE WITNESS: Yes, sir.

DIRECT EXAMINATION

BY MR. TIGAR:

> Q: Will you state your full name, please, and spell out your last name for the reporter?
>
> A: Dennis James Conti. C-o-n-t-i.

Notice, Tigar does not ask Conti to merely give a *pro forma* statement, "for the record." The witness is introduced with solemnity. As a suggestion, given *whom* Tigar represents, he might have improved even this by saying, "The United States calls Dennis Conti."

Next Tigar goes on to authenticate the witness by making a human being out of him, with a background and a history, although he is of course limited by the bounds of the problem he has been given. But when he wants a detail of the background, he takes it by leading without leading through the use of alternatives. Watch:

> Q: Mr. Conti, I'm going to ask you, if you would, sir, to keep your voice up as we're talking so that all of the people within this room can hear you, sir.
>
> A: Yes, sir.
>
> Q: How old are you, Mr. Conti?
>
> A: Twenty-eight.
>
> Q: What is your business or occupation, sir?

A: I'm a truck driver.

Q: Where do you drive a truck?

A: For the Bishop Shipping Company in Providence, Rhode Island.

Q: Is that a delivery truck or an over-the-road truck, or what kind?

A: Over the road.

Very neatly done! No one would suspect that Tigar was guiding the witness by the alternative form of the question. Now it is time for Tigar to change topics. And he does so gracefully, guiding the witness into the next topic and, unfortunately, into the first error—an error not of technique, but of principle.

Q: Did you serve in the Armed Forces of the United States of America, sir?

A: Yes, sir. I did.

Q: And were you honorably discharged?

A: Yes, sir. I was.

If, as I suggest, it is true that the jurors seek to learn what the lawyer is trying to tell them through the witness, then what is the message that Tigar is sending with that last question and answer? Is it that Conti is a nice man, a decent man, one whom Tigar respects and the jury should as well? Because if that is the message he *is* sending, it surely is the wrong one and perhaps the worst one. It is a message that, far from protecting Conti on cross-examination, will make him more vulnerable as the jurors learn the details of his sexual misconduct, his venereal disease, his drug abuse, and his other failures as a soldier. In terms of our four levels of advocacy, what level is Tigar on right now (*see* Volume I, pages 170–182)? I suggest that to present Conti as a decent man to this jury is to be at Level I, "Let's Pretend." And what is such a man doing with an honorable discharge anyway?

Now Tigar changes topic, and then, to play a joke on me, changes topic again.

> Q: Directing your attention, sir, to March the 16th, 1972. Were you serving with the Armed Forces of the United States in Vietnam?
>
> A: Yes.
>
> Q: Let me ask you, sir. Where did you take your basic training?
>
> A: Fort Dix, New Jersey.

The last was aimed at me. I was then a United States District Judge, from New Jersey, and I was presiding over the exercise. Tigar, completely cool and in command of himself, although performing in front of several hundred lawyers and a video camera, without a single question on a pad before him, looked up at me, smiled, and sent me a joke.

Then he brought the witness right back. How did he do it? By leading without leading. How did he do that? By giving the witness a choice.

> Q: Did you enlist in the Army or were you drafted?
>
> A: Enlisted.

On a craft or a technique level that is just wonderful! Tigar takes what he wants by his alternatives. But what of the content of the message? Again, the wrong message is being delivered, albeit clearly. First we are told that Conti was honorably discharged. Now we are told that he volunteered to serve. Can anyone doubt that we are being told that this man Conti is a *good* man?

We must shortly ask ourselves the question, if this is the wrong message for us to give to the jury through the witness, then what would be the right one? The fact is that we already do know the avenue (*see* Volume I, page 322, 323). We learned it when we constructed our opening for the prosecution. But now we will have to study the technique necessary to deliver that identical message to the jury, this time arguing through the witness on direct examination rather than through our opening. But first we must complete the analysis of the remainder of what Tigar has done, which is nearly flawless.

Q: When were you assigned to Vietnam?

A: It was about late November, 1970.

Q: All right. Coming back to March of 1972. Did you have occasion, sir, to be in the village of My Lai?

A: Yes, I did.

Q: When did you arrive in the village of My Lai?

A: It was early in the morning of the 16th.

Q: How did you get there?

A: By helicopter. There were about six helicopters that were sent out to My Lai.

Q: And did there come a time on that day, sir, when you saw Lieutenant William Calley?

A: Yes.

Q: And do you see Lieutenant William Calley in this courtroom, sir?

A: Yes, I do.

Q: Will you point him out, please, for his Honor and the members of the jury?

A: Right there.

MR. TIGAR: May the record reflect that the witness has identified the defendant, Lieutenant William Calley.

Q: Where did you run into Lieutenant Calley on that day, sir?

A: Now—

Q: The first time?

A: Shortly after I got into My Lai, itself. It was on a—along a trail that ran east-west through the hamlet.

The early physical identification of Calley in the courtroom is excellent, and entirely necessary if Tigar is to have Conti refer to Calley by name as he goes through the accounts of what occurred in the village. Notice the next question: "Where did you run into Lieutenant Calley on that day, sir?" Tigar, one of the leading law professors in this country, a man who as a law student was first in his class and offered a United States Supreme Court clerkship, an author of numerous learned articles, surely has to exercise discipline in his other customary role as leading trial lawyer to say "run into" rather than "encounter."

Q: Did he say anything to you, sir?

A: Yeah. Right after I saw him he said, "Round up the people." And I went back into the village and did that.

Q: Who did you round up in response to Lieutenant Calley's *order* to you, sir? (Emphasis added.)

Notice, within the looping Tigar has used the word "order" in recasting what Calley said.

A: About four or five Vietnamese. I found them in the village of—women and kids.

Q: *Were they all women and children, or were there any men?*

A: Well, when we got back to the trail, and I went down the trail a little bit and found Lieutenant Calley, there were about 30 or 40 Vietnamese there. I remember one old man. The rest were all women and children. (Emphasis added.)

Notice the repetition of "women and children" and then the use of an alternative to prevent leading. Notice also that the direct is now more than just the antiseptic presentation of material. This is an argument through the witness to the jury.

Q: Who was standing there in addition to Lieutenant Calley and yourself? I mean military people, if anybody.

A: Corporal Meadlo.

Q: What happened then?

The reader cannot see the videotape and therefore does not know that immediately before the last question Tigar's head went down and there was a pause. In my opinion, as will happen to *every* examiner—certainly myself included—Tigar's muscles weakened momentarily. He had no handle. And so he passed the baton to the witness. He gave the witness a wide-open question, "What happened then?" Now Conti answers at greater length than before, and now he has several events in just one answer.

A: Well, Lieutenant Calley told us to push the people into a rice paddy, to try to keep them under guard. So Meadlo and I took them down the trail a little bit. Took them off the trail and put them in the rice paddy and made them squat down and bunch up together so that they wouldn't run away.

While this is far from a run-on narrative, this particular answer is much broader than the others. To that extent it loses pointedness . . . and commensurate clarity and memorability. But watch Tigar brilliantly climb back into the saddle and slam the point home, *by his questions*.

Q: Did Lieutenant Calley give you another order thereafter?

A: Eventually, yes, sir.

Q: About how long after all these people were sitting there bunched up so they couldn't run away did Lieutenant Calley give you another order?

A: Probably a half hour.

That is simply wonderful. The videotape shows Tigar's hands in motion, even while he repeats the last answer, which itself calls for a detail he only could have cared to call for in order to provide a vehicle for the wonderful question itself.

But, now, let us carefully examine the next portion of the testimony. It commences with an open question, which calls for a conversation. It provides an accounting of that conversation, which the court reporter (completely unguided by me) has in actual quotations marks.

> Q: And what did he tell you to do?
>
> A: Well, he—he told us to take care of those people. And we said, "Fine."
> And he left and he came back a little while later, maybe ten minutes, maybe 15 minutes later, and said, "I thought I told you to take care of those people."
> We said, "We are."
> He said, "I mean kill 'em."
>
> Q: *After Lieutenant Calley said "kill them," sir, did he say anything else?*
>
> A: Well, he said, "Come on around here to the side and we'll get in—get in a line and fire into 'em." (Emphasis added.)

The repetition of the last answer in the next question was excellent. But, that aside, I believe it is highly dangerous to elicit conversations in this form. Witnesses should be discouraged from attempting to repeat conversations verbatim. We shall deal with this at greater length later. But now Tigar is back in total command. His questions are not inquiries. They are body blows to the defendant through the witness *by the lawyer*.

> Q: Did you obey that order?
>
> A: No, sir.
>
> Q: Did Corporal Meadlo obey that order?

A: Yes, sir.

Q: Did he kill some of those people?

A: He was—he, along with Lieutenant Calley, was firing into 'em. Yes, sir.

Q: Could you see them firing and the people?

A: I was standing right behind Lieutenant Calley and Meadlo—yes, sir.

These blows are well timed and well delivered. Now it is time for Tigar to vary the force. Short answers must be relieved by a longer one. And so Tigar opens the sluice gate to let more of Conti's words out.

Q: Will you tell his Honor, please, and the members of the jury what you saw?

A: Well, they, they began firing into this group of people, which sounded like both automatic and semi-automatic fire to me, and there was screaming and yelling and people trying to get up and it lasted about two minutes.

Q: Did there come a time, sir, when Corporal Meadlo stopped firing?

A: Yes. After about two minutes—he started to cry. Then he said, "I can't do it any more. I can't kill any more people." And he handed me his weapon. And I said, "Oh, no. If they're going to be killed, let Lieutenant Calley do it. I'm not going to do it."

The last answer was not responsive to the question. At least not after the "Yes." The witness is pouring out information and verbatim conversations. Time to close it up again.

Q: Did Lieutenant Calley kill any more of the people there?

A: Well, shortly after that, yes, sir.

And now to open it up again.

> Q: Please, as best you can, sir, describe to his Honor and the members of the jury what you saw Lieutenant Calley do?
>
> A: Well, right after I handed Meadlo's weapon back to him, I saw there were a few kids left. I don't know, three or four kids still alive and Lieutenant Calley killed them one at a time.

And now to close it with perhaps the most punishing question imaginable. Watch Tigar use the same technique of calling for a detail, again a time interval, in order to repeat an answer, after he has first rephrased it!

> Q: Did there come a time later that day, sir, when you encountered Lieutenant Calley again?
>
> A: Yes, sir.
>
> Q: About how long after he shot these children did you encounter him?
>
> A: About a half hour.[3]

That is absolutely magnificent! And make no mistake, that is simply *not possible* from written down questions! Could you—as an examiner—even dream of reading out such a question? It must be delivered spontaneously. It must be delivered with lethal sincerity, with murderous quietude, and by a lawyer with his head up.

The next question, narrow as it is, however, emboldens the witness, who has by this time become quite comfortable in the stand and is now jumping all over the court, ready with his answers and eager to chuck them in from three-point range. Watch:

> Q: Where was he?
>
> A: Well, it was on the—on the other side of the village. I had gone over there because I had heard some rifle fire. And I looked up and saw two men

> standing on top of the dike. It was Lieutenant Calley and Sergeant Mitchell. And they were firing down on the other side of that dike.
>
> So I—I moved to the left where I could see behind the dike to see what was there. And there were people there. And they were firing directly down into the people.

Tigar now brings Conti under discipline with sharp, pointed, narrow questions that simultaneously keep the witness confined even as the detailed questioning keeps the prior described event before our mind's eye.

> Q: Were these people Vietnamese, so far as you could see, or were they Americans, or what?
>
> A: All the ones I could see were Vietnamese.
>
> Q: What sex were they? Could you tell?
>
> A: Looked to be—it was hard to tell with the children. But the older people looked to be women.
>
> Q: And there were some children down there?
>
> A: Yes.

Tigar had now nearly exhausted the paltry time he had been given for his demonstration. And so he went into his *end game.*[4] He had the witness finish with a flourish. As we go over it, we can see that Tigar knew exactly where he wanted to end the examination. But he used one word that should almost never be used on direct: the word "exactly."[5]

> Q: Will you tell the jury exactly what you saw there as you walked up by where Lieutenant Calley was standing on the dike looking down at these people?
>
> A: Lieutenant Calley and Sergeant Mitchell had their weapons up on their shoulders and they were firing down into the dike again with their automatic and semi-automatic fire. And there were people

screaming and yelling and trying to get up and they kept firing. And, finally, I remember an older woman got up and Lieutenant Calley shot her and hit her in the head and blew it off.

MR: TIGAR: Pass the witness.[6]

In many respects it was a nice way to end. And yet I would counsel against ending at that spot. It was a dramatic point, to be sure. And yet the witness ended with a peroration by the witness. As we shall see, it is usually more effective to make points in staccato, particularly in the end game.

For example, after Tigar's direct, Benjamin Civiletti, the former Attorney General of the United States and a most able trial lawyer, cross-examined. And he hit Conti on some of Conti's misconduct while in the military.[7] Tigar redirected for just one minute. Watch the cadence of the questioning.

REDIRECT EXAMINATION

BY MR. TIGAR:

Q: Mr. Conti, you remember when counsel for Lieutenant Calley was asking you about the search that you had made of the Vietnamese people for weapons? Do you remember that, sir?

A: Yes, sir.

Q: And that was a strip search that you performed, is that correct?

A: Yes.

Q: And you searched, pursuant to your orders, men and women. Is that right, sir?

A: Yes.

Q: Did you kill them?

A: No, sir.

MR. TIGAR: No further questions.

For an example of what I mean by an ending to a direct in staccato, with the attorney in command rather than the witness in peroration, let us again turn to the master, to Edward Bennett Williams, and to the case of John Connally.

DIRECT EXAMINATION—EDWARD BENNETT WILLIAMS

Williams, as we have seen, has carefully introduced Connally and guided him.[8] Now Connally is at the end of his testimony. Let us watch Williams as he goes into the conclusion of the testimony. And if anyone doubts that Williams knew how to use direct as an argument, what follows should end all doubts.

> Q: Did Mr. Jacobsen ever get into your car with you?
>
> A: Absolutely not.
>
> Q: Did you give Mr. Jacobsen anything on November 25th?
>
> A: I did not.
>
> Q: Did you give him anything, any package?
>
> A: No, sir.
>
> Q: Did you have $10,000 in cash?
>
> A: No, sir.
>
> Q: You heard his testimony on that subject, did you not?
>
> A: Yes, sir.
>
> Q: Did anything like that happen?
>
> A: It did not. Nothing like that happened.
>
> Q: Did there come a time when you testified again before the grand jury?
>
> A: Yes, sir, I testified again before grand jury on April 11th, 1974, I believe.

Q: For how long were you before the grand jury this time?

A: Oh, about three hours.

Q: And who interrogated you on this occasion?

A: Mr. Tuerkheimer, Mr. Sale, Mr. Quarles.

Q: Now, have you computed approximately how many hours of testimony you have given on the milk subject?

A: Approximately 10 hours.

Q: And have you counted the number of pages of testimony you have given?

A: Several hundred pages.

Q: Now, have you turned over your records to the prosecutors?

A: So far as I know we have turned over every record they have asked for that is germane and some that weren't. We have given them all of my appointment logs, we have given them my telephone logs, they have had my bank records.

They have had every record that they have ever asked for as far as I know. I have not withheld one single thing from them to my knowledge.

Q: Did you turn over your appointment books?

A: Yes, I did.

Q: Your logs?

A: Yes, I did. While I was in the government and while I was in private life.

Q: Your telephone records?

Q: Yes, sir, all my telephone records, my telephone bills.

Q: From the home?

A: From the home, from the ranch, from the office, from every other source. Those are the only ones.

Q: Have you turned over your bank records from Houston, Florisville?

A: Yes, I think we have, yes.

Q: Have you turned over your itineraries?

A: All of them, everything we have, every phone call I ever made, every trip I ever made, every person I ever saw that was logged anywhere has been made available to them.

Q: Did you turn those over voluntarily?

A: Yes, sir, we did.

Q: During what months were they turned over?

A: We started turning over documents at the time of my first appearance on November 11th, before the grand jury, and before the Ervin Committee the next day, on November 12th, 1973.

We started turning over months of detailed records of office appointments, phone calls and then subsequently thereafter almost weekly if not daily sometimes they were requesting additional information, all of which we made available to them.

Q: I will ask you four final questions, Mr. Connally.

The allegation in this case is that on May 14th of 1971, he gave you $5,000, is that true or false?

A: That is absolutely false.

Q: You heard the testimony of Mr. Jacobsen that on October 29 you gave him $10,000 in your office in a cigar box.

Is that true or false, sir?

A: That is false. I did no such thing.

Q: And that on November 25th, 1973, the date about which we have been just inquiring, that you gave him another $10,000 in your automobile.
Is that true or false, sir?

A: That is absolutely false. I did no such thing.

MR. WILLIAMS: I have no further questions, your Honor.

It may be seen that Williams—as did Tigar—knew *exactly* where he wanted to end his direct examination. For the defendant on the witness stand it must be with a direct, clear, and unequivocal denial of guilt. And this is done by the lawyer with the witness in staccato—not in a peroration by the witness on his own.

ENDNOTES

1. *See* Volume I, page 287 *et seq*. It may profit the reader to turn back to the problem and to reread the factual statement and the opening arguments of Best and Goldstein.
2. In light of the critique that follows, I emphasize that Tigar was only asked to put on a brief demonstration of "how to" do a direct. These videotapes are part of a videotape lecture series, The University of Virginia Trial Advocacy Tape Series.

   The transcript is reproduced verbatim with one exception: I have used the same spellings of Meadlo and My Lai as used in Volume I.
3. Here Tigar has a couple of "encounters." But he uses a little jargon here—I believe—to normalize in terms of the courtroom language this effective technique of repetition and of argument.
4. Every exercise in the courtroom, whether an argument or an examination, has an "end game"—a pre-thought-out place to end up—even as every such exercise should have a place to begin.
5. This will be explained later. Enough for now to note that such words on direct make the witness more vulnerable to cross.
6. In real life, of course, the direct of Conti would have taken many, many hours, not just a few minutes—which is all Mike Tigar had.

   The jurors would have seen the details of the horrors—the mothers pleading for the lives of their children, the grandfathers holding hands over the eyes of grandchildren so they should not see their murderers. In real life, using the techniques of direct that we have studied, the possibilities open to the lawyer would be limitless.
7. This is for a later work on cross-examination.

8. However, a close review of the entire transcript reveals a little too much Connally narrative for my taste in places.

Chapter Six

The *Bank of the United States* Case

We return to 1931, and to two of the greatest advocates in the history of the American Bar—Emory R. Buckner and Max Steuer—three, actually, if we include Isidor J. Kresel, the man Buckner called to the stand for direct examination and who was then cross-examined by Steuer in the *Bank of the United States* case: *People v. Marcus and Singer*.

The history of the case, and of the feud between Steuer and Kresel, has been told, and a portion of the opening statement for the prosecution has been reproduced (*see* Volume I, pages 49–61). However, I present a brief review here for convenience.

In December, 1930, the Bank of the United States failed. Many lives were crushed in its fall. There were the nearly 400,000 depositors. But there was also Martin T. Manton, the corrupt chief judge of the United States Court of Appeals for the Second Circuit who was unmasked as in desperate need of funds.[1] And there was Isidor J. Kresel, counsel to the bank.

Kresel was then at the flood tide of his career. His practice was lucrative. But his fame as a trial lawyer had been established in the public service he had been in and out of from 1901 until 1930. He had held positions ranging from head of the probe of ambulance chasing by lawyers in New York City, to chief prosecutor at the successful impeachment of William Sulzer, governor of New York, in 1913. At the moment that the bank failed, in 1930, Kresel was acting as chief counsel to Special Prosecutor Samuel Seabury, and the two men were devastating the Tammany Hall organization of New York City in a series of investigations that would ultimately lead to the resignation of Mayor James J. Walker.

Max Steuer, as we have also seen, was at that moment perhaps the most renowned criminal defense attorney of the era. In a later volume we will study his technique of cross-examination. He was "Max the Wonder Worker," "Max the Demon

Defender," "Max the Greatest Criminal Lawyer in the World." He was also closely connected with the Tammany organization, which Kresel was about to destroy.[2] And Max Steuer had another reason to hate Isidor Kresel.

Seventeen years earlier, in 1913, Kresel had sought to have Steuer disbarred on grounds of subornation of perjury. Steuer tried to return the compliment in 1929, charging Kresel with perjury in another case.[3] But Steuer missed his target. Nothing came of the charge. But when the Bank of the United States failed in 1930, Steuer had another chance at Kresel. And this time Steuer was determined not to miss.

Steuer, who professed a distaste for all prosecutors, observing that "my experience at the Bar . . . has taught me that prosecutors, as a rule, are persons who love human blood,"[4] volunteered to be the unpaid prosecutor in the *Bank of the United States* case.

He went before the grand jury and procured an indictment against Bernard Marcus, president of the bank (and a former Steuer client until Marcus switched to Kresel). Steuer obtained the indictment of Saul Singer, vice president, and, of course, Isidor Kresel, counsel to the bank. Steuer also indicted Herbert Singer, Saul's son, who was working as a young lawyer in the Kresel office.

Upon the return of the indictment, Kresel immediately resigned from the Seabury investigation into the Tammany organization and began to prepare his defense. He retained the services of the great John W. Davis, former Democratic candidate for president in 1924 against Calvin Coolidge and, as much as anyone, the recognized leader of the American Bar.[5] It would have been a legendary matchup, Steuer versus Davis, but it was not to be—at least not then—for Kresel fell ill before trial and his case was severed. And so the remaining defendants stood trial without him.

Their selections of counsel were from the best of the Bar. Young Herbert Singer retained Harold Medina, then a Columbia law professor—who taught the bar review course at night to my father's generation of New York lawyers—later to become one of the most famous judges in the country, first on the Southern District of New York bench and then on the United States Court of Appeals for the Second Circuit.

Saul Singer was represented by Charles H. Tuttle, who had just been defeated by Franklin D. Roosevelt for governor of New York. But it was Bernard Marcus' lawyer who was expected to provide the greatest challenge to Max Steuer.

Marcus selected Emory Buckner to represent him. Buckner, who had been the most famous United States attorney of his era, was an old adversary of Steuer.[6] A founder of the firm of Root, Clark, Buckner and Howland—now Dewey, Ballentine, Bushby, Palmer and Wood—he was assisted at the trial by his long-time second chair and principal assistant John Marshall Harlan—future Justice of the Supreme Court of the United States. Buckner and Harlan had been together for many years.

Buckner's ingenuity was legendary. As an example, when he was retained by Heavyweight Champion Gene Tunney, who was sued for 10 percent of the 1926 Tunney-Dempsey fight purse, he found himself opposite the great trial lawyer Martin W. Littleton—in my opinion easily on a par with Steuer if not the greatest trial lawyer of all time.[7]

Tunney's principal witness was a James P. Eagleton, proprietor of a speakeasy in the Bronx. This was—at the height of prohibition—an illegal enterprise. Buckner and Harlan expected Littleton to cross-examine the witness on his occupation, and, or so Harlan later reported, he reassured the witness in this way.

> I took him to see Buckner, and Buckner said, "Don't worry. If Mr. Littleton asks you about your business, you'll have in your pocket a piece of paper from Mr. Harlan you can read in reply." I wrote out for him the statement, "I refuse to answer on the grounds that it might incriminate me," and he took the piece of paper with him.[8]

Indeed, Littleton's first question on cross-examination was: "Mr. Eagleton, what is your business?"

Eagleton responded that Littleton's client "knows my business. He has been in my place of business."

Quick as a cat, Littleton was on him.

> I do not know what Mr. Mara knows. I know some of the things he knows. I do not know all that he knows. Perhaps I never aspired to that, but I have asked you a question, which I expect you to answer, unless you are unwilling to answer it. Are you unwilling?[9]

Eagleton was not willing. He drew the Harlan note from his pocket and invoked the Fifth Amendment.

In a moment, Littleton was finished and Buckner was on his feet. Harlan professed 40 years later, "I couldn't imagine what Buckner would do."

Buckner's first question was, "Before the prohibition laws were passed, what was your business?"

"Liquor dealer," Eagleton responded, and the jury relaxed.[10]

Such was the breed of trial lawyers of the day—nimble on their feet, ready of tongue, with rapier repartee. But that sort of facility comes with lots of doing. The open question for us now, however, is whether they thought about the meaning of what they did—as well as doing it—and whether we today can do better direct examinations than they did if we study and train.

And so we go to the courtroom in New York City in February of 1931 where Steuer, the volunteer prosecutor, faces Buckner.

The two men, Buckner and Harlan, had often tangled with Steuer in the past. As his biographer notes, "Buckner in the late 1920s and early 1930s was, with the possible exception of Max Steuer, the highest-priced trial lawyer in New York."[11] And this shared prominence had brought them head to head in a number of significant cases.

As United States attorney, in 1925 Buckner had prosecuted Harry Daugherty—President Harding's attorney general of the United States. Steuer had defended him. Verdict: hung jury.

As a mark of the cleverness of Steuer, his verbatim statement to the press after the trial is here produced. Notice how he tries to achieve two goals: to explain that his client—although not guilty—was not fully exonerated because of the brilliance of the prosecutor; and, by that glowing tribute to Buckner, to simultaneously give Buckner every reason not to prosecute the case again.

Thus, as he left court after the hung jury, Steuer told the New York *Times* that the jury had been confused by the:

> masterly presentation of the case by District Attorney Buckner. He omitted nothing. His opening address was so masterly that we had the comfort of assuming that he would be unable to do anything that would be more injurious to the defense. He presented the evidence in so fair a way that some of the jurors believed it convincing, and, finally, he summed up the case in so persuasive a manner that some of the jurors accepted his argument in lieu of proof. In short, the one great reason why General Daugherty was not acquitted was Buckner.[12]

That is Level IV advocacy—directed at both the public and the prosecutor—with a vengeance.

In 1927, Buckner—then in private practice—assumed the role of special prosecutor to prosecute Maurice E. Connally, borough president of Queens, New York. Connally had taken bribes from Lockjoint (a pipe company that figured in payoffs to the mayor of Newark when, as we shall see, I tried his case some 43 years later). Steuer defended Connally. Verdict: guilty.

But now we are in court in 1931, some four years later. Steuer has opened to the *Bank of the United States* jury brilliantly. We have seen a portion of it. Buckner waived his opening. This, I think, was error.[13]

The trial has dragged on for many weeks. But the passions of the ruined depositors have not cooled. Every day they crowd into the courtroom. Sometimes there are outbursts in court. Indeed, they ring the courthouse—hissing the comings and goings of the defendants.

The theory of the prosecution has been that the defendants violated the banking laws of the state of New York by means of a rather complicated transaction between the bank itself and its own affiliated companies, in which money was borrowed and loaned back and forth between the bank and its wholly owned safe-deposit companies and other companies set up by the defendants. Suffice it to say that the prosecution contended that the transaction was illegal and highly profitable to Marcus and to Singer.

The defense contends that the entire transaction had been presented to and approved by the State Department of Bank Accounts, by the bank's counsel—Kresel—who had himself counseled the defendants that the transaction was lawful. It was upon this disclosure to the state and particularly upon the opinion of the bank's counsel that the entire defense of Bernard Marcus and Saul Singer rested.

To make that defense, Buckner called Kresel to the witness stand in June of 1931. The trial had been underway for two months. This Kresel direct was to be the key evidence for the beleaguered defendants. It is that direct examination we will study.

DIRECT EXAMINATION BY MR. BUCKNER:

Q: Mr. Kresel, we have great difficulty in having witnesses speak loud enough to hear in this room, which you know is the worst room in the city from the acoustics standpoint. Will you make a special effort to raise your voice, and keep it raised? You are a member of the Bar of New York City?

A: I am.

Q: And you are one of the defendants indicted in this case?

A: I am.

Q: At the time this case started on March 30th, of this present year, were you ill?

A: I was.

Q: Confined to your home?

A: I was.

Q: Where?

A: Scarsdale.

Q: When were you taken ill, Mr. Kresel?

In style, it is a nice tight beginning. In substance, it infuriates Steuer, who wants no opportunity for sympathy for Kresel. The pages smoke with the vehemence of Steuer's objections.

MR. STEUER: Is that of significance here?

THE COURT: I don't think so.

MR. STEUER: He has been ill. He wasn't able to be present in court. The indictment against him has been severed, and he is now here as a witness.

THE COURT: No, it isn't significant.

MR. BUCKNER: I don't think that it would take very much in a 10 weeks' trial to find out whether a man got ill Tuesday and then got well Wednesday.

THE COURT: There is no question—

MR. STEUER: It doesn't make any difference about whether it is a 10-hour or a 10-year trial. It can have no purpose that is legitimate.

THE COURT: There was no question but what this witness was ill at the time this trial was started, and that is the reason his case was severed as to him.

MR. BUCKNER: I want to show that he couldn't go back to work until the 4th of May; that is all.

MR. STEUER: I will concede he couldn't go back to work until the 4th of May.

MR. BUCKNER: All right. That is the only purpose.

Buckner has lost. Or has he? Watch his next question knit right back into Steuer's concession and make exactly the point he wanted to make—which he made anyway since the entire colloquy has been in the presence of the jury.

BY MR. BUCKNER:

Q: From the 30th day of March down to the 4th day of May, when you returned to the city to work, did you from time to time see some of these counsel for defendants, who called on you to see you?

A: I did.

Q: To get information?

A: I did.

Q: And the defendants as well?

A: Yes, sir.

Neatly done as to the time frame, but why does Buckner bring out from Kresel that Kresel is in contact with Marcus and Singer? He does it because he has to—sooner or later—because if he doesn't Steuer surely will. Steuer will anyway—indeed, they will be his opening questions on cross, some days later—but Buckner wants to do it first so as to blunt the blow. But why here? Why on the nose of his presentation? And why in this episodic and unconnected way? This should—as we shall see—have been part of the "end game,"[14] and should have been made part of an explanation for this contact and need "to get information" on Kresel's part. This mere dropping of information into the record to get there first and avoid a claim of concealment is amateurish. But—as we shall see—there is one lethal piece of information Buckner does not know that Steuer possesses, so Buckner cannot deal with it in any form. And this failure of information and consequent failure of both technigue and strategy is to have terrible consequences for all the defendants—and for Kresel himself.

But now Buckner introduces Kresel to the jury. And he does it exceedingly well, holding the reins of the examination and using his questions to remain in control.

> Q: When were you admitted to the bar, Mr. Kresel?
>
> A: In July, 1900.
>
> Q: Have you held any public positions during the time you have been a lawyer in New York City, up to the present moment?
>
> A: I have.
>
> Q: What? Very briefly.
>
> A: From January, 1902, to January, 1910, I was an Assistant District Attorney of New York County under Mr. Jerome. I started in as a Deputy Assistant, was promoted to a full Assistant, and then became the chief of staff. That's the only public office that I have held, although I have performed other public service.
>
> Q: Have you had any public positions of a temporary nature, such as just indicated, which is not a statutory position?
>
> A: Yes, sir.
>
> Q: What, very briefly?
>
> A: In 1911 or 1912—I am not certain of the year—I was counsel with Judge Lymbruze, to a legislative investigating committee that was investigating insurance. In 1913, with John Stanchfield, and with ex-Senator Brackett, and with ex-Judge Parker of the Court of Appeals, I was of counsel to the managers of the Assembly in the impeachment of Governor Sulzer. In 1928 I was designated by the Appellate Division to conduct what was commonly known as the Ambulance Chasing proceedings before Judge Wasservogel of the Supreme Court.

> In the fall of 1930 I was designated by Judge Seabury as his counsel in what is known as the Magistrates Courts investigation.
>
> Q: That position you resigned when?
>
> A: The day after my indictment in this case.
>
> Q: And what day was the indictment in this case, if you recall?
>
> A: It was on the 10th of February of this year.

Very nice. And now watch Buckner loop with his next question, making the testimony tongue and groove in a seamless presentation:

> Q: During these 30 years, when you were not employed in the public office or public works that you have just indicated, have you been an active practicing lawyer?
>
> A: I have been in active practice since I came out of the District Attorney's office in 1910. At that time I formed a partnership with Mr. Jerome, who was my chief during my public service. The name of the firm was Jerome & Rand, at first,—Colonel Rand was one of the partners. Then it was changed to Jerome, Rand & Kresel. And subsequently, Mr. William D. Guthrie joined our firm, and the firm name was changed to Guthrie, Jerome, Rand & Kresel. And that continued until 1925, when the firm was dissolved. Subsequently I formed a firm with ex-Judge Clark, of the Appellate Division, and since January, 1930, I have been practicing alone.

An impressive introduction indeed, all the more so because the advocate was in control. Now Buckner desires to change topics, and to introduce the witness to the defendants. Remaining in absolute control, Buckner does this easily.

> Q: Do you know the defendants, B.K. Marcus, Saul Singer, Herbert Singer and Mr. Pollock?

A: I do.

Q: How long have you known B.K. Marcus?

A: I should say about 24 years.

Q: Did you know his father in his lifetime?

A: I did.

Q: Did you represent the father of B.K. Marcus as a lawyer in any way?

A: I did.

Q: I don't wish any details, but can you fix about the time of your professional connection with Mr. Marcus's father?

A: I think it was in 1907.

By that question, Buckner signals that he wishes a short answer, and so he gets one. But it is not true that he wants no detail. The truth is that he wants to *take* it from Kresel rather than have Kresel offer it.

Q: And was that professional work in connection with any financial institution?

A: It was.

Q: What?

A: It was in connection with the organization of a state bank called the Public Bank.

Q: And what was Mr. Marcus's father's connection with the Public Bank?

A: He was the president of it and was the organizer of it and the chief stockholder.

Q: After the organization of the Public Bank in 1907—did you say it was?

A: 1907.

> Q: Yes. After the organization of the Public Bank, did you or did you not have any further legal work for Mr. Marcus's father or that institution?
>
> A: Not until 1910 or 1911, after I left public office.
>
> Q: Yes. After you left public office, did you have professional work for that bank?
>
> A: I did.

It is now time to move Kresel to the Bank of the United States. Buckner transitions those next dozen years in one question and answer.

> Q: When did you have any professional connection with the Bank of United States?
>
> A: I find that it was in November, 1923.
>
> Q: And from that time until the close of the bank last September, did you continue to have professional relations with the bank?
>
> A: Yes, sir.
>
> Q: In addition to being counsel for the bank, were you also counsel for the Bankus Corporation, City Financial Corporation and so forth?
>
> A: I was.

Buckner, by his questions, has skimmed, skipped over, while taking what he wishes.

And now watch Buckner transition and tie into previous testimony given by other witnesses so that everyone in the courtroom will follow the exact point.

> Q: Reference has been made here by several witnesses to a room in the City Financial building, which was referred to as Mr. Kresel's room. Was there a room set apart for your use in the City Financial Corporation for such time as you might have occasion to be there and use it?

> A: You said, "The City Financial building." There was no such building.
>
> Q: I mean the offices.
>
> A: The offices of the City Financial were at 475 Fifth Avenue, and in that suite of offices there was a room that I occupied whenever I was there, although it was also used for other purposes when I was not there.

Back and forth Buckner goes. Skipping ahead, or moving back, he is in entire control. Watch.

> Q: That is right. Do you recall when you became a director of the Bank of United States?
>
> A: I do.
>
> Q: When was that?
>
> A: In May of 1928.
>
> Q: And remained a director throughout, did you?
>
> A: I did.
>
> Q: Skipping ahead—when Bankus Corporation was organized, did you become a director of the Bankus Corporation?
>
> A: I did.
>
> Q: And did you continue throughout, until the closing of the bank?
>
> A: I did.
>
> Q: In addition to the room that was set apart for your use on such occasions as you should be there, in the office of the City Financial Corporation, was any other room there occupied by any employee of yours?
>
> A: There was a room occupied by Herbert Singer.

Buckner wanted to introduce the subject of young Herbert Singer, and he did so easily. Now he wishes to develop that, and so he does—as much as he pleases—keeping Kresel under tight rein.

> Q: Was Herbert Singer an employee of yours?
>
> A: He was in my employ.
>
> Q: In what capacity?
>
> A: As a clerk.
>
> Q: Can you recall, without looking up any records as to when Herbert Singer was employed by you as a law clerk?
>
> A: I can recall, yes.
>
> Q: When?
>
> A: September of 1928.
>
> Q: And did he continue to be employed by you as a law clerk up to the present time?
>
> A: He did. He is still in my employ.
>
> Q: He is still in your employ?
>
> A: Yes, sir.

Buckner is done with all that and tells us so. Now he is ready to move to a new topic and transitions us to it, without a single herk or jerk.

> Q: I now wish to take up the organization of the City Financial Corporation. Did you do any professional work in connection with the organization of the City Financial Corporation?
>
> A: I did.
>
> Q: Were you the attorney that handled all legal details in connection with the organization of that corporation?

A: I was.

Q: Do you recall approximately, without now looking at records, the date of the organization of City Financial Corporation?

A: I do.

Q: When?

A: August 31, 1927.

And now for a little leading without leading by the use of alternatives.

Q: Had the question of organizing such a corporation as the City Financial Corporation been a subject of discussion at which you were present before that time, or was it an extemporaneous discussion?

A: It had been a subject of discussion before that time.

Q: For how long and between whom, please?

A: It had been a subject of discussion for about a year before that, and it was discussed by me with Mr. Marcus, Sr., and Mr. B.K. Marcus, and with Mr. Singer.

Buckner has forgotten something. He has forgotten to introduce us to how it was that Kresel was introduced to Saul Singer. We have heard all about Marcus, but nothing about Singer. So Buckner simply tells us that he forgot and then introduces the witness to Singer.

Q: I forgot to ask you whether you had any acquaintance with Mr. Saul Singer before he sold out his business and devoted all his time to the bank, which has been placed as 1925?

A: I did not.

Q: Your acquaintance with Mr. Singer dates from that day?

A: It dates from the time when he became connected with the bank officially.

Q: Yes. He was a director of the bank, before he became an officer, wasn't he?

A: I think he was.

Q: But in those early days you, yourself, were not a director?

A: I was not.

Now Buckner moves on to a new point, and evokes a kind of confrontation in 1931 that we still hear today. And as we listen to these long-dead masters of our trade, we will surely see that nothing has changed much from then until now.

> Q: Will you tell us in the briefest possible way, the substance of the discussion between B.K. Marcus, yourself, Saul Singer, and Mr. Marcus' father that had begun for about a year, which finally led up to the City Financial Corporation? As briefly as possible.
>
> MR. STEUER: I object to that, merely because it is entirely irrelevant.
>
> THE COURT: What bearing has that? The corporation was organized for certain purposes and it functioned.
>
> MR. BUCKNER: Well, it is like a good many things in this case that the prosecution has put in by way of background. Also, I at least have rather caught some intimations here that once Mr. Marcus died these younger men went off on a frolic of their own, violated traditions which should have been inherent—

Buckner has been teeing off right in front of the jury. This infuriates Steuer, who justifiably interrupts him.

MR. STEUER: Are you summing up now? I am perfectly willing to sum up right from here on—

MR. BUCKNER: I am not summing up. I am repeating Mr. Steuer's summation which began the day we started the case.

That last by Buckner is a direct reference to Steuer's powerful opening, some of which we have seen. But the record reflects that there was no objection to Steuer's opening and, the reader will recall, that Buckner waived his own.

Steuer smashes back—all in front of the jury. And the judge tries to get on with the whole business:

MR. STEUER: Now, it is only when a man hasn't got any sense to utter that he utters nonsense of that kind, and it is when he is breathing to catch his breath.

THE COURT: This witness has testified that he talked with the father of B.K. Marcus concerning the organization of the City Financial. I think it is in evidence that the old gentleman died in July, 1927. The City Financial was organized the following month. It is all in evidence.

MR. BUCKNER: All right.

It is plain that Buckner *knew* how to control a witness on direct examination, how to get testimony out in small digestible bites, and how to achieve the Wimbledon effect. What is not plain, so far, is that he really did not believe that this was the best and most effective method to examine. He believed—as most of his generation did—and many of our generation still do, that when you get to the critical points of the testimony, or "story" as many think of it, the witness should be turned loose to "tell it his own way."

A few months before his death, Buckner summed up his philosophy of how to open a case and how to conduct direct examination in yet another Wellman book, *Success in Court.*[15] His words are reminiscent of the philosophy of the writers and the doers of trial work of his time, and of several generations of trial lawyers before him. His words also explain in the clearest possible terms why he conducted the kind of direct examination of Kresel that he did, and perhaps even why he waived his opening statement: "[O]penings are not so difficult as cross-examinations and summations, but they are important."

Already we see that Buckner is a man of his times, extolling the dessert of trial work over its meat and potatoes. Buckner counsels against detailed openings. He would leave the "facts" to the client and his witnesses:

> [T]he lawyer simply outlines the general nature of the case . . . then the client and his witnesses will be the first to tell about the facts and will consequently receive even more attention than if the lawyer had already been over it in great detail, leaving the witnesses to serve cold turkey on Friday. If the case is to be won, the plaintiff or defendant must in the end set the sympathy of the judge or the jury and this can best be accomplished by the party himself and not by his paid advocate.

Here, we see, the repudiation of the concept of the powerful opening, and of the concept of advocacy on opening, and also the harbinger of the emasculation of the direct examination as a platform for the advocate. And Buckner goes right for it:

> This naturally leads up to the second important step in the trial of a case and that is direct examination. Direct examinations are *of course easier* than cross-examinations and much of what I have said about opening applies to direct examination.

We can already see the end of Buckner's point—even as we understand why Buckner used Kresel to present Buckner's case.

> The point is that the plaintiff and his witnesses should unfold the case *in their own language, in their own way*, whereas the lawyer should only be a modest guide to get them to talk loudly enough and

> explain to them, when in difficulty, some of the technical rules of evidence . . .

And so, as the testimony went on in the *Bank of the United States* case, and the substance of it got close to the core of the case, Buckner, true to his philosophy of direct, more and more turned the reins of the examination over to the witness. As a result, questioning began to take this tone:

> Q: You testified before luncheon as to how you felt in the matter of policy of making the City Financial Corporation an independent company instead of an affiliate of the bank: do you remember that testimony?
>
> A: I do.
>
> Q: Now, we are up here to the end of 1928. I wish to ask if you discussed with B.K. Marcus and Saul Singer the question of the Bankus with reference to an affiliate.
>
> A: I did, and with others.
>
> Q: And with others. Now, will you just state, *without my leading you*, with whom you discussed the question of an affiliate of the bank at that time, namely, near the end of 1928, *in your own way*, please?
>
> A: I discussed—
>
> MR. STEUER: I object to that as being entirely immaterial and irrelevant and not bearing on the issue. (Emphasis added.)

The objections to the content of the conversations were ultimately sustained and the jury did not hear them. But what is obvious is that the tenor of the questioning began to change—and, as it did, the length of the answers began to change. As Buckner more and more turned the examination over to Kresel, Kresel's answers grew long, then longer, then finally into diatribes. After the last flurry of objections, lunch was taken. Then, the deluge began.

After Recess.

ISIDOR J. KRESEL, resumed the stand.

DIRECT EXAMINATION (CONTINUED) BY MR. BUCKNER:

Q: As to the organization of the Bankus Corporation, will you please explain to the jury in non-legal words the machinery by which the Bankus came into existence as an affiliate of the Bank of United States, that is, the exchange of stock and whatever was done—in non-legal phraseology, as I don't wish to read any documents on that subject.

This question is nothing but a cry for help from Buckner to Kresel. So Kresel responded. And when he finished, he asked Buckner if it was good enough.

A: At the time when Bankus Corporation was organized, the Bank of United States had outstanding approximately 90,000 shares of stock of $100 par value. City Financial Corporation had outstanding 720,000 shares of stock of which 300,000 shares were B stock and 420,000 shares were A stock.

One of the first steps that was taken was to organize Bankus Corporation with 720,000 shares of stock of $5 par value each share, so that Bankus and City Financial Corporation had an equal number of shares.

Then the 90,000 shares of bank stock were converted into 360,000 shares of bank stock, by reducing the par value from $100 to $25, so that each stockholder of the bank who held a share of the old stock received four shares of new the stock without any further compensation.

The next step that was taken was to double the capital of the stock as converted, that is to say, there were created 360,000 new shares of bank stock of $25 par value. That new stock was to be issued to the stockholders of the bank, the then stockholders of the bank, each stockholder being entitled to receive for each share of stock that he then held, another share of stock by paying therefor $25 per share.

Now, Bankus Corporation with this 720,000 shares of stock in its treasury first made an offer to the stockholders to the bank to this effect: That if the stockholders of the bank would assign to Bankus Corporation their rights to subscribe to the new bank stock, Bankus Corporation would give to such stockholder for every such right assigned, one share of its stock, so that, assuming that every stockholder of the bank had exercised that privilege, each stockholder or all of the stockholders of the bank would have received 360,000 shares of the stock of Bankus Corporation, which joined to their then stock of the bank, made 360,000 units of stock, each unit consisting of a share of bank stock and a share of Bankus Corporation stock.

I take it, you will ask me later how much was exercised that way. I will go on with the plan.

Then Bankus Corporation made another offer, this time to the stockholders of City Financial Corporation, and that offer was substantially as follows: that Bankus Corporation would give to the City Financial Corporation stockholders for every two shares of City Financial Corporation, one share of Bankus Corporation stock, and that without distinction as to Class A or to Class B stock of City Financial. Assuming now that all stockholders of City Financial had gone into the plan, 720,000 shares of City Financial converted on a basis of two shares of that stock for one of Bankus would have taken up the balance of the Bankus stock that it had in its treasury.

Now, have I sufficiently explained that? (Emphasis added.)

Kresel, it may be seen, had just been drafted as co-counsel. His torrential answer was not likely to be understood. Steuer did not object to any of it.

Buckner climbed back into the saddle for a few more questions. But then the deluge began again, as Buckner even had Steuer's cross-examination questions to the defendant Saul Singer read to Kresel, and asked Kresel to answer the questions that Steuer had put to Singer.

> Q: Mr. Steuer asked Saul Singer the following question, which I wish to read to you to and make it my question, at S.M., page 3688:
>
> "Now, with City Financial Corporation being prosperous at this time when that swap was made"—referring to the Bankus swap—"with City Financial Corporation having the power to do every item of business that Bankus could do, with City Financial paying all the expenses for the business that Bankus was doing, you take your own time, because I am going to ask a wide open question. You tell this jury every reason there was for creating Bankus Corporation except to equalize the A and B stock so that you could put your B in at the same price with the other man that paid $85 for his A stock."
>
> Will you answer that question, if you know?
>
> And the next question is:
>
> "Why didn't you make the City Financial an affiliate?"
>
> A: Bankus Corporation was organized for the reason that the stockholders of the bank and the stockholders of City Financial, particularly those of the bank, represented to the officers of the bank that this bank which then was a large one—that was after the Central Mercantile merger, and after the Cosmopolitan merger—that that was one of the large banks in the City, one of the few large banks in

the city that did not have an affiliate. At that time it had become sort of a style among banks in the city to have affiliates; it was thought that affiliates could do certain kinds of business, perfectly legitimate business, but which a bank under its restricted powers could not do. And the officers of the bank, in consultation with me, advised them that large stockholders of the bank had approached them with representations that they thought it was about time that our bank had an affiliate.

Now, the question of having City Financial act in that capacity was considered, and I advised that it could not be done, and for these reasons: In the first place, City Financial had two classes of stockholders. It was desired to have units of stock; in other words, it was desired that every holder of stock of the bank was at the same time to be a holder of stock of the affiliate—just like the Chase Bank and its Chase Securities, or the National City Bank and the National City Company.

Steuer could no longer restrain himself. He saw quite clearly that Buckner had turned the duty of advocacy over to Kresel. Steuer had not objected much before. He would not do much again—for this kind of testimony really helped him rather than hurt him. But this time he could not restrain himself.

MR. STEUER: I would like to know whether this witness is now arguing this case to the jury or whether he is stating now what he said at that time in the meeting.

THE WITNESS: Shall I answer the question?

THE COURT: Yes.

THE WITNESS: I am stating now what I said to these men.

After that smart—but patently untruthful—answer to the judge and to Steuer, Kresel launched forth again.

> A: (Continuing) Now, with a Class A stock of the City Financial and the Class B stock of City Financial, there would have had to be two kinds of units. Now, you could not trade in a Class A unit and a Class B unit; and the natural legal procedure, as I advised these men was to organize a new corporation with broad powers—powers to do the kind of business that an affiliate naturally would do, and then, in view of the well-established business of City Financial at that time, to make this proposal to the City Financial stockholders.
>
> I pointed out to these men that the City Financial stockholders were not compelled in any way to come into this plan if they did not want to, any more than the bank stockholders had to come into this plan; that it was an entirely voluntary matter for these stockholders to decide for themselves.
>
> The reason why I advised that the same number of shares of stock was to be for the Bankus Corporation as there were for City Financial Corporation was because it was required to make units to acquire half of the increase of the stock of the bank and the 720,000 shares of stock of City Financial.
>
> Now, that, substantially, as I recall it, were the conferences that I had with these men when this thing was being planned.

And so it went. Not all of the questions and answers were of this ilk, of course. But as time went on, more and more of them were. For example, Buckner, in a plain appeal for narrative help, asked Kresel:

> Q: Will you state what you know *of your own knowledge* concerning those negotiations and particularly *as to why* Marcus, Mitchell and Singer made

> the undertaking in their individual capacities as part of this proposed merger?[16] (Emphasis added.)

This sort of question is rank amateurish. It calls on the witness to segregate hearsay from nonhearsay ("of your own knowledge") and it requests Kresel to explain the motivations of Marcus, Mitchell, and Singer.

Nonetheless, Steuer did not object. And Kresel droned on. Perhaps Steuer did not object because he did not believe that this advocacy from the witness stand hurt him. Or perhaps it was because Steuer knew he could destroy Kresel—and thereby the defendants—on cross-examination, as indeed he did.

During the several days of direct examination, Buckner sometimes took over the lead of the examination. But as it went on, more and more his questions asked for longer and longer narratives, until the answer to just one question began to consume as much as 20 pages of the record.

For example, when Buckner brought Kresel to a critical meeting between Kresel and the defendants and the state banking authorities at the Bar Association, he turned the entire case over to the witness.

> Q: Do you have a distinct recollection of the first meeting at the Bar Association?
>
> A: I have.
>
> Q: Who was present?
>
> A: Mr. Broderick, Mr. Egbert, Mr. Marcus, Mr. Singer, Mr. Mitchell, Mr. Kugel, the two McArdles, young Herbert Singer and I.
>
> Q: Have you any notation or any recollection as to how long the conference lasted on the 14th of September?
>
> A: I have no recollection, but my diary says all afternoon. Now, that may mean from three to five or half past five, something like that, I cannot tell exactly.

> Q: I want you—did you say anything at the conference?
>
> A: I did.
>
> Q: Did you have any notes prepared from which you carried on your discussion?
>
> A: I did.
>
> Q: Have you still preserved your notes from which you made your statement to the Superintendent and Mr. Egbert?
>
> A: I did.
>
> Q: Now, I want you *without any interruption from me* at all, to start at the beginning and state everything which you can recall that took place at the Bar Association conference on September 24th,—what the various people said? I mean September 11th; what the various people said, *without any interruptions from me* and today we are competing with the fans on account of the heat, so make a special effort to keep your voice up.
>
> A: I can give you, of course, the substance only, not the exact words that I used.
>
> Q: *I do not want you to leave anything out*, Mr. Kresel, *no matter how long it takes*. I want everything that you can recall that took place; everything that you said and everything that everybody else said. (Emphasis added.)

The incredible length of Kresel's outpourings at that point make their inclusion in this chapter impossible. However, the complete Kresel answer is included in Appendix A for any who care to see how far this "tell your own story" technique can take us.

Kresel's answer must have taken an hour or more. And while that was his longest, there were many others that went on for five, ten, or more pages of record, as Buckner kept calling Kresel for narrations, and Kresel kept giving them to him.

In sum, Kresel's role in the trial was to establish two main points of defense. The first was that the state banking authorities knew all about and approved the transactions on trial during the meetings at the Bar Association office. The second, that the defendants relied upon their lawyer—Kresel—in going ahead and that neither they nor he believed that the transactions were unlawful.

As to both points, Steuer toyed with Buckner before the jury.

When Buckner, desperate to put Kresel's notes of his meeting of the second conference with the authorities into evidence, was confronted by a disapproving judge, Steuer was magnanimous before the jurors.

> Q: Have you the memorandum there which has your notes that you wrote while Mr. Broderick was giving his statement at the second conference and which you wrote down?
>
> A: Yes, here it is (indicating).
>
> MR. BUCKNER: I offer this memorandum in evidence.
>
> MR. STEUER: Is there anything in there that he has not testified to?
>
> MR. BUCKNER: No. But I would like to be heard for a moment, if I may. Here is the memorandum written by Mr. Kresel, as Mr. Broderick was speaking, at the time before any indictment or any other troubles could have been thought of; and I appeal to your Honor's discretion for the probative force of his notes made at that time, to admit this in evidence. It seems to me that it is in evidence.
>
> THE COURT: Isn't it a self-serving declaration?
>
> MR. BUCKNER: Not a self-serving declaration.

The judge was not inclined to let it in. But he turned to Steuer—the sometime, one-time district attorney—for aid in keeping the document out.

> THE COURT: Hasn't he testified in full as to what it contains? I don't know whether the District Attorney objects or not.
>
> MR. BUCKNER: I would like to have the jury see the very notes.
>
> THE COURT: Does the District Attorney object?

But Steuer was inclined to play the patronizing role.

> MR. STEUER: Do you think it helps you?
>
> MR. BUCKNER: Yes.
>
> MR. STEUER: You would like to have it in?
>
> MR. BUCKNER: Yes.
>
> MR. STEUER: All right.
>
> MR. BUCKNER: Thank you.
>
> (Memorandum made by Mr. Kresel at conference with Mr. Broderick, consisting of four sheets, received in evidence and marked as Defendants' Exhibit 7-R.)

But when immediately thereafter Buckner wanted to show the document to the jury by giving each a copy—which, as we shall see, is the best way to do it—as had been repeatedly done by the prosecution, Steuer decided to bring down the curtain.

> MR. BUCKNER: Your Honor, I wish to interrogate the witness as to one point in this memorandum which was not discussed, and I would like to have the jury examine this memorandum.
>
> MR. STEUER: No. Just a minute; wait just a minute. They are not going to have one piece of testimony picked out of this case emphasized. This is not in the form of an exhibit. I was perfectly willing

to have them use that exhibit and to read it. I object to the use of any photostat with respect to it, because that is making the emphasis of one piece of testimony out of a trial, and that is highly improper.

THE COURT: What is this photostat you are going to offer now?

MR. BUCKNER: I am about to examine the witness on one thing, on this exhibit which has now been admitted into evidence; and I wish the jury to have photostats of this exhibit, just as in this case—why, your Honor recalls that the prosecution has had photostats.

THE COURT: But you cannot bolster up this exhibit with the photostats made of it.

The judge did not know what he was talking about. All Buckner wanted to do was to show copies of an exhibit in evidence to the jurors. This is a commonplace today and was then. Unfortunately, however, Buckner lost his cool. And he let his anger at the judge show:

MR. BUCKNER: I take exception to your Honor's use of the word "bolster."

THE COURT: What?

MR. BUCKNER: I take exception to your Honor's use of the word, "bolster," when I want the jury to see, as has been done repeatedly in this case, photostats of an exhibit, so that they can look at it.

THE COURT: The photostats of exhibits were admitted where the originals were not available.

MR. BUCKNER: No, your Honor, we have had duplicates over and over again in this case. We have had duplicates given to the jury.

This business of taking "exceptions," while in the 1930s undoubtedly *sometimes* necessary to preserve a point for appeal, was not done for that purpose here. No appellate court would care about this point. It was done to express displeasure by one lawyer with the judge, and this in front of the jurors. And, of course, it evoked a Newtonian reaction from the judge—gaining Buckner nothing.

But it gained Steuer something—a chance to again appear magnanimous.

> MR. STEUER: Won't you wait half a second?
>
> MR. BUCKNER: And very properly so.
>
> MR. STEUER: Once more and you will get it in.
>
> THE COURT: He won't get it in without the Court's consent.
>
> MR. STEUER: I understand that. Since he emphasizes it so much, I want this witness and I want counsel, with the Court's permission, to get all the advantage from the use of the photostats as well as the exhibit. I am sorry that I protested against it, and I would like now your Honor to exercise your discretion.[17]

When it came to Buckner's second point—that the defendants had relied on Kresel's advice that the transactions were legal—Steuer was not so generous.

> Q: You were still a director of the Bank of United States on January 11th, 1930, weren't you?
>
> A: I was.
>
> Q: And you were still counsel for the bank?
>
> A: I was.
>
> Q: And for Bankus?
>
> A: I was.
>
> Q: And a director of Bankus?
>
> A: Yes.

Q: Did you tell Mr. Marcus or Mr. Singer, or the McArdles or anybody in that conference, on January 11th, that the plan as described by yourself—I don't want to try to repeat it—as you have just testified, was illegal or unlawful?

A: No.

That was delivered well—with Buckner in full control, making his point *through* Kresel—but Steuer was objecting. And the judge seemed inclined to agree with him—as he usually did.

MR. STEUER: I object to that, because nobody claims that any such plan as that described by the witness is unlawful or illegal. Now, and I also—

MR. BUCKNER: That is what we are indicted on.

MR. STEUER: Wait a minute. That is an outrageous statement, that that is what you are indicted on,—a most outrageous, unwarranted statement, and absolutely untruthful. And no other words suit the situation.

Buckner was so obviously stung that Harold Medina tried to shield him. But Buckner would have none of it.

MR. MEDINA: I object to that, your Honor, and ask that Mr. Steuer be directed to refrain from such comments as that.

MR. BUCKNER: I will take care of myself.

MR. STEUER: I have no objection to this witness stating whatever he said. But this calls for a negative: did you tell them it was illegal? Anything that he did tell them, I make no objection to.

THE COURT: You have first got to show that this witness knew that the plan actually went through—that he knew all the details of it. And then ask him whether or not he said they were illegal. But if he doesn't know the actual plan that went through, then I sustain the objection to the question.

MR. BUCKNER: All right.

And, despite repeated attempts by Buckner, Steuer prevented the answer to every question the answer to which would have demonstrated that the defendants relied on their counsel—Kresel—in consummating the transaction in the belief that it was an entirely proper one.

Not that Steuer should necessarily have bothered, for the defendants were doomed men. They were doomed because of the spirit of the times—and the hundreds of former depositors of the Bank of the United States who ringed the courthouse every day and hissed the defendants when they entered and left the building.

But what most doomed the defendants was the cross-examination that Steuer would conduct of Kresel, a cross-examination that Buckner could not make provision against because it was based on Kresel's grand jury testimony Steuer had taken in the investigating stage—*and only Steuer had access to.*

While we deal with cross-examination separately later, the reader is entitled to the completing of the account.

On cross-examination, Steuer confronted Kresel with his grand jury testimony. Behind the closed-door secrecy of the grand jury room, Kresel had told the grand jurors something thst impugned his entire trial testimony that he saw nothing illegal in the transactions under indictment:

> . . . I have nothing to do, and did not know the course that this transaction took. I do not understand why it should have been necessary to have this devious way of having these two corporations . . . But the very fact that it was passed through that way indicates that there was something suspiciously wrong about it. I would have nothing to do with that sort of a transaction. It is unfortunate that the man who was in my employ [Herbert Singer] was the man who had charge of it.

Those words condemned the accused at trial. Had they known that Steuer had gotten that testimony from Kresel in the grand jury, they never would have called the man at trial—or, at the very least, would have dealt with it on direct examination.

The remainder of the tale is as exotic as the beginning of it. Under cross-examination Kresel denied making the above statement to the grand jurors, in spite of Steuer's heavy cross.

Both the foreman of the grand jury and the grand jury stenographer were called to testify to the veracity of the grand jury minutes. Then Steuer took the stand himself, to attest to the accuracy of the minutes of his grand jury questioning of Kresel.

The defendants Bernard Marcus and the Singers, father and son, were convicted. These convictions were affirmed—except for young Herbert, whom Medina saved by portraying him as a self-important youngster. "You know how these boys in law school are—these law clerks of yours—" Medina argued to the New York State Court of Appeals, "They think they know everything."[18]

Herbert Singer became a very successful lawyer in New York City. He later established a Medina Chair at Columbia Law School, with an initial $50,000 contribution from the estate of Saul Singer, who made a fortune in Texas oil after his release from prison. Medina became one of the most famous federal judges in the United States.

The Marcus family remained prominent. Its most famous contribution to the legal profession was Roy M. (Marcus) Cohn, whose mother was Bernard Marcus' sister.

As for Emory Buckner, this was his last case. He fell ill not too long after the trial and, although he was to live until 1941, did not try another jury case.[19]

Kresel, however, had a long road ahead. Shortly after the convictions, Steuer had Kresel indicted for perjury for his denial at the trial of his grand jury testimony.

John W. Davis represented Kresel without fee and cross-examined Steuer, who testified—but did not prosecute the case—against Kresel. Near the end of the trial, Kresel reported that one of the jurors approached him for a loan, and a mistrial was declared.

Davis again served Kresel without fee in the second trial. His defense was that Kresel had really used the subjective—had said not that the transaction *was* suspicious, but that "it would appear that this was a devious transaction" and that "if it was I would have had nothing to do with it."[20]

Where does the truth lie? For the interested reader who wishes to make an independent judgment, I have produced that portion of the Steuer cross of Kresel in the Appendix B. For me, it is clear that Kresel, in the grand jury, was doing all he could to persuade that body not to indict him—even to the point of washing his hands of his former clients. Certainly that was Buckner's view, who summed up to the jury, "Because Kresel did not want to be indicted . . . These defendants are condemned, deserted, betrayed by the lawyer on whom they relied."

In any event, Kresel's second perjury trial resulted in a directed verdict of acquittal for him on the ground that Kresel's words to the grand jury had not been material.

But Kresel had one trial left, the original indictment in the bank case from which he had been severed because of ill health. Again Davis served as Kresel's counsel. And again without fee. For 38 trial days the case dragged on before a jury and a nearly empty courtroom. The public was no longer interested. Steuer had gone on to other things. It was just a long, dull, technical bank case.

Kresel was convicted. Two weeks after the verdict, Kresel's wife died. A few months later, Kresel was disbarred. One of the most extraordinary careers at the Bar had apparently come to an end.

Nonetheless, two weeks after the verdict, Kresel wrote to Davis:

> It isn't often that it is given to a man to see the soul of another. I have seen yours . . . it is divine. You have given to the Bar an example of professional brotherhood and fine chivalry never before equalled

> in our jurisprudence, and you have done it at great personal sacrifice and in an atmosphere that I knew was repugnant to you. Yet you stood by me these many weeks because of your sense of justice and because you believed that a brother lawyer was being persecuted.[21]

Davis took on the Kresel appeal. On January 16, 1935, the conviction was reversed, and thereafter Kresel was re-instated to the Bar. He remarried and flourished professionally until his death in 1957. But the scars remained. Kresel's unpublished 1955 autobiography, which exists only in typescript, ends with the words that should end this story—for Kresel should have the last word, after all.

> TAMMANY'S REVENGE
>
> The heads were falling. The fire was getting too close for comfort, too close to Tammany and its overlords. Where would it end? Who knows what a weak-kneed vice cop or magistrate caught in the clutches of the ever-spreading investigation might be forced to reveal? . . .
>
> Using the power of subpoena we had laid bare the Vice Squad's graft from prostitution. What was to stop us from using the same power to subpoena the bank accounts of the District Leaders, the high-ranking officers of the Police Department, the magistrates, the head of Tammany, and even the Mayor; and what might those accounts disclose?
>
> Such were the fears of Tammany and such its thinking. What was to be done? Could the investigation be stopped? Clearly not. It had gone too far. The public was too aroused and a sudden cessation of its activities would be blasted by the newspapers as a sell-out to the grafters.
>
> Well, if the investigation couldn't be stopped could it be hampered in any way? Yes, by buying the man who had sparked the investigation and was its

head and front. What could he be tempted with? By a judgeship. Several vacancies on the Supreme Court were to be filled at the coming election. One of them could be offered to me.

A trusted Tammany stalwart came to see me. I knew him and knew that he was one of the inner council. I could have the Tammany nomination for the Supreme Court, he said, provided I resigned as Chief Counsel in the investigation. He stated further that although nominations to the Supreme Court had already been made there was still time for nominees to file declinations, and that if I would accept the nomination one of the nominees would file a declination and I would be substituted in his place. I promptly declined the offer.

They tried another approach. The District Attorney of New York County was in an embarrassing position vis a vis the investigation. We had laid before him stenographic records of the testimony of the Vice Squad members, Magistrates and others, putting the responsibility up to him, where it rightfully belonged, to determine whether the testimony warranted prosecution of any one. This resulted in the indictment of a number of the members of the Vice Squad. Now he was confronted with the necessity of trying these policemen. Here was his embarrassment. If he tried and convicted them it would not please Tammany. If he tried them and failed to get convictions it might be claimed that he deliberately let them out.

So he sought to put the burden on me. He offered to appoint me as an Assistant District Attorney, and to put me in charge of all prosecutions growing out of the investigation. This would relieve him and get me out of the investigation for, obviously, if I accepted the offer, I would have to resign as Chief Counsel in the investigation. I could not fill both positions. Needless to say, I declined that offer.

Tammany is not so easily thwarted. Since they couldn't win me by wooing they would try to undermine and destroy me. In that effort they found a ready-made weapon. It was at this time (early in 1931) that the Bank of the United States of which I was a director and counsel failed. The failure created a great stir in the community and Tammany took full advantage of it. They caused their adherents to fan the flame of prejudice against those connected with the bank. It engulfed me as well as the officials. Right, fairness and common sense were thrown to the wind. The same District Attorney who but a few weeks before offered to appoint me as his assistant, now caused me to be joined as a defendant in an indictment against certain officers of the bank, although my only connection with the transaction on which the indictment was based was to give legal advice to the bank officials.

In this situation I resigned as counsel in the investigation, and to this extent Tammany succeeded. But no man is indispensable. The investigation continued without me and developed into a city-wide overhauling, resulting in the resignation of Mayor Walker, the eclipse of Tammany, and the advent of LaGuardia.

The indictment against me was tried and resulted in a conviction. Upon appeal the conviction was reversed and the indictment dismissed. . . .

This conviction, though later reversed, was my only reward for a public service voluntarily performed without compensation. I was asked to conduct the investigation by the three Bar Associations; and yet, in my darkest hour, none of them uttered a word of encouragement to me, none of them voiced confidence in my innocence and integrity, and none had the courage to publicly proclaim that I was being crucified because of my participation in the investigation.

> Only one man and his partner had the courage and the fealty to defend me against this unjustified and cruel prosecution. I speak of the late John W. Davis, may God grant him eternal peace, and of his partner Theodore Kiendl. Without compensation and purely as evidence of their belief in my innocence, they acted as my counsel throughout my travail, and succeeded in vindicating me. Publicly I do now acknowledge the great debt I owe them which I can repay only in undying thanks.
>
> I write with bitterness of this episode in my career because the love of my life died as a result of it. Dear girl, why couldn't she have lived to see my vindication! There was never a moment during the almost three years of the cloud which enveloped me when I lost faith in my ultimate vindication, and that faith helped me to survive, but my darling, like the tender sweet flower she was, succumbed to the wind of adversity.
>
> During these many years since her death I have tried to observe the injunction not to hate but to forgive. If retribution is in the prerogative of God alone, I can only hope that those responsible for my sufferings will get their deserts. All but one of the Tammany cabal who plotted against me have passed on and that one's paying his debt here in drink and disease.

And so we leave the *Bank of the United States* case, with its examples and its teachings—its legends and legendary lawyers. Some of them we will meet again when we see them cross-examine and sum up. But as we go we leave a question: would the outcome of the case have been different, and consequently the lives of all of these people been changed, if Buckner had known about the impeaching material that Steuer would use to cross-examine Kresel. What would have been the impact on the case, on the defendants, on Kresel, and on the lawyers, if Buckner had known what Kresel had said to the grand jurors—or at least what the grand jury transcript revealed that he had said—and armed with that knowledge had dealt with those matters during his direct examination of Kresel—before Steuer hit him on cross?

ENDNOTES

1. We shall study the transcript of his trial in a later volume.
2. The interested reader might wish to consult the following works on the Seabury-Kresel investigation of Tammany: Herbert Mitgang, *The Man Who Rode the Tiger: The Life and Times of Samuel Seabury* (Philadelphia, 1963); Milton MacKaye, *The Tin Box Parade* (New York: McBride & Co., 1934).
3. Interestingly enough, the 1929 case involved the estate of Abraham L. Erlanger, the same Broadway producer who had been the central figure in the 1912 matter in which it was alleged that Steuer procured Miss Edith St. Clair's perjurious testimony.
4. Trial record in *People v. Marcus and Singer*, cited in M. Mayer, Emory Buckner 270 (1968).
5. The reader interested in the life and professional career of this wonderful lawyer is enthusiastically referred to William H. Harbaugh's magnificent biography of Davis, *Lawyer's Lawyer* (Oxford University Press, 1973).
6. For an excellent account of Buckner's life and career, see Martin Mayer's biography, *Emory Bucker* (Harper & Row, 1968).
7. Perhaps my view is colored by the accounts of my father, Samuel Stern, who "second chaired" Littleton in one of his last cases in the late 1930s. My father regaled me with stories of the legendary trial lawyer. I remember his account of Littleton's summation on behalf of their client, charged with murder, against whom a man named Ryan had testified.

   "Ryan, Ryan," my father would intone in Littleton's voice, "Ryan, Ryan, his soul will go hissing and howling into Hell." Nevertheless, my father and Littleton lost the case.

Stories like that, of course, propelled me toward the law. But for those who think I view Littleton through rose-colored glasses, I refer them to Lloyd Paul Stryker's famous work, *The Art of Advocacy*, and his references to Littleton, whom Stryker clearly believed to be the greatest advocate of his time. One of Littleton's greatest victories came in 1908. It was in his defense of Harry K. Thaw, who had shot and killed America's greatest architect, Stanford White, as he dined at a table in the Roof Top Restaurant of the original Madison Square Garden—which White had built. Littleton won an acquittal on the grounds of insanity. The prosecutor was the then-District Attorney William Travers Jerome, whose chief assistant and later law partner was . . . Isidor J. Kresel.

The fame of the case endures. It inspired novels and films (*The Girl in the Red Velvet Swing* and *Ragtime*). For an account of its history, see Richard O'Connor's *Courtroom Warrior, Combative Career of William Travers Jerome* (Little Brown, 1963).

8. M. Mayer, Emory Bucker 264 (1968). We can be certain that the story is accurate because Mr. Justice Harlan had much to do with authorizing the Mayer book, and wrote its introduction—while a sitting member of the Court.
9. *Id.* at 265, citing page 618 of the record on appeal.
10. *Id.* at 265, quoting Harlan and the record on appeal, *Tunney v. Mara*, page 626.

    Buckner won before the jury, but the appellate division reversed. So Tunney paid Mara $30,000 to settle. The more things change, the more they stay the same.
11. *Id.* at 245.
12. *Id.* at 271.
13. *See* Volume I, pages 59–61; *see also* n.36, at 68.
14. "End game" is defined at page 106 n.4 *supra* and demonstrated at page 386 *et seq. infra*.

15. F. Wellman, Success in Court 357, 358 (1942). The emphasis is mine.
16. For the interested reader, the entire question and answer are reproduced below.

> Q: Will you state what you now know of your own knowledge concerning those negotiations and particularly as to why Marcus, Mitchell and Singer made the undertaking in their individual capacities as part of this proposed merger?
>
> A: Mr. Kugel at this time was chairman of the Board of Directors of the Municipal Bank. He was also attorney for Mr. Barnett who was the president of the bank. Mr. Barnett was then on his death bed and he was actually confined at Johns-Hopkins Hospital in Baltimore. Mr. Kugel stated that he felt as representing Mr. Barnett, that he would not advise and could not advise Mr. Barnett to agree to the merger of the two institutions unless Mr. Barnett, who realized that he was on his death bed, could be assured that at least a part of the units that he would get in the merger of the two institutions in exchange for his stock in the Municipal Bank would be taken off his hands.
>
> At that time the units were selling at $225 per unit. Mr. Kugel therefore insisted as a condition precedent on him, Kugel, agreeing to the merger of the two institutions, that at least 10,000 units of those that Barnett was to get out of the exchange should be bought from him at $225. Mr. Kugel asked for a higher price, but finally the $225 price was agreed to.

> Mr. Kugel was advised that the agreement would be made by Bankus Corporation to take these units. Kugel said no, he was acting in a fiduciary capacity, he didn't know much about the Bankus Corporation, he did know Mitchell and Marcus and Singer, he thought they were rich men, and so he said that for the protection of his client he wanted the obligation of these individuals rather than of a corporation.
>
> That is the reason why this agreement was made by these men. But before it became operative the matter was presented to the Board of Directors of Bankus, as you have read, and passed on by them.

17. For those interested, the remainder of the exchange is as follows:

> THE COURT: I would like to know what the purpose of the photostat is. What is the purpose of it? If you have one photostat of an exhibit admitted you might just as well offer 50 different ones that have been taken at different times. What is the purpose?
>
> MR. BUCKNER: Does not your Honor recall that over and over again that you ruled—
>
> THE COURT: I do not care what I ruled on other matters. I want to hear you on this matter.
>
> MR. BUCKNER: On this particular matter I want the jury to see a photostatic copy of the memorandum of Mr. Kresel made at the time, to see what it looks like, to see what is there, just as any other exhibit in the case. I can ask each juryman to look at it.

THE COURT: Has there been any evidence that this witness did not make this memorandum at that time? Are you anticipating some evidence that has not been introduced up to the present time, that it was not made at the time of the interview?

MR. BUCKNER: Not the slightest. But I have—

THE COURT: What is the purpose of offering a photostat? There is no dispute up to the present time that this was not made by him right at that interview.

MR. BUCKNER: The purpose of offering the photostats is so that each juryman can see the exhibit, instead of passing it from hand to hand.

THE COURT: That is the only purpose?

MR. BUCKNER: Yes, sir.

THE COURT: Well, that is a different matter. All right. I thought, Mr. Buckner, you were anticipating some testimony that the witness had not made this memorandum at that time. That is what I thought. If it is only for the purpose of convenience so far as the jury is concerned, of course, I do not see any objection to it.

MR. BUCKNER: Well, we are saving time.

THE COURT: Well, we lost a lot of time through misunderstanding. Then I will withdraw the characterization given to the photostatic copies as bolstering up the original exhibit. It was said under a misapprehension of the facts.

MR. BUCKNER: All right. I do not think your Honor understood it.

THE COURT: Well, I did not. If it is only for the convenience of the jury, all right, have 20 photostats of every exhibit so that they can all have one.

MR. BUCKNER: I want to read it out loud, but I would request the jurymen to examine it for just a moment before I ask another question.

THE WITNESS: Mr. Buckner, may I have one of those, because I have nothing before me.

MR. BUCKNER: Yes.

THE WITNESS: Thank you. I have one now.

THE COURT: Now, have you offered this in evidence?

MR. BUCKNER: It has been received, your Honor.

18. The court agreed and set aside Herbert's conviction. M. Mayer, Emory Bucker 277 (1968).
19. Of all the *dramatis personae*, Buckner is the one best remembered. Perhaps this is due to his founding one of the great New York City law firms—Dewey, Ballentine. Even more likely, his name has endured best because of the devotion of his young lawyers—men like Harlan, who rose to the nation's highest court, and J. Edward Lumbard, who became chief judge of the United States Court of Appeals for the Second Circuit. These men and others like them kept Buckner's name alive and his memory fresh.

    Today, most of Buckner's "boys" are gone. Few are the lawyers who remain who saw him work—or even knew him. The Federal Bar Association gives an Emory R. Buckner Award at its annual Thanksgiving luncheon in New York City. Today more than 1,500 lawyers attend. But few of them know anything much about the life and career of the man in whose name the medal is each year presented to an outstanding lawyer or judge in New York, New Jersey, or Connecticut.

20. W. Harbaugh, Lawyer's Lawyer 306 (1973).

21. *Id.* at 310, quoting letter of Kresel to Davis, November 23, 1933.

Chapter Seven
Exhibits

PURPOSE

There are two basic purposes to your exhibits: (1) to put information into the record and (2) to corroborate oral testimony in order to give the testimony greater weight in the direct and to make cross-examination more difficult. Of the two, the second is more often the reason for an exhibit, or should be.

Exhibits should be used as footnotes to authenticate what your witness is relating—much like footnotes to the text of a law review article—and they should be used in profusion. We have seen Emory Buckner employ this technique during his direct of Kresel as he used the Kresel notes of conferences with the banking authorities to footnote the truth of Kresel's testimony about those conferences.

If your witness says he was in Chicago on May 11, produce the canceled ticket, or the hotel bill. No matter that it is not a critical point. If you thought it important enough for him to swear to it, it is important enough for you to *demonstrate* to the jury that the testimony is truthful and accurate *and that you have checked*! It is also thereafter virtually impossible to impeach your witness on that particular point.

This sort of corroboration of even unimportant details is significant because it gets the jurors used to crediting the witness and because when it comes to the big issue of the case you may not be able to offer that kind of corroborative evidence. Then the jurors will have to go just on the testimony—and you want them in the groove. The deeper and longer they are in that groove, the more difficult it will be for an adversary to move them on cross-examination.

To achieve this footnote quality with exhibits, the trial lawyer must learn how to authenticate them with ease and speed. Lengthy, detailed "foundations" are boring, turgid, and dull (the name of America's largest law firm) and form arteriosclerosis in the arteries of advocacy.

AUTHENTICATION—LAYING A FOUNDATION

A hallmark of the inexperienced attorney is his belief that authentication is a difficult task, or one that should be done with detailed precision. Nothing could be further from the truth. Indeed, as we shall see, experienced attorneys learn that fixing on details of anything they do not have to is frequently *dangerous* to a witness and bogs down the testimony.

Nonetheless, the inexperienced attorney believes that "laying a foundation" is a mountainous task, one that requires a myriad—or at least a pyramid—of questions, and he is encouraged by "how to" primers in this creation of stumbling blocks to his own free passage on direct. And so, the inexperienced lawyer stands in the well of the courtroom laying on cement with a trowel, layers upon layers of "foundations," building a veritable Tower of Babble, to the immense boredom if not the outright pain of all within the room.

How to Lay a Foundation

In truth, most exhibits can be foundated with just two questions. This is the first one:

1. I show you what has been marked (plaintiff's/defendant's/government's/state's) exhibit for identification and I ask you whether or not you can identify it?

The witness will of course (one hopes) answer in one word, "yes." The next question is even shorter and simpler:

2. What is it?

And then the witness says—and, hopefully, says it briefly—and that does it! In the overwhelming majority of cases, you have now done all that you *legally* need to do to have the exhibit admitted. At this point the spotlight swings to the other side of the courtroom. It becomes the other lawyer's problem to do something to *stop* the admission. And if he does not do that something (which we will come to later) after you next say, "I offer exhibit ____ into evidence," your exhibit will almost surely be received into evidence. And that is all there is to it.

But, the inexperienced doubter may ask, how can that be? Isn't the witness's answer authenticating the exhibit likely to be conclusory, and doesn't that answer itself have to be authenticated by showing how the witness knows what he is talking about—something like this?

> Q: Mr. Jones, I show you what has been marked plaintiff's exhibit 32 for identification and I ask you whether or not you can identify it?
>
> A. Yes.
>
> Q: What is it?
>
> A. That is the airplane ticket I bought to go to Chicago on May 11.
>
> Q: Who did you buy it from?
>
> A. The Bergenfield Travel Agency.
>
> Q: Who at the agency did you deal with?
>
> A. Roger Badou.
>
> Q: When did you buy the ticket?
>
> A. On May 10th.
>
> Q: Did you order it by mail or by phone or did you physically go in?
>
> A. I ordered it by telephone.
>
> Q: Well, how can you identify this particular ticket as the one that you bought on the 10th and used on the 11th of May?
>
> A. *Because, you idiot, my name is on it! See, it's right there!*

It must surely be obvious to everyone that a great deal of time has been wasted preparing the way for the receipt of a scrap of paper whose significance to the case is likely to be little more than a footnote of credibility to the testimony of the witness, who has sworn that he did in fact travel to Chicago on

May 11th. Nonetheless, and as turgid as it is, the *legal* explanation for why the first two questions and answers alone suffice to authenticate the document must be given. And so we turn to two of the Federal Rules of Evidence, 901 (which deals with how to authenticate) and 104 (which tells us who decides whether something has been authenticated, and how and by how much he does it).[1]

Rule 901 begins by providing us with a test for admissibility that is no test at all. Watch:

> 901(a): *General Provision.* The requirement of authentication or identification as a condition precedent to admissibility is satisfied by evidence sufficient to support a finding that the matter in question is what its proponent claims.

Ah, but who makes the finding, and by how much evidence? In other words, how much evidence must there be, and what kind of evidence need it be before whoever makes the "finding" of admissibility is allowed to move it? The rule itself is silent. But the notes of the advisory committee refer us to Rule 104(b).[2]

Rule 104 governs the issue of admissibility. While not generally recognized or understood, Rule 104(a) and Rule 104(b) set forth two entirely different tests and procedures for admissibility. Under Rule 104(a) the judge makes all necessary factual findings, or is supposed to, as to whether the evidence is admissible under the rules. Under Rule 104(b), the judge makes no factual finding but admits the evidence if the jury could find that the legal evidence is relevant (although the differences between the two tests are not, in my view, capable of precise definition in terms of which test applies to what kinds of evidentiary offers).

Rule 104(a)provides:

> (a) *Questions of Admissibility Generally.*
> Preliminary questions concerning the qualification of a person to be a witness, the existence of a privilege, *or the admissibility of evidence shall be*

> *determined by the court, subject to the provisions of subdivision* (b) . . . . (Emphasis added.)

This provision clearly applies, for example, if one offers a hearsay statement as an excited utterance under Rule 803(2). Who decides if the declarant was excited? The judge, under Rule 104(a). How sure does the judge have to be that the declarant was excited?

The rule is silent as to the burden of proof under Rule 104(a) or as to how sure the judge must be as to disputed facts before making a finding, but the cases now conclusively hold that the judge need only be satisfied by the preponderance standard.[3]

What sort of material may the judge consider in his "determination" that the test of 803(2), the excited utterance exception to the hearsay rule, has been met? Anything that he wants to! In making the 104(a) determination, the court is not bound by the rules of evidence—and so Rule 104(a) *specifically* provides:

> In making its determination it is not bound by the rules of evidence except those with respect to privileges.

Suppose, in our little hypothetical, the out-of-court declarant says, "I just saw the defendant run a red light and run into the plaintiff, *and I am very excited*!"

In deciding the issue of whether the declarant was excited, the judge may utilize the contents of the proffered statement in determining its admissibility because the Rules of Evidence do not confine the judge to legal evidence in making evidentiary determinations.

That means, for example, when the judge considers the admissibility of an out-of-court declarant's statement under the co-conspirator rule, 801(d)(2)(E),[4] the judge decides by a preponderance of the evidence whether that evidence is admissible and in making his determination includes the proffered out-of-court statement. He then decides if he believes the conditions of 801(d)(2)(E) have been met; that is, is it more likely than not that there was a conspiracy and that this was a statement in furtherance of that conspiracy, based on all the evidence in the case, *including the proffered statement itself.*

So much for 104(a). But Rule 901, the rule of authentication, refers us to Rule 104(b), and that is a *different* test.

> Rule 104(b) *Relevancy Conditioned on Fact.* When the relevancy of evidence depends upon the fulfillment of a condition of fact, the court shall admit it upon or subject to, the introduction of evidence sufficient to support a finding of the fulfillment of the condition.

The first difference between 104(a) and 104(b) is that while the judge makes a finding of fact under 104(a) by a preponderance (that the declarant was excited 803(2); that the declarant was a co-conspirator with a party and his statement was in the course of and in furtherance of a conspiracy, 801(d)(2)(E)), under 104(b) *the judge makes no factual finding.* He decides only whether there is sufficient evidence in the record from which the jury could conclude that the evidence is relevant. What does all this gibberish mean?

Well, let us take an example. A witness on the stand says she recognizes the defendant's handwriting on a document, and the document is offered into evidence. If it is the defendant's writing, the document is admissible.[5]

If it is not the defendant's writing, it is not admissible. But who decides? Not the judge. This is a 104(b) determination. All the judge does is to decide whether there is sufficient evidence in the record of the witness's familiarity with the defendant's handwriting from which the jury can conclude that it was the defendant's. The same 104(b) analysis would apply if the witness claimed to recognize the defendant's voice on the telephone and was asked to testify about the conversation.[6]

901 authentications of physical evidence and oral communications *tend* to be 104(b) determinations. That is, the judge decides whether the jury *could* find that the conditions of

admissibility are met. And under this analysis the issue is *usually* the personal knowledge of the witness on the stand. In other words, a Rule 602 issue. Rule 602 provides:

> A witness may not testify to a matter unless evidence is introduced *sufficient to support a finding* that the witness has personal knowledge of the matter. *Evidence to prove personal knowledge may, but need not, consist of the witness's own testimony.* (Emphasis added.)

Notice the similarity between the language of 901(a) and 104(b) and 602, "evidence sufficient to support a finding."

Finally, we turn back to Rule 901, the rule of authentication. What kind of evidence is "sufficient to support a finding" that the preferred evidence is what the proponent claims?

> Rule 901(b) *Illustrations*. By way of illustration only, *and not by way of limitation*, the following are examples of authentication or identification conforming with the requirements of this rule:
>
> (1) *Testimony by a witness with knowledge*. Testimony that a matter is what it is claimed to be. (Emphasis added.)

Notice also the confluence between the personal knowledge test of 602 and the illustration of 901(b)(1). The witness may by his own bold statement authenticate his own knowledge by his own proclamation. Then, *it is for the jury, not the judge, to decide*.

We have threaded our way through these rules to provide the intellectual underpinnings for our earlier conclusory statement (which all seasoned lawyers know to be true based on experience) that most exhibits can be authenticated with two questions, and nearly all of the rest of them can be done in three, in which the witness claims in conclusory terms that he recognizes the proffered exhibit and the attorney then offers it on that basis.

Photographs

No photographer need be called. All that is needed is a witness with personal knowledge of how the depiction looked at the time of the photograph who swears that the photograph is a truthful and accurate reproduction. This never requires more than three questions:

> Q: Mr. Brown, I show you what has been marked plaintiff's exhibit 32 for identification and I ask you if you can identify it.
>
> A: Yes.
>
> Q: What is it?
>
> A: It is a photograph of my Buick car.
>
> Q: Is that photograph a fair and accurate depiction of the way your Buick looked on May 11th?
>
> A: Yes.

And that is that. Nothing more *needs* to be done before offering the photograph. Of course you may do more if you *elect* to, but do not ask more questions because you think you have to. All you will achieve is a bogging down of your own examination.

You might decide you want to ask more questions in order to use the authenticating process as an argument and an opportunity for causing repetition. For example:

> Q: Now, you say this is an accurate depiction of the way your Buick looked on May 11th?
>
> A: Yes.
>
> Q: Well, was the right side of the car caved in the way it is shown on May 11th?
>
> A: Yes.
>
> Q: Was the car in that condition on May 10th?
>
> A: No.

> Q: Well, how about today? Is the car still in the condition depicted in this photograph today?
>
> A: No. We have since had it repaired.

And so it goes. The authentication process becomes a tool in the arsenal of the advocate.

Unfortunately, that is not the way we teach the young students at the bar. Here, for example, is a passage from Professor Edward J. Imwinkelreid's *Evidentiary Foundations*. Note as we go through the various exercises that the problem of authentication is laid out in four tasks by the Professor, and that the student or novice lawyer is given a script to follow, with each task numbered.[7]

> THE VERIFICATION OF PHOTOGRAPHS
>
> I. *Still Photographs*
>
> Like other articles, still photographs must be authenticated or verified. In the past, some courts insisted that the photographer appear as the sponsoring witness. Modernly, the prevailing view is that any person familiar with the scene or object depicted may verify the photograph.
>
> The foundational elements are as follows:
>
> 1. The witness is familiar with the object or scene.
> 2. The witness explains the basis for his or her familiarity with the object or scene.
> 3. The witness recognizes the object or scene in the photograph.
> 4. The photograph is a "fair," "accurate," "true," or "good" depiction of the object or scene at the relevant time.

The student is now given the problem and is also given a script to work from:

> Our fact situation is a civil tort action arising from a collision. The collision occurred at the intersection of A and Third Streets. The plaintiff calls a

witness to verify a photograph of the intersection. The witness has already identified himself as Mr. Donald Adams. The accident occurred in 1977.

P WHERE do you work? (2)
W Downtown.
P WHERE downtown? (2)
W I'm a teller at the First National Bank on Third Street.
P WHERE is the bank located on Third Street? (2)
W I think it's the 400 block. The bank is between A and B Streets.
P HOW long have you worked there? (2)
W A good seven years.
P Your honor, I request that this be marked plaintiff's exhibit number three for identification.
J The record will so reflect.
P I request permission to approach the witness.
J Permission granted.
P I now hand you plaintiff's exhibit number three for identification. WHAT is it? (3)
W It's a photograph of the intersection of A and Third Streets.
P HOW can you recognize it? (2)
W As I said, I've worked in that area for years.

The witness knows what the lawyer has apparently forgotten—that this testimony is repetitive. That is what he means by the "as I said." That does not, however, deter our scripted advocate.

P HOW often have you passed that intersection? (2)
W I couldn't give you a figure. I've been there hundreds of times.

Again and again we hear the same thing. The witness already said he knows the corner and has worked in the area for years. But we go on and on and on, in a never-ending stream of discourse. One must wonder how interesting this material can be for the jurors and, if it is boring them, what those jurors are doing throughout.

P WHAT perspective or viewpoint does this photograph show? (3)
W Let's see. Third Street runs north-south. A Street runs east-west.
P WHICH corner are you on? (3)
W You're on the southwest corner.
P In WHICH direction are you facing? (3)
W You're facing north; you're looking up Third Street.

No one can possibly follow this. Only the lawyer and the witness can see the photograph. It is forbidden to the jurors because it is not yet in evidence. But we go on and on some more.

P HOW accurate is this photograph? (4)
W Very. It's a good, true depiction as far as I can tell.

This last question is incomprehensible. But the answer saves it. But the examiner does not agree to be saved. He must turn clarity into murkiness.

P HOW accurate does it show the intersection as it was in 1977? (4)
W Well, it's a good photograph for that purpose. I worked downtown then, and I think it shows roughly how the intersection looked then.

The lawyer who doesn't know when to quit is back in trouble. And that leads him to bury us all in a mass of unwanted detail. We can only imagine the state of mind of the hapless jurors who are listening to this close examination of something that they cannot see.

P HOW has the intersection changed since 1977? (4)

W Some of the signs have changed; businesses come and go. However, the intersection itself really hasn't changed. As best I can recall, it's the same size, the street markings are the same, and traffic flows the same way.

In my opinion, the lawyer has diminished his evidence. He should have stuck with just the three questions that were necessary to get the exhibits in. If he wanted to do more, he could have done more after it was in evidence and while showing it to the jurors.

This overquestioning and overfoundating is recommended in the same work for even the most simple exhibits, and even if they are distinctive by reason of their markings and thus easy to identify. Here is the recommended procedure by Professor Imwinkelreid, replete with the tasks and the checkoff list.[8]

ELEMENTS OF THE FOUNDATION

The foundation for ready identifiability is very short:

1. The object has a unique characteristic.
2. The witness observed the characteristic on a previous occasion.
3. The witness identifies the exhibit as the object.
4. The witness rests the identification on his or her present recognition of the characteristic.
5. As best he or she can tell, the exhibit is in the same condition as it was when he or she initially received the object. . . . .

SAMPLE FOUNDATIONS

The fact situation for the ready identifiability foundation is a civil tort case. The complaint alleges that the defendant assaulted the plaintiff with a knife. The witness is a police officer who investigated the complaint. The proponent is the plaintiff. The officer has just testified that he reported to the scene and began inspecting the scene.

P WHAT did you do during this inspection?
W I was looking for any evidence.
P WHAT, if anything, did you find?"

Not "What did you find?" or "Did you find anything?" but "What, *if anything*, did you find?"

W I found a knife answering the description the plaintiff, Ms. Brown, gave me.

How he is allowed to say this is puzzling. It sounds enough like hearsay to surely draw some fire.

P WHERE did you find it?
W Right at the corner of the building where the alleged assault occurred.

How the witness is allowed to say this is doubly puzzling. Whether or not what Mrs. Brown said to him earlier was hearsay, this testimony is a mass of hearsay topped with a conclusory cherry.

P WHAT did you do with the knife? (1)
W I followed standing operating procedure.

Very helpful. Note, up until now no tasks have been achieved. We are now on task (1). Let us hope we can pick up some speed.

P WHAT is that procedure? (1)
W I marked it for identification.
P HOW did you do that? (1)
W In the case of a relatively inexpensive item such as this one, I scratched my initials and the date onto the wooden handle.

His view of the value of the item may be right or it may be wrong. It is not clear how he gets to say this. After all, for all the officer knows this may well be Jim Bowie's knife. In any event, we are ready to get on with task (2).

P WHEN did you do this? (2)
W As soon as I found it.
P HOW much time passed between your discovery of this knife and your marking it? (2)
W No more than a couple of minutes.

Why do we have to ask this—or for that matter any of this? Only because the attorney is insecure and continues to nail down what has been proven beyond a shadow of a doubt.

P Your honor, I request that this be marked plaintiff's exhibit number two for identification.
J It will be so marked.
P Please let the record reflect that I am showing the exhibit to the opposing counsel.
J It will so reflect.
P I request permission to approach the witness.
J Permission granted.

It may be seen that the judge is an automaton intoning permission to requests framed in legalese, which demonstrates that the lawyer is a real lawyer and the jury should not be somnolent. In any case, we are now ready for task (3).

P I now hand you plaintiff's exhibit number two for identification. WHAT is it? (3)
W It's the knife I found.

The lawyer has done it . . . finally. But is he content? Of course not.

P HOW can you recognize it? (4)
W As I testified, I marked my initials and the date on the handle. They're right there.

The witness is correct to treat the lawyer as deaf and blind. In any event, task (4) is done. And now for task (5), which is totally unnecessary.

P WHAT condition is the exhibit in? (5)
W It's in good condition.

Very helpful indeed. Just what this means is beyond understanding. But is the examiner done? Of course not.

P HOW has it changed since you found it at the scene? (5)
W It doesn't *appear* to have changed at all. It *seems* to be in the same condition. (Emphasis added.)

The lawyer by this last useless salvo has done nothing but perhaps weaken his own position. At long last he is ready to offer the exhibit to the comatose courtroom.

P Your honor, I now offer plaintiff's exhibit number two for identification into evidence as plaintiff's exhibit number two.
J It will be received.
P I request permission to hand the exhibit to the jurors for their inspection.
J Permission granted.

No one can teach or do trial work by the numbers. Trying cases is not a paint-by-number exercise. In the end, handling a witness cannot be blueprinted any more than an angler can diagram the process of catching and landing a fish. There are general rules, to be sure. But at some point you have to learn how to feel what is happening at the other end of the line.

Laborious and tedious authentications will foul your line. And, once the witness states in conclusory terms that he does know and can identify the object, it is usually pointless and frequently dangerous to probe these statements by asking detailed questions like, "How do you know?" or, "Are you sure?" or, "Has it changed in the last 2 years?" and so forth and so on. That sort of probing ties witnesses to details and places their feet in cement. These interrogations are the work of the cross-examiner, not the direct examiner.

Remember, once a bare foundation has been laid, that is, once the witness has said enough under Rule 104(b) cum 602, cum 901 to support a finding by the jury, the item is admissible—*and then it becomes the adversary's problem*!

When you offer the item, the adversary has only three choices. He may not object, in which case the exhibit will come in. He may object, in which case it will either come in, or the judge will ask for more foundation—in which case you will get another opportunity. Or, finally, the adversary may ask for a voir dire, that is, a junior cross in the midst of your direct that is—or at least is supposed to be—limited to testing the admissibility of the preferred exhibit.[9]

Most voir dires are unsuccessful. In the great majority, the end of the voir dire sees the admission of the exhibit. The cross-examiner plows through most of the detailed, petty, and boring questions—which the wise direct has avoided—searching for minor handholds, uncertainties, and so forth in a general waste of time. For in the great majority of the instances, *as long as the witness insists that he knows whatever is being offered is what he claims it to be, it will be a jury question under Rule 104(b) and the exhibit will be received.* It is for precisely this reason that wise cross-examiners begin their voir dire examinations something like this, "It may be that I will have no objection to the exhibit, your Honor, but I would like to have a few questions on voir dire (or admissibility, etc.)." And then the examiner, as we shall see, often takes the voir dire as an opportunity to do far more than merely challenge the particular offer of evidence.

As I went through some years of cases, I began to learn these lessons and kept my authentications down to a minimum of questioning, recognizing that they were usually the side and not the main show. I also would sometimes challenge my adversary. Let us use Professor Imwinkelreid's last hypothetical to demonstrate this technique.

> Q: Officer, after you arrived at the scene did you examine the area?
>
> A: Yes.
>
> Q: Did you find anything?
>
> A: Yes.

Q: I show you what has been marked plaintiff's exhibit one for identification and I ask you if you can identify it?

A: Yes. That's the knife I found at the scene.

Q: Officer, do you have a way of knowing that? That this is the knife that you found?

A: Yes.

COUNSEL: I offer plaintiff's one for identification into evidence.

And now what will happen? In just three questions we have nailed down what might otherwise have taken a dozen. And what is the adversary going to do? He knows the cop has his initials on the handle. Is he really going to be so suicidal as to appear to challenge the exhibit, knowing that he will meet a sure and certain defeat at the end of the exercise? Well, then, suppose he says "No objection," and either because the judge looks uncertain or because I do not want some worry wart on the jury to be uncertain, I desire to nail the point away. Then even after the knife is in evidence I go ahead anyway.

Q: Officer, will you please tell his Honor and the jury how you know that this is the exact knife that you found on that street nine months ago?

And then it will roll in like the Mississippi.

A: Because I put my initials and the date on the handle.

There are, however, some exhibits that absolutely require careful foundating. As to these there is no choice. To meet the legal necessity for admissibility, a careful chain of custody must be forged, link by link, to admit fungible exhibits.

Fungible Exhibits

If an object has no distinctive characteristics it cannot be identified on the basis of appearance. If it cannot be identified on the basis of its bald appearance, then it cannot be authenticated solely on the basis of memory. If the policeman had not placed his initials on the knife, then—unless this was a very unusual looking knife indeed—he would not be able to single out this as the one and only knife that he found from the world's storehouse of knives. The same is true for characteristics of objects that can easily be changed.

Suppose, for example, the policeman had found an ordinary glassine envelope containing drugs and merely placed his initial on it. If a half year later he were to attempt to identify that envelope solely on the basis of that marking, it might cause problems. Not that it necessarily should. We often forget that on the offer of evidence we are not required to prove anything to a certainty or even beyond a reasonable doubt. All that is required is evidence sufficient to support a finding by the jury (Rule 104(b)) by a more-likely-than-not standard that our particular burden has been met.

Nonetheless, because judges as well as lawyers tend to forget that we are dealing with a standard that is hospitable to the receipt of evidence, courts frequently require a fair amount of evidence to support the admission of exhibits that the authenticating witness could not possibly remember and therefore cannot have the requisite personal knowledge about under Rule 602.

The introduction of these "fungible" types of exhibits requires—heaven help us—the establishment of a chain of custody. The attorney must trace the possession of the item from the time of its discovery to every hand that touched it and through every depository wherein it reposed. Procedures for withdrawing evidence from safes may have to be gone into. Discussions of locked cabinets may have to be undertaken. All in all, if there is anything that can be done in the pretrial phase of the case to "distinctivize" such an object, one would be well advised to do so and to thereby save the agony of "the chain." One technique is to keep the exhibit in the custody or control of just one person. At least that will limit the number of witnesses necessary to call in order to establish the chain of custody.

Tape-Recorded Conversations

No chain of possession need be established for a spool of tape or a cassette of a recorded conversation. All that is needed is a participant, or an overhearer prepared to testify that he has listened to the recording and that it is a fair and accurate recording of the conversation that he participated in or overheard. Foundating can be accomplished in less than half a dozen questions. The answers will be conclusory, to be sure. And it is also to be doubted that anyone can remember word for word a conversation they participated in or overheard for comparison purposes with the tape. Nonetheless, if the following testimony is given, the odds are that the offer will be accepted.

> Q: Now you told us that you participated in a conversation with A and B on May 11th, is that correct?
>
> A: Yes, that is true.
>
> Q: I now show you what has been marked _____ exhibit ____. Have you listened to that cassette?
>
> A: Yes.
>
> Q: Is that a fair and accurate recording of the conversation which you yourself participated in on May 11th?
>
> A: Yes.
>
> COUNSEL: I offer it in evidence.

It will now likely become the adversary's problem. And it is fair that it should. For while the witness cannot indeed recall every word from May 11th to compare it against the recording that he did hear, he was not asked to. He was asked if the recording was a fair and accurate one. He certainly can remember if significant parts have been edited out or inserted. No one is required to prove that the tape is word-for-word accurate *beyond a reasonable doubt*—just that it probably is.

The same is true for transcripts of the conversations. In just a few questions a transcript can be authenticated by having someone testify that he compared the transcript to the audio version and that the transcript is accurate.

EXPOSING JURORS TO THE CONTENTS OF EXHIBITS

There are only two ways to transmit the contents of exhibits to jurors: to read them or to show them to the jury.

The more important the exhibit, the more you will want to show it to the jurors. Recall Buckner, in 1931, fighting with the judge for the opportunity to show his exhibit to the jurors. As we have seen, under the principles of vividness, we retain more of what we see as well as hear (*see* Volume I, pages 121–123). There are many methods of showing exhibits to the jurors, and some of them are not mutually exclusive.

To begin with, exhibits can be passed hand to hand. This is not a preferred way if there are a number of exhibits to be passed throughout the examination, because the examination should pause until the exhibit has made the rounds of the last juror. The reason for that is simple: if you keep your examination going during the passing of the exhibit, you are by implication suggesting that one of the two, the exhibit or the testimony, is expendable, since the jurors cannot both listen and read at the same time. Therefore, testimony should usually be halted until the viewing is completed. For that reason, the individual passing of exhibits should be held to a minimum, if possible. And for that same reason, many judges will not be inclined to permit large numbers of exhibits to be passed among jurors, one by one, if the direct examination will thereby be unduly extended.

In my opinion, the best method to introduce exhibits into the jury box is to make enough copies so that each juror can have one. Then there is no delay while exhibits are passed hand to hand. Again, recall Buckner in 1931 with his photostatic copies ready to pass out amongst the jurors. If the exhibit and the testimony warrant it, the jurors may be permitted to keep hold of the exhibit—after their initial reading—as testimony concerning or utilizing the exhibit is developed.[10]

Of course, the individual practices of courts and even judges within the same court vary. Some judges permit jurors to have exhibit books in which copies of the exhibits are compiled, while others do not. Some courts permit jurors to make notes, while others do not. The practice of the judge must be learned by the trial lawyer *before* he begins his case.

Some trial lawyers, myself included, like to use blowups of evidence during their examination of witnesses. Such enlargements can be very useful illustrative aids placed in a large stand or easel in plain view while testimony concerning the exhibit is developed. It is even possible for the attorney or the witness to accent portions of the blowup with a grease pencil as the testimony is given. These markings on the blowup may confine it to being only an illustrative aid, rather than "evidence," although I have seen courts admit marked-up enlargements into evidence as well.

The various methods of showing exhibits to jurors are *not* mutually exclusive. Nothing in the rules prevents an attorney from both passing out copies of an exhibit *and* using an enlargement of that exhibit during the examination—even as the jurors hold copies in their hands.

Some lawyers have become fond of overhead projectors, using screens and so forth to project copies of documents after they are in evidence. I see no principled objection to such devices, although I do not use them myself. First, they seem a bit fancy and contrived. Second, I find them harder to manage than good old fashioned blowups. Third—and most important—mechanical devices do not work for me and I do not know how to deal with them when they fail. I therefore try to keep things simple, particularly in the well of the court—where I find that Murphy's law reigns supreme.

In the interest of saving time, trial lawyers learn that not every exhibit can be shown to the jurors. Many documents—or portions of them—will have to be read to the jury in the interest of keeping things moving along.

If something is to be read to the jury, there is only one person who should read it—*you*! On the odds, you are the best reader that you have in the courtroom. If you entrust this task to your witnesses, you can bank on the fact that they will tangle up the reading—miss a word, mumble, leave something out, and so forth. And when they do, you may not be able to have the exhibit re-read. "Asked and answered!" your adversary will cry. And from that point on, the future is in the lap of the gods.

On the other hand, if during your reading you do make an error—as will happen—you can offer an apology, "Gosh, folks, I guess I messed that up. Let me see if I can get that right." On the odds, you will be able to immediately launch into a re-reading.

Where should you stand when you read something to the jury? At the same spot as where you opened. Face the jury. Stand *at least* six feet back. Position yourself in the middle of the box, favoring neither juror 1 nor juror 6, and read the material to them.

TIMING THE OFFER OF YOUR EXHIBITS

It is essential to learn when *not* to offer an exhibit into evidence. Many of us are so mesmerized by the task of sufficiently foundating that we almost automatically make the offer the moment that the foundating is complete. But once the foundation for a successful offer has been completed—usually with just two questions, as we have seen—the exhibit may be offered any time thereafter.

The timing of the offer is critical. Why? Because the offer of an exhibit on direct-examination opens the door to a voir dire examination by the adversary. At a *minimum*, this can cause an unwanted and distracting breach in the presentation of the direct testimony. At a maximum, however, such mini cross-examinations may provide your adversary opportunities to raise subjects and issues at a time when you do not want the jury to hear them. For remember, "the organization of what you present is as persuasive as what you have to say."

The Dangers of Voir Dire

The subject of cross-examination in general is reserved for a later work, but it is impossible to discuss the dangers of voir dire to direct examination without invading some of the provinces of that land.

Whenever evidence is offered against a party, his attorney has a right to challenge its admissibility. And, although many trial lawyers do not think in these terms, that right exists as to the offer of evidence by *oral* testimony as well as by documentary or physical evidence.[11]

There is no specific provision in the Federal Rules of Evidence authorizing a cross-examination on the offer of evidence.[12] Nonetheless, the right to a voir dire to test the admissibility of the proffered evidence is universally recognized in virtually every federal and state court.

Such cross-examinations—for that is what they are—can take one of two basic forms: the first is an examination in the presence of the jury; the second is an examination with the jury out of the room. Each of these represents separate dangers to the direct examiner, and to his witness.

If the jury remains in the room while the cross-examiner does his voir dire, the cross-examiner has an opportunity not merely to break the flow of the direct but to score affirmative points as well. Consider for a moment the method and the scope of such voir dire examinations.

To begin with, they *are* cross-examinations, in which adversary counsel are indeed permitted to use leading questions. And leading questions are *not* designed to elicit information *from* the witness. Leading questions are—or should be—designed for the lawyer to *give* information to the jury *through* the witness. In short, by utilizing a voir dire, your adversary can seize control of your witness in the midst of your direct examination.

And what of the scope of this cross-examination? Well, clearly, the adversary may ask any question that relates to the admissibility of the evidence he is challenging. Does that include the material that goes to the credibility of the witness's answers? Most attorneys would instinctively respond, "No!" But why not? As we have seen, the majority of exhibits will be identified on the basis of the personal knowledge of the witness. And the credibility of that identification will be at issue.

Be that as may be, however, if the jury is excused from the room during the voir dire examination, then that proceeding can be converted into a discovery deposition by an adversary in the midst of the case. Why? *Because with the jury out of the room no answer to any question can hurt the cross-examiner on the merits of the case.*

That is why adverse attorneys love to get the jurors out of the courtroom during their voir dire examinations. With the jury absent, they exercise the typical cross-examination techniques of leading and control only on the narrow issue of admissibility. But then they can *explore* other material with open-ended questions designed to ferret out the witness's positions, all without risk to the examiner because of the empty jury box. Any answer under such questioning is of no use to the direct examiner—since it would at best be only a prior consistent statement once the jurors return to the room—but can be useful to the cross-examiner as a prior inconsistent statement when he conducts his cross-examination in chief.

To be sure, judges are reluctant to excuse juries during voir dire examination because much of the questioning will later be repeated in the presence of the jury during the cross-examination in chief. And to be sure, as well, judges do *try* to confine voir dire examinations to the narrow question raised by the issue of admissibility. But in practice voir dire examinations *are* conducted outside the jurors' presence—and should be so conducted when the examination must delve into the substance of the challenged evidence.[13] And lawyers *do* routinely get to question more broadly than the strict limitations of the issues. In any event, even a highly limited voir dire in the presence of the jury in the midst of the direct examination is often undesirable to the attorney examining.

LESSON: Do not offer an exhibit into evidence merely because you are entitled to. You can frequently obtain all that you need from that exhibit by the mere act of authentication. The actual receipt of the exhibit may be superfluous!

Here is an illustration. The witness is on the stand. He has testified that he was in Chicago on May 11th. You want to demonstrate to the jury that the witness is accurate.

> Q: Where were you on May 11th?
>
> A: I was in Chicago.
>
> Q: I show you what has been marked plaintiff's exhibit 12 for identification and I ask you if you can identify it.
>
> A: Yes.
>
> Q: What is it?
>
> A: That is my receipted bill from the Palmer House Hotel in Chicago for my stay on May 11th.

At *this point* there is no need to offer the exhibit into evidence. You have achieved all that you wished from the act of authentication. The offer into evidence will not do any more for you. And it could harm you by giving your adversary the *opportunity* to interrupt your examination with a voir dire on the offer.

Experienced lawyers learn that they have a spigot in hand. If they loosen that spigot with numerous offers, they admit the possibility of numerous interruptions—and worse. But by controlling the timing of the offer of the exhibit, they also control the timing of their adversaries' ability to object and to intrude.[14] That is not to say that the exhibit is never to be offered. To the contrary, your bias ought to be to offer into evidence whatever you have identified. The question is only one of timing. At the end of the examination you may offer all of the previously foundated exhibits—and offer them in a body.

This technique also has the advantage of forcing your adversary to confront the offer and possible challenge to a group of exhibits at a moment when he would rather begin his cross-examination in chief at the place of his own choice.[15] But that is an incidental benefit. The main reason for this technique is to prevent the adversary from getting even his nose into your tent during your direct examination and thereby to provide greater protection for your witness.

Of course, the danger of this technique is that by the end of the examination the court may not recollect that you have authenticated the unproffered exhibits sufficiently to support their introduction into evidence. But that risk is minimal, because the re-authentication is but the work of a moment and a flip of the wrist of the examiner. So if the judge forgets that you have done it once, why, just go ahead and do it again.

There is one time when you cannot employ these techniques. If you need to expose the jurors to the contents of the exhibit, then you have no choice but to offer it into evidence. You will simply not be permitted to expose the contents of exhibits to jurors unless those exhibits are received into evidence. In that instance you no longer have a choice. If you do not offer the exhibit, you can be prevented from showing or reading it to the jurors.

INTEGRATION OF NOTES AND EXHIBITS FOR DIRECT EXAMINATION

I am enchanted by the current proliferation of lectures and writings on the subject of "the trial notebook." It seems to me that if all the proscriptions and prescriptions in this were followed, the trial lawyer would need bearers to bring his trial notebooks in court. There are so many parts and subparts to this recommended "book" that my mind boggles at the handling of it. I never have anything that I will need in court anyplace other than ready at hand.

For myself, I always use a three-hole looseleaf book for my courtroom work. The notes for my openings are on the pages, front and back, so that there are always two pages of notes displayed. And, of course, those "notes" are abbreviated reminders of the next subject to be argued to the jury.

For direct, I use the same notebook, with abbreviated notes on the two display pages of what the witness will talk about. My exhibits rest by my side in a pile on counsel table, arranged top to bottom *in the order* that I will offer them for identification. My notes reflect that there is an exhibit. By use of the pile of exhibits—at least the one on top—and my notes of the next line of answers, I have a perfect outline of what is next to be done.

As my exhibits are offered into evidence and received, I try to deliver them to the custody of the court clerk or reporter—if the local custom permits. For the exhibits I do not offer, or that are offered but not admitted, I begin a separate pile. By the end of the examination, that is the only pile that remains. It is my checklist of what remains to be done.

The exhibits that I intend not only to offer into evidence but to question from as well, I photocopy and integrate into my notes. On these photocopies I make marks as reminders of the points to be made with the document during the examination or the portions to be read to the jury.

This has proven an infallible system for guiding me through even the most complicated direct, one lasting as long as five days and dealing, as we shall see, with hundreds of documents without having to ask for numerous pauses or "indulgences" from the court.

CHARTS AND SUMMARIES AND HOW THEY CAN ARGUE YOUR CASE FOR YOU

The Federal Rules of Evidence provide for the use of summaries of voluminous evidence. Rule 1006 provides:

> The contents of voluminous writings, recordings, or photographs which cannot conveniently be examined in court may be presented in the form of a chart, summary, or calculation. The originals, or duplicates, shall be made available for examination or copying, or both, by other parties at reasonable time and place. The court may order that they be produced in court.

This rule does nothing more than state the common law and practice of most courts, with one major exception. Charts and summaries have historically been used with great commonality. What this rule adds, however, is permission to introduce into evidence charts and summaries of masters that themselves *are not in evidence—or even in court*—provided the adversary has been given a reasonable chance to inspect them. For reasons that follow, the last permission, in my opinion, should only rarely if ever be invoked.

The ability to create exhibits that organize and summarize your case is an opportunity for advocacy without limitation. Let me offer an illustration from the *City of Newark* case—a case I tried, which we will deal with at great length later.

In that case, we introduced a witness named Irving Kantor, who from his deathbed testified that he had created a phony bank account in the name of Kantor Supply. Into that account he had run checks totaling over one million dollars. From that account he had withdrawn over 900,000 in cash and given the currency sometimes to a Joseph Biancone (a defendant at the trial) and sometimes to an Anthony Gagliano, known as "Tony G."

The government's theory was that this was a payoff scheme whereby contractors and suppliers doing work for the City of Newark were forced to kick back 10 percent of the city payments to a ring of mobsters and public officials—including the mayor of the city—for whom Biancone and Tony G were bankers.

Checks from the city, totalling nearly 10 million dollars (on just one 1965 project), to the contractors were put in evidence—in bulk. The checks from the main contractor, C. Salvatore and Sons, Inc., to the subcontractors and from them to their subcontractors were put into evidence, again, in bulk. Then, the checks from all subcontractors to Kantor Supply were put into evidence. Finally, the chart on the following page was offered and received in evidence.

Notice that the chart is more than just a compilation of exhibits. It combines the physical checks from the city, the contractors, and the subcontractors with *oral* testimony of Irving Kantor to his conversion of the checks into cash and the delivery of the cash to the two men named at the bottom of the chart.

APPENDIX

Exhibit 1300

FLOW OF CASH

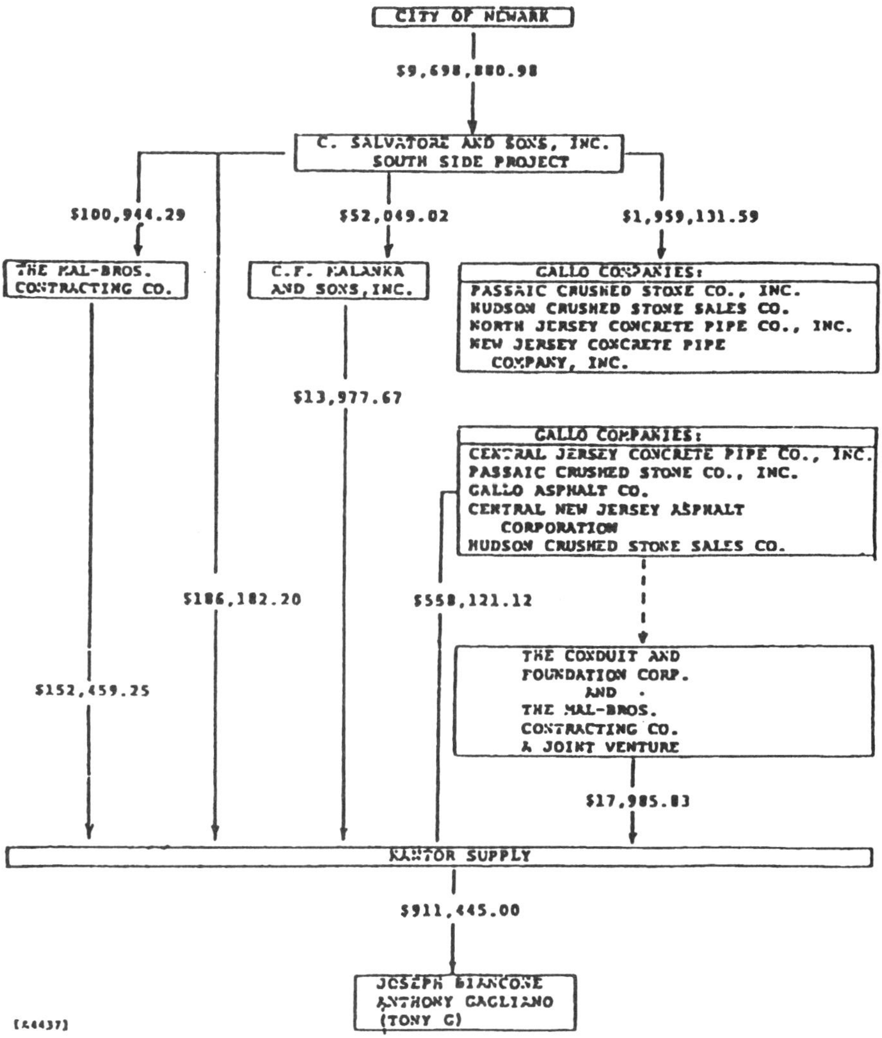

[A4437]

The court of appeals not only approved of this exhibit; it liked it so well that it made this chart, which was Government Exhibit 1300 in evidence at trial, the appendix to its opinion affirming the conviction. The chart is reproduced here as it appears in the court's opinion.

LESSON: Your "summary" can summarize more than physical evidence. It can combine oral testimony as well, making your exhibit into an argument that, because it is in evidence, will be carried into the jury room itself at the end of the case and that is also immune to cross-examination.

What cannot be displayed is the exhibit size. Exhibit 1300 stood higher than a man, at least seven feet tall. It dominated the courtroom ("Big is beautiful," a lesson I learned from Simon Rifkind during the *Colonial Pipeline* trial). In addition, each juror had a miniature copy to follow the testimony with.

Not that the testimony was extensive. It took but few questions to authenticate this chart:

> JOHN A. De AMICUS, called as a witness by the government, being duly sworn, testified as follows:
>
> DIRECT EXAMINATION BY MR. STERN:
>
> Q: What is your business or occupation?
>
> A: I am a special agent of the Federal Bureau of Investigation.
>
> Q: And how long have you been a special agent for the Federal Bureau of Investigation?
>
> A: Approximately twelve and a half years.
>
> Q: Are you assigned to any particular squad in the Federal Bureau of Investigation?
>
> A: I am on the accounting squad.
>
> Q: For how long have you been assigned to accounting duties within the Federal Bureau of Investigation?
>
> A: At least 10 years.

Q: Have you had any formal training in accounting?

A: Yes, I graduated from college majoring in accounting.

Q: Prior to joining the Federal Bureau of Investigation, did you work as an accountant?

A: Yes, I worked in a CPA firm for approximately three years, and I worked with an international airline as an internal auditor for two years and in the comptroller's office of that airline for another year.

Q: And subsequent to that time you had joined the FBI, is that correct?

A: Yes.

Q: Now, Agent De Amicus, did I make a request of you to analyze certain documents which have since come into evidence in this case?

A: Yes.

Q: Well particularly, did I ask you to analyze certain checks from the City of Newark to C. Salvatore & Sons, the joint venture on the South Side Project?

A: Yes.

Q: Did I also ask you to analyze certain checks now in evidence flowing from the joint venture to individual joint venturers and to Kantor Supply?

A: Yes.

Q: Moreover, did I ask you to analyze certain checks now in evidence emanating from the joint venturers to certain Gallo-related companies?

A: Yes.

Q: Did I ask you to analyze certain checks now in evidence from individual companies which comprised the joint venture and from Gallo companies to Kantor Supply Company?

A: Yes.

Q: Finally, did I ask you to analyze certain checks now in evidence emanating from Kantor Supply Company, which were ultimately turned into cash?

A: Yes.

Q: Did you perform that analysis?

A: Yes, I did.

Q: Have you also read the testimony of Irving Kantor?

A: Yes, I have.

Q: Did you, pursuant to that study and analysis and the reading of Mr. Kantor's testimony, prepare a chart which would summarize these checks now in evidence and Mr. Kantor's testimony?

A: Yes.

Q: Will you indicate which chart you prepared in reference to this series of questions?

A: I prepared these three charts. One is a flow of cash, and the other is an analysis of those particular checks as they apply to the Kantor Supply account.

MR. STERN: I would ask that the large chart which stands up on the easel be marked Government's Exhibit 1300 for identification and the other chart 1301 for identification.

(Exhibits G-1300 and G-1301 were marked for identification.)

Q: Agent, would you kindly take the pointer and if you can conveniently do so will you take

Government's Exhibit 1300, the large chart, and explain it to the jury?

A: What the chart shows is a movement of cash, checks and cash. The block on top represents the City of Newark. The figure $9,698,880.98 is the amount of money paid by the City of Newark into C. Salvatore & Sons, Inc., South Side project, which is the joint venture. The figure $100,944.29 represents a number of payments paid to the Mal Bros. Contracting Company by the joint venture. This represents services rendered. Mal Bros. is blue because this is one of the joint venturers.

The amount of $ 52,049.02 represents payments made to C.F. Malanka & Sons, Inc., another member of the joint venture, and this also was apparently for services rendered.

The Gallo Brothers were apparently suppliers to the joint venture, and they received from the joint venture $1,959,131.59. The figures in this portion of the chart represents payments from Mal Bros. Contracting Company into Kantor Supply. That figure is $152,459.25.

This line represents payments directly from the joint venture into Kantor Supply's account of $186,182.20.

The line from Malanka down to Kantor Supply represents the payment of $13,977.67 paid by that company into Kantor Supply.

These lines emanating from these particular Gallo companies represent the payment of $558,121.12 paid by these companies into Kantor Supply.

This figure of $17,985.83 represents the Conduit and Foundation Corporation and the Mal Bros. Contracting Company, which was another joint venture in and of itself into Kantor Supply account. The figure of—

MR. STERN: Excuse me. There is a broken line from the Gallo companies connecting it with the Conduit and Foundation Corporation and the Mal Bros. Contracting Company. Can you explain the significance of that broken line:

THE WITNESS: As I understand it, the payment of $17,935.83 was made by this company at the request of Mario Gallo.

Q: And that is the significance of the broken line?

A: Yes. The money didn't move directly from the Gallo companies into this particular company.

Now, the $911,445 represents payments out of Kantor Supply. This is cash checks—checks that were cashed out of the Kantor Supply account for the ultimate production of cash.

Q: And the box underneath that?

A: That represents the individuals that Mr. Kantor has stated he paid the money to, Joseph Biancone, Anthony Gagliano.

Q: Also known as Tony G?

A: That is correct, yes, Tony G.

Q: If I understand your testimony correctly, agent, the figures which appear on that chart were determined by you based upon checks which are now in evidence, is that so?

A: Yes.

Q: Is there any figure on that chart which does not represent accumulated checks now in evidence?

A: Not that I know of.

Q: And if I understand you correctly ultimately from these sources you were able to ascertain that

> $911,444 was taken out of the Kantor Supply account in the form of cash?
>
> A: Yes, ultimately produced in cash.
>
> Q: Now, in reference to the other exhibit, can you explain what that exhibit is?

And that was all the questioning there ever was regarding Exhibit 1300. The defendants reserved their cross for another day. But that day never came, and the exhibit went into evidence, into the jury room, and into the opinion of the United States Court of Appeals.

And that brings us to the final point. Although we did not have the Federal Rules of Evidence in 1970 when I introduced Exhibit 1300, if we had I would not have invoked the provision of Rule 1006, which would permit the introduction of the exhibit without the necessity of introducing the hundreds of checks and invoices that were the predicate for that chart. Why? Well, it was the simplest matter to introduce these exhibits—even though their volume was great—and their physical presence in the courtroom was not only imposing; that presence added weight to the exhibit and demonstrated to the jurors just what had gone into the enterprise, that is, the illegal enterprise of kickbacks. Equally important, it showed the jurors what had gone into the enterprise of unravelling the scheme and presenting the case in the courtroom.

Of course there is much, much more to the subject than this overview.[16] Charts may be far simpler than Exhibit 1300—or more elaborate. They may be prepared prior to trial, or they may be created by a witness using an easel in the presence of the jury during trial. The possibilities are legion. The point, for now, is that both vividness and frequency—as well as protection from cross-examination—require the consideration of the use of such charts and summaries in almost every case, at least on damages if not on liability.

ENDNOTES

1. Whether a state has these rules—and a great many do—or not is immaterial. The universal practice is to follow them.
2. "The requirement of showing authenticity or identity falls into the category of relevancy dependent upon fulfillment of a condition of fact and is governed by the procedure set forth in Rule 104(b)."
3. U.S. v. Bourjailly, 483 U.S. 171 (1987).
4. Rule 801(d)(2)(E) in pertinent part provides: "(d) a statement is not hearsay if—(2) the statement is offered against a party and is (E) a statement by a co-conspirator of a party during the course and in furtherance of the conspiracy."
5. *See* 801(d)(2)(A). *See also* 901(b)(2).
6. *Id. See also* 901(b)(5).
7. E.J. Imwinkelreid, Evidentiary Foundations at 85 *et seq.* (1980).
8. E.J. Imwinkelreid, Evidentiary Foundations at 82 *et seq.* (1980).
9. We will return to this subject when we discuss the timing of the offer of exhibits.
10. We will see a major exception to this advice in the *City of Newark* case shortly, wherein I had to pass hundreds of individual checks among the jurors. It was not possible to duplicate them all—and there would have been no saving time if I had, because the passing of one individual check to be glanced at would have been necessary in either case, whether by me or by the jurors. This is different from the use of a document that has to be read and digested for a few minutes. As will be seen, when those sorts of documents were used—particularly the Rigo diaries—copies were given out to each juror.

In any event, at least initially, we did stop the testimony while jurors passed the checks. Anything less would have been foolish.

11. That means that one can demand a voir dire on the offer of oral evidence if there is a good faith basis to believe it inadmissible.
12. Perhaps the basic authority for such proceedings is found in Fed. R. Evid. 103(B) and 104(C), which enjoin the presentation of inadmissible evidence in the hearing of the jury.
13. *See, for example*, voir dire examinations on confessions, and other matters covered by Fed. R. Evid. 104(c).
14. The most graphic illustration of this technique will shortly be demonstrated from the transcript of my most important and difficult direct examination.
15. The strategy of cross-examination is for later, but the observation must now be made that the cross-examiner would be foolish to immediately confront a cascade of exhibits at the outset of his cross-examination. For him, too, the order of what he has to present is as important as the content of the presentation. His best tactic would be to ask the court to reserve ruling on the offer, promising to do his voir dire in the context of his cross-examination. Such a request should be seasoned with the promise that its granting would save the court time. Courts are always avid to save time.
16. For an excellent work on the entire subject of visual evidence, see Joseph, *Modern Visual Evidence*, published by Law Journal Seminars Press, Inc., in 1984, which has an annual update service.

Chapter Eight

Making a Witness Invulnerable to Cross-Examination

The first rule in protecting witnesses from cross-examination is to deal with their weaknesses during your direct of them. That is not only what made Kresel vulnerable to Steuer, it is what will make Conti vulnerable to whoever cross-examines him at the conclusion of Tigar's direct.

The main problem with the Conti direct is not the use of quotations in the testimony about conversations, although that is a problem. It is not even the tendency of the witness to seize the bit and gallop off, although that too is a bit of a problem.

The central problem is that the direct did not even touch on any of the misconduct of the witness, which the jury was certain to hear about on cross-examination: Conti's use of drugs, Conti's molesting of women, Conti's failure on guard duty, Conti's sexual misconduct when he was suffering from venereal disease, Conti's threats against Calley.

Perhaps Tigar expected to be able to prevent some—but surely not all—of this material from coming out by objecting during cross. But, then, the best course would have been to move in limine before the direct to edit this material out from the cross. And whatever he was unable to persuade the judge to keep from the jury on cross, the direct examiner *had* to deal with himself before the cross-examination began.[1] But in no case should Conti have been presented as a decent man. The job of the direct was to present the "bad" material about Conti in the best way for the prosecution, not to pretend that it did not exist by introducing the witness as a volunteer who had been honorably discharged.

THE MOTION IN LIMINE

No one desires to shoot himself in the foot, much less in the heart. When the examiner knows that his witness may be impeached depending on rulings by the judge during cross-examination, the direct examiner seeks to anticipate the ruling *before* direct. If the judge will let the evidence in on cross, then the direct *must* deal with it before the direct ends and the cross begins. But if the trial judge will not permit the cross to embrace the material, then the direct must stay as far from that subject as is possible, to avoid "opening the door."[2] Enter the motion in limine.

We were introduced to this supple tool earlier, in the context of opening statements (*see* Volume I, pages 161–164). The motion is a device to raise issues for decision before they would otherwise arise. In this instance, the attorney asks the judge to rule on the limits of the cross-examiner's impeachment *before* he does the direct. If the judge will cooperate, the attorney goes down the list of possible impeachments—in this case, the venereal disease, the drug abuse, and so forth—and argues against its admissibility. Presumably, the other side argues the contrary view. The judge then rules, and the examiner conducts the direct examination informed by the judicial decision.

Unfortunately, many judges refuse to cooperate. Whatever their real reasons, many *say* that they cannot give an advisory ruling on the scope of cross-examination until the direct has been presented. And no offer of proof as to what the direct will be will ever satisfy such a judge, because what he really desires is to force the direct examiner to bring forth the harmful material himself. Once this is accomplished, there is no further need for a ruling and therefore no possibility that an appellate court may find error. And so the judge withholds his ruling, hoping that the examiner will not dare to forbear to bring out the material himself, on direct. The judge counts on the direct examiner's fear that if he fails to prevent his adversary from using the material later, his failure to have brought the material out himself on direct will be doubly harmful. And so it will.

There is only one antidote to the judicial refusal to rule on a motion in limine addressed to the cross-examination until after the direct examination has been completed. After the refusal, the direct examiner should present his examination entirely, but, before concluding, he should say to the judge:

> Your Honor, I can well understand the court's prior difficulty in ruling on the motion addressed to the scope and content of the cross-examination until after the court had heard the direct. But that is now completed, except for just one area which depends entirely on your Honor's ruling. If my motion is granted, then I am done. If not, I naturally have a few more questions.

While no advice or device is foolproof in any courtroom, since uncertainties and unpredictabilities always exist, this technique is about the best that can be offered to help the judge who sincerely could not rule without first hearing the direct examination or to smoke out the judge who was improperly attempting to evade his duty to decide. This device does, however, cost you the ability to place the material anywhere other than at the very end of the direct examination.

THE ORGANIZATION OF THE DIRECT EXAMINATION

It is now time to confront the direct examination as "argument," for we have now identified enough of the tools of speech on direct to be able to appreciate that it is not extravagant to claim that a lawyer can argue through a witness on direct. And so we now deal with the organization of your argument on direct. Even as with openings, the organization of what you present on direct is as persuasive as what you have to present. This is true for directs for the same reasons it is true for openings—not the least of which, of course, is that, just like an opening, a direct examination is an argument.

To be a persuasive argument, the direct examination must be organized to take account of its weaknesses as well as its strengths. Even as the witness must be properly introduced at the outset of the examination, the examination must not conclude without the examiner at least attempting to present the most unattractive aspects of the witness and his testimony in the most favorable light—and that means at Level IV (*see* Volume I, pages 175–182). At Level IV those aspects become affirmative aids to your case rather than glitches to be explained away. Where in the scheme and order of the direct should such material be presented? The beginning? The middle? The end?[3]

This is a difficult question to address without reference to the particulars of the witness, the testimony, and the particular potential impeachment. But I do believe in a general rule for dealing on direct examination with potential impeachment that goes to a witness's character or motive to lie.

Most of us would opt to place this testimony in the middle of the examination, relying on principles of primacy and recency (*see* Volume I, pages 115–120). The theory behind this choice is to try to make the "bad stuff" as inconspicuous as possible by keeping it away from the primacy and recency of the examination.

But this kind of testimony will not be inconspicuous, no matter where it is placed. Moreover, if the examiner will *use* it as affirmative rather than negative evidence, then there is no reason to try to conceal it. And if its ugliness cannot be camouflaged, then the best place for it is at the end, that is, at the final phase of the examination. Why? *Because it is the furthest from the beginning.*

You do not want that sort of material at the outset, forcing your jurors to hear and to sift the remainder of the testimony through the strainer of the witness's bad character. You want the jury with you, believing the witness as much and as long as possible before you must touch this explosive stuff. The longer they have been on board, rowing with your witness, the more they will want to—and thus will be able to—forgive the blemishes and believe the explanations of your witness. This material, then, should not be in the middle, for that is still too close to the beginning.

Let me illustrate this point by returning to the Calley problem. We have studied and learned how to deal with the character of Conti, that is, how to use it affirmatively on Level IV (*see* Volume I, pages 322, 323[4]). That means we have already done the strategy—the architecture. We know *what* to say and *why* we need to say it. All that is left is the technique of *how to* say it—the crafting of the questions—to deliver the message through the witness to the jury on direct examination. As an exercise, try crafting the questions by forming the answers that will deliver to the jury precisely the message you need.

Whether or not you have tried it out yourself, here is how I would proceed. First, I want the witness to say that Calley picked him to kill the people because he knew that Conti smoked dope and suffered from a venereal disease. But I cannot ask Conti that question directly. The rules do not permit him to testify as to what was in Calley's mind.

I might take a shortcut using Rule 701, which permits lay people to give opinions on many subjects. For example:

> Q: Mr. Conti, do you have an opinion as to why Lt. Calley, here, selected you to shoot the children in the ditch?

That would be an easy way. If the judge allowed the question—and he probably would not—the testimony would roll on like the Mississippi.[5] It would be an easy way—and would suffer from that vice. The witness would have to carry the arguments. Why not do this instead?

> Q: Mr. Conti, while you were in Vietnam did you or did you not use drugs?
>
> A: Yes.
>
> Q: Was that in Mr. Calley's presence or in his absence?
>
> A: In his presence.
>
> Q: And while a member of Lt. Calley's company, did you suffer from any venereal disease?
>
> A: Yes.
>
> Q: Which one?
>
> A: Syphilis.
>
> Q: Did you require medical treatment for this syphilis while under Lt. Calley's command?
>
> A: Yes.

Q: Did you know whether or not Lt. Calley, as your commanding officer, received reports of your treatment for syphilis?

A: Yes, I did.

Q: Did he?

A: Yes.

Q: Now, let me return to the moment that Lt. Calley selected you to order to shoot the civilians in the ditch. As of that moment, Mr. Conti, can you tell the judge and the jury whether or not Calley was aware of your drug use and your treatment for venereal disease?

A: Yes, he was.

Q: Notwithstanding all that, Mr. Conti, did you obey Lt. Calley's order?

A: No.

Q: Did you kill any of those babies or those women in that ditch?

A: No!

Q: Will you tell this judge and this jury why you refused to obey Lt. Calley's order to kill these civilians?

A: [The reader may fill in his own answer. It may be a long one, for Conti has now earned the right to answer at length.]

Q: Mr. Conti, when you refused to kill these people, what did Calley over there [pointing] do?

A: He shot them himself.

This testimony belongs at the end of the examination. To be sure, the jury has already heard of the shooting once, but that is hardly a vice. And, to be sure, the examiner might have tried to weave this material into the initial account of the shooting, but it really would not have fit there.

First, the examiner would have had too many jobs to do at once at that point; and it is hard enough to clearly communicate even one point at one time on direct examination (or anywhere else in court, for that matter). But even more important, it would simply not have sounded fitting there. It would have sounded like an excuse there. The jury would not have been quite ready there. It had to wait for the end.

Indeed, we notice that Mike Tigar did something like that when he started in on redirect examination to rehabilitate Conti after Conti's cross-examination. The point, of course, is that this should be done on direct, not just to take the wind out of the sails of the cross, although it does, but to turn weakness into strength—in short, to reach Level IV. And from this we draw the final observation, one to which we will return again and again.

LESSON: While chronology is important to clarity, it is not the invariable outline of the direct. Facts must be grouped together to make points, and this often requires the grouping of widely time-separated events.

PRIOR INCONSISTENT STATEMENTS

Most impeachment will not be based on anything as dramatic as the Conti background. The overwhelming majority of impeaching material is based on the witness's prior inconsistent statements.

Did the witness testify before? Was it in the grand jury or in a deposition? In either event, there is likely to be at least some small inconsistency between that prior testimony and the testimony on direct at the trial.

Rare indeed is the witness who can tell the same story twice, particularly over a six-month—or longer—hiatus, without at least some inconsistencies creeping in. Then, too, testimony given early in the investigating processes of the case is likely to have mistakes and errors, however honestly made, which are revealed by later exposure to after-found documents and subsequent testimony. For that reason, witnesses often find that their early testimony, pretrial, contains errors they wish they had not made, particularly months later when they are called to take the stand at the trial.

By the time the direct examination is blocked out, and certainly before the direct examination is concluded, the examiner must have a plan for dealing with the inconsistent prior testimony.

If It Isn't Broken, Don't Fix It

The primary lesson is, *minor inconsistencies are immaterial.* Jurors simply do *not* expect people to tell faultless stories or to be error free. Indeed, the hallmark of unsuccessful cross-examinations is the nit-picking over minor inconsistencies that clearly make no difference whatever to the integrity of the story or to the credibility of the witness.

After learning about the existence of any and all inconsistencies, the first task of the direct examiner is to evaluate *objectively* whether the inconsistency matters. Is it a trivial point, or a critical one? Does the inconsistency go to a central theme of the case, or is it in one of the back alleys of the litigation? If the matter is trivial, leave it alone. The best service your adversary could do for you is to make much of such minor matters on his cross-examination. Such cross-examinations are the telltales to a tribunal that the examiner has no case.

If It Is Broken, Do Fix It

But if the inconsistency is a serious one, then the direct examiner *must* deal with it on direct. For reasons that should not need further exposition by this stage of this work, it is foolish for the advocate to permit the adversary to first acquaint the jury with the inconsistency on cross-examination in the hope that he will thereafter put matters to right on redirect. To be sure, sometimes this cannot be avoided—particularly when the advocate does not know of the impeaching material or the judge will not permit reference to it on direct examination—but if the direct examiner has his druthers, he should address such matters on his direct examination. And how is that to be done?

Most of us are nervous, frightened, and often confused when we are called upon to give testimony. Jurors readily understand that. Over the past 30 years I have seen witnesses repudiate past testimonial mistakes on just that basis, and I have seen jurors readily forgive past testimonial glitches on just such explanations. For example:

> Q: Now, Mr. Smith, do you recall testifying in deposition on this case some nine months ago?
>
> A: Yes.
>
> Q: By the way, Mr. Smith, had you ever testified before in any kind of a proceeding?
>
> A: Only one, in traffic court.
>
> Q: Well, then, during the deposition in this case, do you recall being asked where you were on May 11th of last year?
>
> A: Yes.
>
> Q: And what did you answer?
>
> A: I said I was in Chicago.
>
> Q: Now, since then have you had an opportunity to review your testimony and your records?
>
> A: Yes.
>
> Q: And were you in Chicago on May 11th?
>
> A: No.
>
> Q: Well, where were you on May 11th?
>
> A: I was in Detroit.
>
> Q: Why did you testify that you were in Chicago [if it pleases the examiner]?
>
> A: I was just confused [or I guess I messed up, or whatever pleases the witness].

Suppose that instead of a testimonial error there was an actual deliberate misstatement in the earlier testimony. It has since been corrected. But now the witness faces an imminent impeachment on cross-examination. What should be done?

It is vital for the direct examiner to bring the earlier misconduct out himself—along with whatever the reasons for it having been committed. The jurors are likely to be far more forgiving if this regimen is followed than if the explanation is given on redirect after the accusation has been driven home on cross-examination.

These principles have been well known in the practice for years. I quote now liberally from a work I earlier criticized, Justice Louis B. Heller's book, *Do You Solemnly Swear*, in which he criticizes a direct examination for failing to follow this principle.

> The manner in which this direct examination was conducted illustrates an important principle frequently overlooked by many lawyers. They labor under the delusion that their obligation to protect the credibility of their witnesses begins only when opposing counsel starts his cross-examination. Often, however, it is too late by that time for a lawyer to do anything effective on their behalf simply by raising objections to the searching questions that his opponent puts to them. The proper time for an attorney to begin setting up his defenses against the cross-examination of his witnesses is while they are giving their direct testimony.[6]

Justice Heller somewhat later gives a perfect illustration of how to deal with earlier misstatements—even deliberate lies—during the direct examination and before the witness can be impeached on cross-examination.[7]

> The accused, charged specifically with vehicular homicide on the New York Thruway, is on the stand and has just finished identifying himself, stating his address, his occupation, and the place where he was

on the night of the alleged crime. His attorney proceeds with direct examination as follows:

Q. After you left your home on the morning of December 8, 1962, do you remember whether anything happened while you were driving out of New York City?

A. Yes, an attractive woman standing on the side of the road put her hand up to thumb a ride with me.

Here counsel took care to avoid asking a leading question like "Did you see an attractive woman trying to thumb a ride?" Instead, he phrased his question in general terms that permitted the witness to supply the details.

Q. What did you do?

A. I stopped my car.

Q. What happened then?

A. The woman asked for a lift.

Q. What did she say?

A. She said, "Mister, are you going upstate?"

Q. What did you reply?

A. I told her I was going to Newburgh.

Q. What, if anything, did she say?

A. "That's just where I am going!"

These are all excellent questions, precise and pointed. Each contains only five or six words, and each calls for a brief response.

But now counsel is coming to a crucial part of his direct examination. There is, apparently, a contradiction between the statement made by his client when he was questioned by the State Police and the allegations made in the defense. Here is how the problem is approached:

Q. What did you tell the State Police after your arrest when they asked you whether anyone else was in the car with you?

A. I told them that no one was in the car with me.

Q. Was that true?

A. No.

Q. Do you have any explanation?

A. I was lying when I said no one was in the car with me. Frankly, I didn't want my wife to know I took a day off from work and that I was driving upstate and had a woman in my car.

Q. Do you realize your predicament now?

A. Yes.

Q. Have you anything further to say?

A. I am sorry that I lied, and that is all I can say.

"Counsel, Do Not Impeach Your Own Witness"

Why is it, as Justice Heller notes, that so many lawyers do not deal with impeaching material on direct examination? Because of an arcane legal doctrine that forbids an attorney from impeaching his own witness.

A little history is necessary. Originally, attorneys were presumed to "vouch" for the testimony of their own witnesses—and the attorney's "own" witness was any witness he called to the stand. That means, of course, that an attorney was not only forbidden to lead on direct examination, but the attorney was "bound by" the answers of his own witness. The examiner could not "impeach" the answers of his own witness, and in many courts those answers were frequently treated like judicial admissions against the party calling that witness to the stand.

All that nonsense was supposedly put out to rest, at least in federal court, with the enactment of the Federal Rules of Evidence in 1975.[8]

Rule 607 provides:

> The credibility of a witness may be attacked by any party, including the party calling him.

To add confusion to confusion, we must ask, what does the ancient rule against impeachment of one's own witness have to do with the direct examiner's efforts to bring out the prior inconsistencies of his own witness *before* the adverse party does in order to *protect* that witness against cross-examination and not at all for the purpose of impeaching the witness?

Unfortunately, courts have historically used the rule against "impeaching" one's own witness to prevent direct examiners from bringing out the prior inconsistencies or the character blemishes of the witness on direct before cross-examination. And in spite of Rule 607, and in spite of the fact that the attorney is *not* impeaching his own witness, the admonition "Counsel, do not impeach your own witness" still rings out in courtrooms throughout the land when lawyers attempt to anticipate the cross-examination to come.

Even in more enlightened courts, such direct examinations are all too often aborted by trial judges who rule that such examinations improperly "bolster" the direct testimony of the witness and may be done only after the testimony has been impeached.

The trouble is that there is no law on the subject upon which an advocate can rely. One judge will permit such direct examinations, while another will not. And no appellate court is likely to be much concerned with how the trial court rules. Provided that the "rehabilitation" of the witness is permitted by the trial judge at *some* point, the appellate court is not likely to reverse because the examiner was forced to wait for redirect to do something he wished to do on direct examination—*even though the timing of the testimony may well be outcome determinative with the jury!*

The Remedy

The skilled direct examination often brings out the explanation for the inconsistency as a natural part of the witness's testimony and without flagging the effort by asking pointed questions that will elicit adversary objections and unpredictable and whimsical rulings. This is often done by simply opening up the questioning to permit some narrative by the witness in which he offers his explanation as a part of his narrative.[9] In my view there is nothing unethical in this. If a lawyer believes he has a good faith basis to elicit certain testimony, nothing requires him to alert the adversary that there may be a good faith basis to object. Whether or not a statement is an exception to the hearsay rule as an excited utterance, or nonhearsay as an admission, or a co-conspirator's or an agent's statement may well be an issue for the court. But it is usually up to the opposing party to object, not up to the offering party to tell the court and adversary that this or that time might be a good time to consider making an objection.[10]

I once discussed this point with Mike Tigar, who related to me that he saw Edward Bennett Williams use this technique when Tigar second chaired Williams at the Connally trial.

Connally was on the witness stand during direct examination. He had to testify to a certain meeting on a certain date. By the time of trial, Connally and Williams realized that Governor Connally had made a mistake about the date of the meeting when he had appeared and testified before the grand jury and that he faced cross-examination on this inconsistency at the trial. So what did Williams do? He had Connally testify as to the error in the middle of a narration on direct, without posing a direct question.

Some years later, I obtained the direct testimony of Connally, and I believe I found the place where Williams employed this technique. Watch.

> Q: Now, I hand you Defendant's Number 31.
>
> A: Yes, sir.

Q: Which you have indicated was your itinerary for that weekend.

A: Yes, sir.

Q: Did you in fact stay with that itinerary or did you deviate from it?

A: No, we deviated from it considerably.

Q: How did you deviate from it?

A: Well, this had us leaving the ranch on Friday morning, October 26th, and arriving at Ragsdale Airport at 9:45 in the morning. George Christian came down on Thursday, October 25th, and so he had to go back that evening, so since he was going back and I was going to send him back in the plane, I just—my wife and I decided we would go back with him.

So we went back, flew up late in the afternoon of the 25th with Mr. Christian to Austin, didn't even go to the hotel, as I recall, we got his wife and the wife of another friend of ours and went and had dinner and checked into the hotel, so actually we checked into the Sheraton Crest Hotel the evening of October 25th as opposed to flying up the next morning.

Then there was substantial changes in the rest of the schedule as well.

Q: I will come to those.

So you spent the night of the 25th of October in Austin?

A: Yes, sir.

Q: At the Sheraton Crest?

A: Yes, sir.

Q: Contrary to your itinerary which had you spending the night in Florisville?

A: That's correct.

Q: On the 26th of October, did you see Jake Jacobsen?

A: Yes, sir, I did.

Q: Would you tell us the circumstances under which you saw him?

A: I saw him at the Sheraton Crest Hotel. My memory was that I saw him in the afternoon, the late afternoon of Friday, October 26th, or while I was dressing to go to this evening ceremony, that was my memory.

I have a vivid memory of dressing while he was there. However, I had heard and I was persuaded that he had to be in the evening since according to this itinerary I had spent the night and I testified before the grand jury that I had spent the night in Florisville at the ranch, and had seen him in the evening.

My memory still is that I saw him in the afternoon. But I heard Mr. Barnett here testify that I saw him, that he saw me and he saw Mr. Jacobsen in the morning of October 26th.

My memory still is that it was the afternoon on the 26th, but I would have to accept Mr. Barnett's testimony over my own memory, very frankly, because I think it would have made more of an impact on him when he said he knew me and I knew him. I know he has no reason to testify to anything that he didn't believe. And I would have to accept—

MR. TUERKHEIMER: Your Honor, I am going to object. Mr. Connally is giving an explanation—

THE COURT: I think you better go to something else. Go on.

> MR. WITNESS: Mr. Jacobsen, in any event, I saw him that day. He came to tell me that he had been or was going to be subpoenaed to appear either before the Ervin Committee or the grand jury, and I can't be certain which, and I said what about. . .[11]

The prosecutor was obviously objecting to Connally giving an explanation before impeachment. The judge, just as obviously, agreed. Why the judge should want to prevent the witness from bringing forth the fact that he made a mistake before the grand jury before he is attacked for having done so is far from clear. But the point is that Williams—not the witness, even though it was his narration—was not about to let the adversary get the first blow.

FLUIDITY—GIVE YOUR WITNESS ELBOW ROOM

Inexperienced trial lawyers not only fail to protect witnesses from the perils of cross-examination; they make those witnesses more vulnerable by nailing the witnesses' feet to the floor by overdetailed questioning on direct. Words like "exactly" and "precisely" are the enemies of direct examination and the friends of cross-examination.

Inexperienced lawyers tend to overprove. They get too detailed. They grope for exactitudes and precisions, and thereby make stationary targets out of their witnesses when it comes to cross-examination.

A proper direct examination must have enough structure, form, and detail to be creditable, of course. But it must not strangle in a miasma of detail. The witness must be clear and definite, at least enough to be believable, but not so definitive as to be a totally immobile target for cross-examination.

Words like "in substance" or "indicate" are the friendly words for your witness on direct. They give enough form for perception but not enough for rigidity. Remember, it is usually the cross-examiner who wants to fix the witness to the *exact* speed of the vehicle or to the *precise* height of the tree. While there may be times when the direct examiner may need to reach an exactitude, this is usually not in his interest.

Nowhere is the problem of overproof on direct examination more prevalent than in the foundating of exhibits, as we saw in the previous chapter, but the same problem also arises in presenting testimony about conversations.

Conversations by Testimony

A witness's testimony concerning his out-of-court conversations is likely to be important evidence in any case. Why? Because for the conversation to be admissible it is likely to have been with a party or his agent. This is the doctrine of admissions.[12]

Admissions in this sense do not require that the statement admit anything or be against the interests of the party declarant. In this sense the word "admissions" is a misnomer. It all depends on who is offering the out-of-court statements of a party. *Anything* said by the plaintiff, or his agent, is an admission if offered *by the defendant*, and vice versa. But the party's own words are *not* an admission when offered by himself. Then they are treated as self-serving hearsay and must be found admissible under an exception to the hearsay rule.[13]

It is precisely because the words of a party, as "recalled" by a witness, are likely to be highly significant to the jury that conversations offered into evidence are likely to be key pieces of evidence. Special care should therefore be taken in presenting this evidence and even greater care in ferreting it out pretrial.

We must first recognize that the rules seem to require us to present this testimony in an impossible and hence implausible way. No one can remember the exact words of any conversation. And yet the orthodox incantation universally intoned to elicit the conversation is as follows.

> Q: You say that you and Jones spoke while standing on the corner?
>
> A: Yes.
>
> Q: Well, what did you say to Jones and what did Jones say to you?

A: [And then the witness is likely to answer in quotes.]

Here, for example, is an illustration Imwinkelreid offers as the proper way to introduce and authenticate a conversation, albeit in this instance a telephone conversation. Once again, watch the checklist approach.[14]

> Introducing conversations into evidence is a common, everyday occurrence during trials, one that can and should be handled routinely and smoothly. Conversations need proper foundations to be admissible. (See FRE 901(b) (5).) The foundation should be established for every conversation, even if the opposing side may not object to its absence. First, opposing counsel can always decide to object, thereby breaking up the flow of your direct examination. Second, the foundation enhances your witness' credibility by demonstrating his ability to remember details.
>
> *Elements*:
>
> The following foundation elements must be established to properly admit in evidence a conversation between two or more persons:
>
> 1. When the conversation occurred.
> 2. Where the conversation occurred.
> 3. Who was present during the conversation.
> 4. Who said what to whom.
>
> It is not necessary that the witness actually participated in the conversation. He may properly testify to a conversation he witnessed between two or more other persons (as long as the conversation is otherwise properly admissible).
>
> *Example*:
>
> Q: Did you personally talk with Frank Jones?
> A: Yes, I did.
> Q: When did that conversation occur?

A: I talked to him on April 25, 1974.
Q: What time of day was that?
A: That was about 3:00 in the afternoon.
Q: Where did that conversation take place?
A: We talked in his office.
Q: What's the address of his office?
A: It's at 150 North Clark Street, Suite 100.
Q: Who was present during that conversation?
A: There was just myself and Mr. Jones.
Q: What did you and Mr. Jones say at that time?
A: I said: "Mr. Jones, you still owe me $2500 for roofing job on your house." He said: "I know I do. I just don't have the money to pay you right now."

Putting aside for the moment the advice to obtain all that detail for each and every conversation—the time of day for example—the *deliberate* and *intentional* eliciting of conversations in *quotations* does not further the goal of credibility, because *no one can remember conversations in that way*![15]

Jurors get nervous when they hear that sort of testimony. And witnesses in your office not only get nervous about giving such accounts; they are likely to protest an inability to do so and to gravely limit what they really could do. This is a lesson I learned to my pain in the most important case I ever tried, as we shall see.

The Correct Way to Develop and Deliver Conversations

Because no one expects or will even believe that anyone can remember conversations verbatim, such testimony must be delivered in the courtroom "in substance." And in the office the witness must be assured that all he will be asked to do is to remember the "substance" of what has been said in the past.

For example, when asking a witness to give such testimony in court, the following is a useful model:

> Q: Now, Mr. Jones, you said you had had a conversation with Mr. Smith six months ago?

A: Yes.

Q: Now in all fairness, Mr. Jones, can you remember word for word what you said to Mr. Smith six months ago and what he said to you?

A: No, not word for word.

Q: But do you remember the substance of the conversation?

A: Yes.

Q: Well, then, in substance, what did you say to Mr. Smith and what did he say to you?[16]

Now, that sort of presentation not only allows the witness greater fluidity, flexibility, and turning-around room for cross-examination later, it goes down better with the jury and has a better chance of staying down during direct examination.

Even before you get into the courtroom, when you are in your office interviewing your witness and you ask him to testify to a conversation with Smith that he had six months before, what are you likely to hear? "No. Don't ask me that. I can't possibly remember."

How often we hear that sort of thing. What you should say to your Mr. Jones is something like this: "Look, don't worry. I'm never going to ask you for the exact words that you and Mr. Smith used. No one could recall that. But remember—words are just the messages of ideas. They are the delivery system that one brain uses to transmit a message to another. I do not expect you to remember the words. All I will ask you about is the message, the substance of what was said between you and Smith."

Almost invariably the witness relaxes. He sees how he can now "remember." He also sees that he has plenty of elbow room to defend what he has remembered. His recollections are likely to be more generous and full than if he had been confined within the narrow box of the exact words.

The point has been made but needs to be made again.

MAXIM: The direct testimony of a witness must be definitive enough to be received in evidence—but not so rigid in form or precise in detail so as to defy belief or be immobile in the teeth of cross-examination.

WITNESSES MUST BE TAUGHT TO DEFEND THEMSELVES ON CROSS-EXAMINATION

Even as witnesses must be taught to eschew unrealistic precisions on direct examination, they must be warned against succumbing to the cross-examiner's efforts to pin them to details during his examinations. Of course the witness must and should give the detail that is recalled. But he must and should resist attempts to force him into exactitudes during cross-examination. Above all, he must be taught to resist demands for "yes" or "no" answers.

Despite what is said in much of the literature and despite the customary practice of many cross-examiners, *no* rule of law requires witnesses on cross-examination to answer in a word, just "yes" or "no."

While it is true that some judges will sometimes confine a witness to a yes or a no if requested to by the cross-examiner,[17] such instructions will be obviated if the witness states that he cannot answer with one word, *consistent with his oath*. That almost invariably ends the dispute. Few judges or lawyers are willing to press the debate beyond that point.

That is not to say that a witness on cross-examination should be encouraged into long narratives, any more than the witness should be on direct examination. Fighting with adversary counsel by making long, self-serving speeches in response to proper cross-examination is as harmful to a witness's credibility as long-winded narratives during direct examination.

A witness must preserve as much impartiality as possible during cross-examination. But the witness should not allow a false impression to be given of what he has to say because his cross-examiner seeks to distort the testimony by artificial constraints. The balance is not easy to describe, nor is it easy to execute. Yet the attempt to explain this to the witness *before* direct examination *must* be made.

Even as the witness should be taught to testify in themes (*see* page 67 *supra*), the witness's understanding of his role in the case, how his testimony helps one side and hurts the other, as well as the objective evidence which supports—or contradicts that testimony—are all necessary ingredients to the preparation of the witness for his testimony at the trial on cross-examination as well as direct examination.

Nothing prevents a witness from calling for or asking to see a supporting document. Nothing prevents a witness from having a better recollection at the time of trial—after he has seen additional materials—than he did six or 12 months earlier when his statement was taken without the benefit of these materials. And no witness should blanch before the question, "Isn't it true that your memory was better a year ago than it is today?"

The answer may well be, "No." And the witness should not hesitate to make that answer, armed with the ability to identify the additional material that he has seen in the interim, which has in fact improved his ability to recall.

Witnesses should not hesitate to repudiate prior inconsistent testimony on the ground that they were nervous or scared at the time—if that is the truth. Juries are usually quite generous in understanding such matters.

The full scope of the subject of how to protect a witness from cross-examination is for a later discussion of cross-examination itself. Now we are concentrating on preparing and delivering the direct examination, and we have touched on this subject briefly only because no pretrial preparation for direct examination can afford to totally ignore it.

THE ORDER OF WITNESSES AND PROOFS PROTECTS WITNESSES FROM CROSS-EXAMINATION

We now enter what I believe to be the most difficult and sophisticated considerations in the entire arena of trial work: the order of witnesses and proofs.

For me, the last major pretrial decision in any case is the order of my witnesses and proofs. It is the last decision because it requires the greatest knowledge about the case. I make the decision only when the last scrap of information has been gleaned and assembled.

Of course, in the real world of courtrooms we do not always have our druthers in the order of calling witnesses. Their schedules may not permit us the luxury of our choice of batting order. In such cases, every lawyer does what he can given what he has to work with. But if we do have the ability to select the lineup of our proofs and our witnesses, here are what I believe to be the key criteria—although very few trial lawyers apply them.

To properly select the order of his witnesses and his proofs, every experienced trial lawyer plays the trial out in his mind over and over again using every conceivable order of presentation. This, of course, is reminiscent of what he does in the earlier process of trying to determine what the jury will believe the "facts" to be so that the trial lawyer can form his theme or theory of the case (*see* Volume I, pages 79–84).

But this much later process is only reminiscent of the first, for its purpose is essentially different. What the trial lawyer is about now is not the initial crafting of the examinations to see how they will be done and to separate what will sell from what will not. What the trial lawyer is about now is the effort to determine the *order* in which he wants the jury to hear the material—because he knows that the organization of what the jury will hear will be as persuasive as what they will hear.

So far, I believe, the majority of the trial bar would be in agreement. But here many of us would part company. There are many rules of thumb that trial lawyers invoke in compiling the order of their witnesses.

1. *Chronology:* Some lawyers begin with the witness who gives the early part of the story so that the jurors will be able to follow the progression of the case and avoid confusion.
2. *The biggest slice of the case first:* Some lawyers begin with the witness who tells the majority of their case their way—so the jury will be educated.

3. *Key witnesses first and last:* Relying on primacy and recency, many lawyers believe that they must begin with a strong witness and end with a strong witness. What they want the jurors to forget, they seek to bury in the middle of their case.
4. *The client should go on first or last:* Some lawyers say to put the client on first. Some say put your client on last, because the client gets to sit in the courtroom—since he cannot be excluded—and he gets educated by the content of the testimony that is presented before he takes the stand.

There is merit to each of these approaches. But, for me, none of them are particularly helpful. There is only one test for me: what order of witnesses *in relationship to each other* will be the most persuasive.

The chronological approach is not necessary—even if it were attainable. After a full and powerful opening, the jurors will not be confused simply because the first witness does not testify to the earliest events. Nor do we need to rely on the first witness to educate the jurors as to the theory of the case. Moreover, witness testimony usually does not fall into these grooves. Witness A has something that leads to Witness B, who has something that leads to Witness C, whose testimony is helpful to understand that of Witness A. Few cases of any complexity permit a chronological ordering of witnesses. And it is a rare witness indeed whose testimony contains the entire theory of a case that has a number of witnesses.

As we have seen, the arrangement of the organization of the testimony that each witness will give is the same point in microcosm. The organization of the order of witnesses is the point in macrocosm.

The key to the ordering of witnesses and proofs is the same as the key to arranging your argument in opening or summation. You want to put that witness on first who helps you the most—while hurting you the least. And those are two very different considerations.

Some witnesses help a lot but will also hurt your case on cross-examination. Some witnesses help only a little but are invulnerable to cross-examination. Helping a lot or hurting a little, which is the more important?

Never put a witness on at the beginning of your case who will deal you substantial wounds on cross-examination. Why? Because that will make the cross-examination of subsequent witnesses by your adversary easier. Why? Because your case will have lost credibility.

Never take heavy blows on the nose of your case if you can avoid them. You want the jury with you—with no substantial reason to be against you—as long as possible before your adversary begins to make hay with them. Why? Because, as we have said elsewhere, they will make up their minds early and begin to root (*see* Volume I, pages 129–132). The longer they have their minds made up, the harder they will root. And the harder they root, the more they will be inclined to fail to see or to forgive the problems in the position of the side they root for.

The relationship of the testimony of each witness to the other is the key ingredient in completing the ordering of your witnesses and proofs. By that I do not mean their chronological relationship or the testimonial predicate that one sets for the other. I mean the testimonial *protection* that one gives to the other.

Put another way, when you reflect on the testimony of your witnesses, I believe you will find that their direct examinations will not vary in any significant way depending on the order in which they are called to the stand. *But the ability of your adversary to successfully cross-examine may depend on what the jury has heard before that witness testifies.*

Take a hypothetical Witness A and Witness B. Both see the same event. A, however, is the more significant witness. He has more information than does B. But he is easier to cross-examine, either because of bias or because of an unfortunate prior inconsistent statement. In which order should these witnesses be called to testify?

Many lawyers would say, "Call A first. Even if he is successfully cross-examined, B will be available to rescue the situation." Thus, many trial lawyers call essentially corroborating witnesses after the main witness has testified, to buttress testimony *after* the attempt to impeach it. But I believe this approach to fly against the odds.

If A is easier to cross-examine than B and is successfully impeached before B takes the stand, then B becomes easier to cross-examine than if A had never been heard. Why? Because the jurors have already made a commitment. Conversely, if B takes the stand first and survives cross-examination—is believed by the jury—then the cross-examination of A on the material already testified to by B and credited by the jury becomes immeasurably more difficult. Why? Because now it is the cross-examiner who must change the jurors' minds. And that is no easy thing to do. Why, then, do so many trial lawyers opt to offer corroborating evidence *after* the cross-examination of the main offer?

The answer, unfortunately, is that no matter what we say about primacy, most of us still opt for recency—for winning the case at the end, in summation, or with the last witnesses, or with the surprise we have saved for rebuttal.

Every case has at least one witness who must be believed, hence protected from cross-examination at all cost if the case is to be won. The order of proofs must be selected to give that witness the greatest protection. If that means calling a party first, so be it. If it is the party who must be protected—as is likely—then the consideration is: what order of proofs will make it harder for my adversary to cross-examine this person, and easier for this person to defend his testimony while being cross-examined?[18]

In the final analysis, most witnesses have at least some information that can help the other side or are in some way vulnerable to cross-examination. That is why one of the most difficult decisions of any trial lawyer is whether to call certain witnesses—even though those witnesses do have helpful information. As a rule, the benefits of a witness's direct testimony should *substantially* outweigh the harm that could be done on cross-examination, else the witness should not be called.

LESSON: The damage done on cross-examination is rarely confined to the witness under cross-examination. The placement of witnesses must be calculated not only to reduce the adversary's ability to successfully cross-examine that witness, but also to reduce the impact of the cross-examination of that witness upon the entire case.[19]

ENDNOTES

1. Again, it must be emphasized that in real life it cannot be doubted that Mike Tigar would have done this, given time. Yet it is also true that his questions about the honorable discharge were hurtful.
2. This is yet another reason for not reaching out to present Conti as a volunteer, which *may* be perceived to open the subject of his character, or for putting his honorable discharge into the record, which *certainly* will open up the subject of his military misconduct, particularly on the issue of a reward for the testimony.
3. By "beginning, "middle," and "end," I do not mean the very first or last question, or the one precisely in the center, but rather the phases of the examination.
4. For ease of use, recall that we decided that we could not present Conti as a good man (Level I). We could not ignore and thus fail to mention the problems (Level II). We could say that we know that he has problems, but promise to overcome his lack of credibility with corroboration, but that would leave us stranded at Level III.

   And so we decided to make affirmative use of what at first seemed to be problems by arguing that Lt. Calley knew that Conti, a private under his command, smoked dope and molested women and that is why Calley selected Conti to shoot the helpless villagers. Calley thought Conti was the kind of man who would do that for him. But even a man like Conti would not murder those helpless souls. And so, in the end, Calley had to pull the trigger himself.
5. The question is, however, far from clearly improper. Laymen may offer opinions on things within their abilities. So can a person offer an opinion as to why he was selected for a particular job? Reasonable people can surely differ on the answer.
6. L. Heller, Do You Solemnly Swear at 231 (1968).

7. L. Heller, Do You Solemnly Swear at 251–253 (1968). I think this is an excellent example. Justice Heller tells us that it came from an actual case. Later, we will see that same technique in an actual transcript. One thing, however, is clear: no one could hope to do that direct examination nearly as effectively as reproduced by Justice Heller if it is to be delivered from the kind of a "script" that Justice Heller earlier advises.
8. I say "nonsense" because that is what it is. Ofttimes a lawyer *must* call witnesses who will say many things, some of which the advocate believes to be true, some of which he does not. Nonetheless, the advocate must call the witness to make a *prima facie* case. To hold that an attorney or his client must endorse *everything* a witness will say in order to put that witness on the stand is the height of imbecility.

   For example, when I tried the *Colonial Pipeline* case, the employees of Colonial and Bechtel and Roland Tompkins were hardly my allies. Indeed, many of them refused to speak to me before I called them to the stand. Nonetheless, I was held to nonleading questions on direct examination and my adversaries sought to have me "bound" by all of the answers of "my witnesses." None of that nonsense would be possible today. As the accompanying note to Rule 607 makes clear,

   > The traditional Rule against impeaching one's own witness is abandoned as based on a false premise. A party does not hold out his witnesses as worthy of belief, since he rarely has a free choice in selecting them. Denial of the right leaves the party at the mercy of the witness and the adversary.

9. Here the direct examiner uses the witness to help him elicit testimony, not because he lacks the skill to obtain the testimony by a close-knit Q & A but because he does not wish to run a gauntlet of objections.

10. I emphatically state that I am *not* advocating the offering of evidence that an advocate knows is improper or even has no good faith belief is proper. *That* would be unethical. But the fact is that some judges do allow a witness to give the explanation before the accusation, while others do not. And there is precious little law on the subject.
11. Trial transcript, pages 997–999.
12. To be sure, there are exceptions to the hearsay rule that deal with one-party declarations. But on the odds most of the out-of-court declarations will come in under 801(d)(2), *Admissions by a party opponent*, or 801(d)(2)(E), *Statements by co-conspirators*. And, again on the odds, these rules will provide some of the most lethal evidence.
13. Probably one of the subdivisions of 803 or of 804. Of course, if the plaintiff should offer only a portion of what the defendant has said, the defendant may insist on the remainder under Rule 106. But this is a rule of completeness, not a basis for independent admissibility.
14. E.J. Imwinkelreid, Evidentiary Foundations at 123 (1980).
15. Trial transcripts do often contain quotation marks. But that can be because the court reporter *elected* to place them there. The quotations should not be sought by the examiner or deliberately conveyed by him. As we shall see, the examiner should strive against this. My trouble with the quoted material is that Professor Imwinkelreid elected to show the quotation marks as desirable.
16. The court reporter may still elect to put the answer in quotation marks when typing the answer. But that is of no consequence to those who hear the testimony and judge its credibility.
17. Indeed, as a further work will explain, I believe that such methods on cross-examination are *harmful to the cross-examiner*.

18. A word on calling adverse parties. This can be a case winner—or a case loser, particularly if the adverse party is called early in the case. If the adverse party leaves the stand disbelieved, you have gone far to winning your case. But . . . if the adverse party leaves the stand believed, what then?

    The practice of calling adverse parties, particularly as the first witness in the case, can be outcome determinative precisely because it makes the remainder of the case more or less susceptible to attack.

    The most critical aspect in the decision to call an adverse party—particularly as the first witness—is the skill of that party's lawyer. Why? Because the issue will be whether that lawyer has prepared his client to testify and, equally critical, whether that attorney is prepared to redirect upon the completion of your cross-examination. For if the trial judge permits a full examination of the defendant by his attorney on the nose of the plaintiff's case, this could poison the entire case of the plaintiff.

19. We will see a practical example of this strategy of ordering the testimony of other witnesses to protect the key witness when we analyze the *City of Newark* case.

Chapter Nine

The Ultimate Protection Is to Prevent Cross-Examination

HEARSAY EVIDENCE

On direct, every sensible trial lawyer uses as much hearsay evidence as he can. Why? Because such evidence cannot be attacked on cross-examination. The adversary is helpless to deal with hearsay evidence except by collateral attack.

Such hearsay, of course, may take the form of documentary evidence, or declarations may be related on the witness stand by a witness, who reports what some third party said or what his own out-of-court declarations were—provided they fall within one of the recognized exceptions to the hearsay rule. And today there are plenty of such exceptions.

Indeed the Federal Rules of Evidence are so hospitable to the receipt of hearsay that today the odds actually favor the trial lawyer's ability to introduce the out-of-court statements of persons who are not witnesses and never will be. While this is not a work on the Federal Rules of Evidence, it is appropriate to note that there are literally two dozen separate justifications for the introduction of out-of-court statements of witnesses *who nevertheless are available to testify*,[1] nearly another half dozen justifications for using hearsay statements of those who are not available,[2] and "catch all" provisions that permit the trial lawyer to offer hearsay not otherwise authorized by the other 28 provisions.[3] The odds favor a skilled lawyer's ability to use hearsay in his case. And when he does, such evidence is by definition uncross-examinable.

Let us take a few examples from the first half dozen of the exceptions to the hearsay rule under Federal Rule of Evidence 803, which applies whether or not the out-of-court declarant is available to testify.

Rule 803(1), the present sense impression exception, authorizes witnesses on the stand to buttress their own testimony with contemporaneous notes made by them of telephone conversations, events they witnessed, and the like.

Rule 803(2), the excited utterance exception to the hearsay rule, permits the witness to repeat out-of-court statements by himself or by others if made in a state of excitement, in relation to a startling event.

Rule 803(3) permits out-of-court statements of anyone whose state of mind is at issue in the trial at the time the statement was made. Is fraud an issue? Then state of mind is an issue. So, too, for intent, reliance, pain and suffering, fear—or the lack of fear. The possibilities are endless.

Rule 803(4) authorizes doctors to testify to the out-of-court statements of their patients if those statements were made for the purpose of medical diagnoses—and those purposes can be rather expansive.

Rule 803(5), the past recollection recorded exception, authorizes the receipt of out-of-court writings of the witness, or another, if the witness has no present recollection of the events described in the writing but does have a vestigial memory that the writing was accurate when written. Now, how do you cross-examine either the document or the amnesiac witness?

For myself, I do not care to use this exception with important witnesses who have large amounts of other testimony to offer. Why? Because it makes them appear almost retarded, as the examiner has them testify that they once had a recollection of an event—which they no longer remember—except that they do recall that the event was accurately described in a writing—which they now recall to be an accurate writing—although they no longer remember anything else about the event itself.

In extremis, one does what one has to do. But, all in all, this exception should be used only sparingly with key witnesses who have much else to testify about.[4]

Rule 803(6), authorizing the receipt of the books and records of regularly conducted business activities, is perhaps the most commonly used and the most lethal exception to the hearsay rule. When 803(6) is properly used, records can flow into court like the Mississippi, with the adversary nearly helpless in their wake.

A prime example of this point is the *Weber* case. It may be recalled that within three months of finishing the *Colonial* case, I began the trial of Peter Weber. Those who have read the openings,[5] will recall that Weber, a labor leader, was accused of accepting four separate payoffs from the H.C. Price Company of Bartlesville, Oklahoma, an employer of his men. It will also be recalled that Roy Burgess, the H.C. Price Company employee who traveled to New Jersey to make the four unwitnessed payments, was dead by the time of trial. Nonetheless, we proved three of the four payments. How?

Harold Price, the president of the company, took the stand. Under the co-conspirator exception to the hearsay rule, he was permitted to testify as to Burgess's reports to Oklahoma that Weber had demanded cash in New Jersey.[6] Using the old shop book rule,[7] all the canceled checks used to raise the cash were introduced into evidence—as well as Burgess's expense account records tracing his movements. Finally, after each trip to New Jersey, after each raising of cash, Burgess would report back to his superiors on the payoff—including the details of when, where, and how much. These reports were also admitted on the basis of the co-conspirator exception to the hearsay rule. There was, of course, no possible cross-examination of Burgess's reports or records or accusations.[8]

The point of this exposition is certainly not to detail the rules of evidence. It is to alert the direct examiner to the tools of his trade, and to emphasize that these tools not only are essential in the achievement of the first three goals of direct examination (clarity, memorability, and credibility), but are particularly helpful in making direct testimony—and, for that matter, the direct case—invulnerable to cross-examination. Nothing I can think of better illustrates this point than the case of Angelo DeCarlo.

The *DeCarlo* Case

Angelo "Gyp" DeCarlo was not an honest man. Indeed, he was a mafia "Capo" whose jurisdiction included the City of Newark, New Jersey's largest city.

DeCarlo was an extortionist—a loanshark. But that was not his only enterprise. He ran numbers and bookmaking operations. He had "points" in a Las Vegas casino. His extensive criminal enterprises required official protection to survive, so his tentacles reached out to politicians in city and county government. Indeed, even the superintendent of state police at the time was not beyond his reach.

DeCarlo's political home base was Newark, where with other mobsters such as "Tony Boy" Boiardo, and the latter's father Ruggiero "the Boot" Boiardo, he had managed to install and maintain Hugh J. Addonizio as mayor.

The Newark mobsters of the day were not the only organized criminals in New Jersey, by any means. In Hudson County Joseph "Bayonne Joe" Ziccarrelli formed a combination with the Hudson County Democratic organization originally founded by "Boss" Hague and, by the late 1960s, led by his successor John V. Kenny, "The Little Guy."

In the middle of the state, Simone Rizzo DeCavalcante, "Sam the Plumber," reigned. On the shore it was Anthony "Little Pussy" Russo. In the south the historically corrupt administration of Atlantic City and Atlantic County thrived in close harmony with the Mafia leaders of south Jersey and Philadelphia like Ray Catena and Angelo Bruno.

The FBI knew of their activities, of course, but it seemed powerless to stop these combinations of mobsters and politicians—joined with corrupt labor leaders like Anthony "Tony Pro" Provenzano of the Teamsters and Peter Weber of the Operating Engineers—who bestrode the state and were strangling it.

When Robert F. Kennedy became the Attorney General of the United States in 1961, illegal bugs and listening devices were installed in the headquarters of DeCarlo, DeCavalcante, Ziccarrelli, Catena, and Bruno. Others were installed elsewhere in the country. For the first time, and for the next nearly three years—until Kennedy resigned to run for the office of United States Senator from New York—information flooded into the FBI about the activities of organized hoodlums around the country, and J. Edgar Hoover, who had a decade before denied the existence of a Mafia, became interested in organized crime.

A particularly ugly example of the recorded conversation of some of these men was picked up by FBI microphones when DeCarlo and DeCavalcante were speaking with the Boiardos, father (the Boot) and son (Tony Boy)—and the son related how he and his father had killed a man.

> "How about the time we hit the little Jew," said Tony Boy.
>
> "As little as they are, they struggle," said DeCarlo.
>
> "The Boot hit him with a hammer," Tony Boy went on. "The guy goes down and he comes up. So I got a crowbar this big, Ray. Eight shots in the head. What do you think he finally did to me? He spit at me and said you [obscenity]."

The FBI recorded a conversation during which DeCarlo actually bribed a Newark councilman not to run against Hugh Addonizio, so as not to split the Italian vote in Addonizio's campaign against the then-mayor, incumbent Leo Carlin.

> "Now, look, you are in this business, ain't you?" DeCarlo asked Michael Bontempo, the President of the City Council of Newark.
>
> "At my age, I am," the microphone recorded Bontempo's answer. "You've got to be reasonable," Joe DeBenedictis, the democratic boss of Newark's North Ward interjected, "We want to win. You've got to sit down with Hughie [Addonizio]."
>
> "I don't care if it's you or Hughie, as long as it's an Italian," said DeCarlo.

But what DeCarlo said wasn't true. It was not that DeCarlo wanted "an Italian." DeCarlo wanted Hugh Addonizio. After Bontempo left, DeCarlo told DeBenedictis, "We'll see if we can raise ten thousand for him [Bontempo]. We'll get all the bookmakers. The Boot will put up five thousand."

The men paid off Bontempo. He did not run. Addonizio was elected in 1962. Later DeCarlo could boast, as picked up by FBI headquarters, "Hughie helped us all along. He gave us the city."

But the eavesdropping devices were illegal, so the information they yielded could be used only for intelligence, not to make criminal cases. So crime and corruption continued to flourish in the cities and the counties of New Jersey, and the state continued to be squeezed by the politicians and the organized criminals, with only occasional cases against the powerful criminal elements.

Then, in 1967, Newark exploded. Race riots engulfed the city. When I was presenting the *Colonial Pipeline* case and the *Weber* case to the federal grand jury in Newark, I saw armored personnel carriers with loaded machine guns rolling down the streets of Newark. Armed soldiers stood on the streetcorners. Buildings, indeed entire city blocks, were ablaze. Soldiers and police had to fire at the roof tops of dwellings—and sometimes into them. When it was finally over, much of Newark was a burned-out shell.

The governor, Richard Hughes, convened a select committee to inquire into the causes of the riots. That commission found that a "primary cause of the riots was a pervasive feeling of corruption . . . the sense that everything in City Hall had a price tag on it." A special grand jury was recommended. That was the beginning of the end.

On September 13, 1968, two months before I opened to the jury in the *Colonial Pipeline* case, a smalltime thief named Louis B. Saperstein was taken to DeCarlo's headquarters. He had borrowed a large sum of money from DeCarlo on extortionate terms, and he could not repay it. Because he was unable to repay the loan—or even the weekly interest—he had gone into hiding in New York City. But he was discovered and brought to DeCarlo. There, he was beaten nearly to death and told to pay $5,000 per week in interest and a lump sum of $200,000 on December 13, 1968. The beating and the threats were not recorded by the FBI microphones, which had long since been removed after Kennedy left the Justice Department.

On November 26, 1968, Saperstein entered the hospital, where he died shortly thereafter. His death was diagnosed as a product of a gastro condition. One day later, the FBI received two letters from Saperstein, both dated and mailed the day before his death.

His body was exhumed. It was found to be loaded with poison. In August of 1969 DeCarlo and several of his henchmen were indicted by a United States Grand Jury for making an "extortionate extension of credits" to Saperstein—a legal term for loansharking.

On September 2 Fred Lacey was inducted as United States Attorney. By then the *Colonial* and *Weber* trials had been concluded and we—former adversaries—were now joined as colleagues, for I accepted the post as Lacey's chief assistant. Our first case was to be the *DeCarlo* case.

It was not a strong one. The only witness to the crime was himself a criminal who had helped the DeCarlo ring first locate Saperstein in New York and then take him to New Jersey for the beating by DeCarlo's people. The letters that Saperstein wrote to the FBI had highly corroborative evidence. We needed them at the trial. And it was a trial that we *had* to win.

The defense had moved to see the results of any illegal eavesdropping to which they had been subject. Immediately after the jury was selected and sequestered, the trial judge, United States District Judge Robert Shaw, publicly filed thousands of pages of transcripts of the overheard conversations of DeCarlo and the other mobsters. New Jersey was rocked to its foundations.

The intimate details of the mob and their conversations with much of the political leadership of the state were revealed. For example, the details of the payoffs demanded by the former head of the state police were listed, and the behind-the-scenes transactions where "Gyp" DeCarlo and "Tony Boy" Boiardo had paid off potential candidates for the office of mayor of Newark not to run against Addonizio were laid out.

To top it all off, on December 17, 1969, just three months after taking office and two weeks before the *DeCarlo* case was due to commence, Lacey and I announced the indictment of Mayor Addonizio and 10 public officials, as well as "Tony Boy" Boiardo and two members of his organization in a 64-count indictment. The federal grand jury had thus accused the administration of Newark of having turned the state's largest city over to the control of the underworld.

It was against this background that the *DeCarlo* trial opened two weeks later, January 2, 1970. Our only witness was himself a master thief.

Gerald Martin Zelmanowitz was a con man's con man. He made a substantial—although highly dangerous—living by stealing from the Mafia. He had introduced both Saperstein and DeCarlo to the wonders of international arbitrage. He opened a Swiss bank account for them. DeCarlo put his money in. Saperstein borrowed money from DeCarlo to put in. But the only one who got money out was . . . Gerald Martin Zelmanowitz.

Saperstein fell behind in his "vigorish" payments—the enormous weekly interest that DeCarlo charged him for the loans. Saperstein became afraid and fled to New York. And it was there, at DeCarlo's behest, that Zelmanowitz found him and brought him back to DeCarlo's headquarters—where, according to Zelmanowitz, Saperstein was beaten until, "He was purple. He was bloody. His tongue was hanging out of his mouth. There was spit all over him. I thought he was dead."[9] Finally, Saperstein managed to drag himself over to DeCarlo, wrap his arms around his legs, and beg him to stop the beating because he could no longer breathe.

To catch the flavor of the testimony, and as a further illustration, the following few pages of Zelmanowitz's testimony are illustrative.

Q: All right. Did you set a place, a time and place? Did he set it with you for that meeting?

A: Mr. Saperstein set a time and place.

Q: What time and what place did he set?

A: Within another hour at the Hilton Hotel lobby.

Q: What, if anything, did you do after Mr. Saperstein set that time and that place?

A: I went outside and told Mr. Cecere that I had moved the appointment up another hour and that we would meet him at the Hilton Hotel later on.

Q: Did you have a further conversation with Mr. Cecere then?

A: I again insisted on some assurance that Mr. Saperstein would be okay, would be given an opportunity to speak and explain what had transpired, what had happened. I was reassured again.

Q: By whom?

A: By Mr. Cecere.

Q: After that conversation did you and Mr. Cecere and this man known to you as Lenny go any place?

A: Yes, we went to the Hilton Hotel, into the lobby.

Q: Was Mr. Saperstein there when you arrived?

A: No. He had not arrived yet.

Q: What, if anything, happened?

A: Eventually he arrived and when he did we started to walk over to him. His back was turned toward us. As we approached he turned and saw us, and he became very frightened and started to move away.

MR. DIRENZO: I object.

MR. QUERQUES: Objection.

THE COURT: What did you observe?

THE WITNESS: I observed him frightened, nervous. He tried to turn and run.

MR. DIRENZO: I object to that and move that that portion be stricken.

THE COURT: Motion denied.

THE WITNESS: It was too late. Cecere had one arm; Lenny had the other arm, and Saperstein was going to scream out. He was spoken to. He was reassured, calmed down, everything would be all right. "We just want to talk to you."

Q: Who was speaking to him?

A: Mr. Cecere.

Q: Was Mr. Saperstein saying anything?

A: There was no—he didn't say anything.

Q: What did Mr. Cecere say?

A: He was just reassuring him, calming him down.

Q: What, if anything, happened next?

A: We asked him what room he was staying in. He told us. We went upstairs to his room and asked him to come back to New Jersey with us.

The testimony was going in clickity-clack. But notice, my questioning has a lot of unnecessary "what, *if anything*," prefixes. I would not do that today. Today I would say, "What happened next?" or, better yet, "After Mr. Cecere calmed Saperstein's fears, what happened?" But this writing is nearly a quarter of a century in courtrooms *later*.

Q: When you arrived at Mr. Saperstein's room what, if anything, occurred?

A: There was a lot of confusion, Mr. Stern. Mr. Saperstein was trying to explain that he had not been to Europe. He was frightened. He was in great fear for his family. Saperstein made the statement that he would take out a $100,000 insurance policy and jump out of this window, "If you don't hurt my family," and he would "make you my beneficiary."

MR. DIRENZO: I move that the answer be stricken.

THE COURT: Motion denied.
To whom was he speaking?

THE WITNESS: To Mr. Cecere.

MR. DIRENZO: I move for mistrial.

THE COURT: Motion denied.

There is that error we mentioned earlier, asking for a mistrial in the presence of the jury (*see* Volume I, page 47). And the attorney doing that was no novice. Mike Direnzo had been defending criminal cases in New York City for at least 30 years as of this time. I had observed him a few years before when I had been a New York County assistant district attorney. As for me, I was still what-if-anythinging.

Q: What, if anything, happened next?

A: He continued to pack his bag and walk toward the bathroom. I was standing there. He had an envelope which he started to tear up and was going to throw it into the bathroom. I observed it, and I saw the word "investigation" was written on it.

Q: That is all you saw, that one word, is that correct?

A: That is all I saw, yes.

Q: Did there come a time when the four of you, the defendant Cecere and this man known to you as Lenny and Mr. Louis B. Saperstein, left the Hilton Hotel?

A: Yes, sir.

Q: What, if anything, happened then?

A: We left. Mr. Saperstein, Mr. Cecere and this Lenny got into Mr. Saperstein's automobile. Mr. Cecere told me to drive over to Mountainside, in back of this Weiland's Restaurant, to the barn, the house in back of Weiland's, DeCarlo's place, and to meet them there.

Q: Did you follow those instructions?

A: I did.

Q: How did you get there?

A: I drove my automobile.

Q: Will you tell the jury what, if anything, happened when you arrived at the little house in back of Weiland's?

A: I arrived and parked my car and started to walk into this house. There was a group of people in the first room as I entered, and I heard my name called, and there is another room attached to this room which I entered, and when I got in there Mr. Saperstein was laying on the floor. He was purple. He was bloody. His tongue was hanging out of his mouth. There was spit all over him. I thought he was dead, and—

Q: Was anybody doing anything to Mr. Saperstein?

A: Yes. He was being kicked and punched.

Q: By whom?

> A: By Mr. Polverino and Mr. Cecere.
>
> Q: What, if anything, happened when you entered the room?
>
> A: Saperstein seemed to come awake, and he started to say things. He said, "Stop hitting me." He pleaded. He pointed to me and said, "He is the cause of this." "Hit him." He was trying to get them away from him onto me.
>
> Q: Did the defendant Cecere and the defendant Polverino continue to hit and beat him?
>
> A: He was lifted up off the floor and placed into a chair, and in the chair he was hit again.
>
> Q: What happened after he was hit while he was in the chair?
>
> A: He was knocked off the chair, Mr. Stern, and picked up again and hit again.
>
> Q: What, if anything, happened *later*? [Emphasis added.]

It was almost *too* much. I had all the repetition I wanted. I was afraid that Zelmanowitz, who was by that time thoroughly at ease and almost enjoying himself, would have Saperstein in and out of the chair a few more times. And so I forced Zelmanowitz out of that groove with the question, "What, if anything, happened, *later*?"

> A: There was some commotion outside and Mr. DeCarlo arrived. Mr. Saperstein saw Mr. DeCarlo standing outside the room, and Mr. Cecere and Mr. Polverino went over to Mr. DeCarlo and tried to explain that Mr. Saperstein had said that he had no money and that he used the money, and Mr. Saperstein was running to Mr. DeCarlo and pleading with him to have a stop, and please don't hit him anymore, he was going to die if he was beaten any more. He couldn't breathe.

> Q: Was Mr. Cecere and Mr. Polverino asking Mr. DeCarlo for anything?
>
> A: Yes, they wanted to kill him.
>
> MR. DIRENZO: Objection, and I move that it be stricken.
>
> MR. QUERQUES: I join in that objection.
>
> THE COURT: What, if anything, was said? I don't want your conclusions.
>
> Q: The exact words, if you can remember them.[10]
>
> A: He said, "This s.o.b. stole our money. I am going to kill him."
>
> THE COURT: Who said that?
>
> THE WITNESS: Mr. Cecere.

This testimony was all well and good, but would the jurors believe Zelmanowitz? Why was he testifying? He had been caught by the FBI attempting to move millions of dollars in stolen securities, and had made a deal. This, coupled with his complicity in the entire Saperstein affair, plus his criminal record, did not exactly bode well for his credibility. We simply could not rely on his uncorroborated testimony. But there was no corroboration . . . except for the Saperstein letters. But that was corroboration that simply could not be impeached.

And so, we offered the Saperstein letters from the grave into evidence. We did this under the theory that the letters went to prove Saperstein's state of mind—that he was in fear of DeCarlo—a necessary element of the crime charged. The trial judge agreed. And so, standing mid point, eight feet back from the jury box, I read Saperstein's letter from the grave to the jurors.

> Federal Bureau of Investigation, Newark, New Jersey.
>
> Gentlemen: I am writing you, maybe others can be helped by my plight. On September 13, 1968, I

> was severely beaten at a place in the rear of Weiland's Restaurant, Route 22, DeCarlo's headquarters. I was then told and given 3 months until December 13, 1968 to pay the entire accumulated amount under threat of death. Cecere, DeCarlo and Polverino, also stated many times my wife and son would be maimed or killed. Please protect my family—I am sure they mean to carry out this threat.
>
> Last night from my home I called DeCarlo and pleaded for time but to no avail. Over the phone DeCarlo stated unless further monies was paid the threats would be carried out.
>
> Louis B. Saperstein[11]

DeCarlo was convicted after less than four hours of deliberation, on January 28, 1970—and the stage was set for the most difficult direct examination of my entire career.[12]

ENDNOTES

1. *See* Fed. R. Evid. 803, subdivisions 1–23.
2. *See* Fed. R. Evid. 804, subdivisions 1–4.
3. *See* Fed. R. Evid. 803(24) and 804(5).
4. It will be very clear later how hard my adversaries in the *City of Newark* case tried to make me use this exception—and how tenaciously I resisted.
5. Reproduced in the appendices to Volume I.
6. The Price people and Weber were deemed co-conspirators because it is illegal for an employer to pay a representative of his men. This co-conspirator exception to the hearsay rule was the precursor to Rule 801(d)(2)(E).
7. 28 U.S.C. § 1732(a), the precursor of Rule 803(6).
8. Weber was convicted of these and other crimes—including extortions of Bechtel and Colonial. He was sentenced to 10 years imprisonment. His convictions were affirmed. *See U.S. v. Weber*, 437 F.2d 327 (1970).
9. Direct testimony of Zelmanowitz.
10. On this rare and exceptional circumstance I called for the exact words—confident that the jurors would believe that the witness had a reason and the ability to remember them.
11. This was not the entire contents of either one of the two letters. The jury was given an expurgated version, with amounts of money deleted.
12. The conviction was affirmed. 458 F.2d 358 (3d Cir. 1972).

Chapter Ten
The *City of Newark* Case

As I said earlier, the riots and the burnings in Newark had led to the Governor's Commission report on corruption. That report led to a county grand jury investigation of the city administration. And that grand jury began to focus on the business of a man named Paul Rigo.

Rigo was an engineer by profession. And he wanted to become a wealthy one. Ultimately he achieved that goal—by becoming the engineer most often employed by Newark on public works, for which he kicked back 10 percent of the city contracts to a consortium of public officials, headed by Mayor Addonizio, and mobsters, headed by "Tony Boy" Boiardo.

In the mid 1960s Rigo formed a company known as Constrad. And Constrad was the vehicle that he used to get the work from the city and to wash hundreds of thousands of dollars out as bribes.

No one lived better than Paul Rigo. Only a year or two before, he had been an employee of the state of New Jersey, an engineer covered by and paid at the wages of a civil service employee. After making contact with the Addonizio-Boiardo ring, Rigo lived on a private compound with his own helicopter. He traveled the world collecting art and antiques. He entertained lavishly both at home and abroad and on chartered yachts. Eventually he purchased his own yacht. He lived an opulent—nearly decadent—existence, hemorrhaging money.

The special county grand jury—convened after the Newark riots—summoned Rigo before them. Rigo obeyed the subpoena. But once sworn before the grand jury, he lied—exonerating not only himself but the politicians and the mobsters as well. But still the pressure increased.

The county investigators were all over his books and his records. His bank accounts fell under scrutiny. Meanwhile, the mobsters kept pressuring him to keep his mouth shut and, together with the public officials, to keep his payments up to date.

Rigo finally broke. By November of 1969 he was under investigation by our federal grand jury as well. He fled to Acapulco. From there, he made contact with a friend in the White House, who in turn made contact with the highest people in the Department of Justice in Washington. On November 17, 1969, slightly more than two months after we had assumed office, Fred Lacey rendezvoused with Rigo in Washington. Two days later, I joined them. One month later, on December 17, 1969, we announced the grand jury indictment of 14 defendants on 64 counts of extortion. The so-called *City of Newark* case had begun—although the trial would not commence for five months, until May of 1970, for the *DeCarlo* case was due to start in January.

When the indictment was handed up, Addonizio, a former seven-term Congressman, was running for re-election against Kenneth Gibson, a young black engineer. In spite of the indictment, Addonizio obtained enough votes to force a runoff election with Gibson—an election campaign that was still underway when the trial opened in May. It was a trial that caught the imagination of the nation. Not only had the DeCarlo tapes been released now, but the federal grand jury had accused the largest city in the state of having fallen into the hands of the Mafia. The mayor and the mob were on trial together—in the midst of his re-election campaign against an opponent who, if elected, would become the first black mayor of a major Northeastern American city. It was a case that Lacey and I *had* to win. And the *only* witness we had against Mayor Addonizio, the *only* witness against "Tony Boy" Boiardo—indeed the *only* witness who could tie the mobsters *and* the politicians to the conspiracy charged in the indictment—was . . . Paul Rigo. It was to be the most important direct examination I would ever conduct.

This background is essential to an understanding of the five days of direct examination I conducted of Rigo. The direct examination is analyzed in the following pages in light of the principles and the techniques of direct examination we have previously tried to isolate and identify. As I have noted earlier, mere doing without an intellectual framework is worthless. By the same token, mere intellectual discussion of principles without a nitty gritty analysis of trial records is vacuous. And so, what follows is as candid and objective an analysis of the trial record as I am capable of giving. And if you find that this is the record from an exciting case at a critical moment in the life of a city, well . . . who is to say that professional study *has* to be dull?

THE ORDER OF WITNESSES

The last and the hardest decision in the trial was the selection of the order of the witnesses. The key witness, indeed the only one that mattered, was Paul Rigo. If he were believed on direct examination, and if he survived cross-examination, the case would be won. If not, the case would be lost. It was as simple as that.

In the first moments of the investigation the choice was easy. In fact, there was no choice at all. For when Paul Rigo fled to Mexico and made contact with us in Washington in November of 1969, he was our *only* witness. For the next month we began to accumulate evidence as quickly as we could.

To begin with, there were the Rigo diaries. In Washington Rigo informed Fred Lacey and me that he had diaries for the years 1964 through 1969, which had coded entries reflecting the payoffs to the public officials of Newark and their Mafia allies. That was essential corroborative evidence. We immediately sent a squad of agents to Rigo's premises in New Jersey to take possession of the Rigo diaries.[1]

The grand jury began to hear evidence. Among the public officials accused by Rigo was Phillip Gordon, Newark's corporation counsel. Rigo revealed that he had given envelopes stuffed with money to Gordon, and additional envelopes for Gordon to pass to another councilman. We subpoenaed Gordon before the grand jury and he confirmed Rigo's story.

But now it was a race against time. With the election campaign underway, we decided that we could not wait to finish a lengthy investigation before recommending an indictment. And so, just one month after Rigo met us in Washington on November 17th, that is, on December 17th, 1969, the grand jury indicted virtually the entire top echelon of officialdom of Newark, along with their mobster allies. The mayor, the corporation counsel—and his predecessor, the public works director—and his predecessor, six present or former members of the city council, each and all were charged with a conspiracy to commit extortion—along with Anthony "Tony Boy" Boiardo and two of his henchmen, Joseph Biancone and Ralph Vicaro. The indictments contained 65 counts, and had an unusual structure.

Sixty-four separate payments from Rigo were alleged—for he was our only witness at that time. But we hoped for more. So we drafted the conspiracy count to allege that the defendants conspired to extort money from *everyone* doing business with the City of Newark. We hoped and prayed that by the time of trial we would develop additional witnesses, and that this open-ended conspiracy count would permit us to buttress the Rigo testimony with these after-found witnesses.[2] And it did.

THE ADDITIONAL WITNESSES

Two weeks after the Addonizio indictment was returned, Fred Lacey and I were trying the *DeCarlo* case. But even as we were in court, teams of assistant United States attorneys paired with IRS agents were hurriedly assembling witnesses and documents to support the 60-plus Rigo counts of payments.

Assistant United States Attorneys John W. Bissell and Garrett E. Brown (now both United States district judges) and Special Assistants Donald Merkelbach and Michael Riccardelli worked for months to persuade witnesses to come forward and to assemble the documentary evidence for a trial that was only a few months away. And they were successful.

By the time of trial we had nearly half a dozen businessmen prepared to testify about the payments exacted from them. Even more critical, largely through the efforts of Jack Bissell, Irving Kantor—dying in a hospital of amyotrophic lateral sclerosis, "Lou Gerhig's disease"—was persuaded to tell the truth about a phony bank account he had set up in the name of Kantor Plumbing Supply, which had been used to wash millions of dollars in checks into cash. It would be his testimony that he received checks drawn on accounts of contractors doing city work, which he would deposit and then take cash out (less 5 percent for himself) and deliver the cash to Joe Biancone or to Tony G—members of "Tony Boy's" organization.

It was dramatic testimony from a man suffering from the last stages of a fatal disease which had so paralyzed his nervous system that he was totally bedridden, unable to move, with tubes conveying nourishment into him and waste from his bladder. Five months before trial he could hardly speak any longer, having lost nearly all control over his larynx. I remember bending over his hospital bed in the final stages of pretrial preparation, straining to catch his words through his blurred speech as, with tears rolling down his cheeks, he struggled to explain to me that he was willing to testify because he wanted to help his country undo the wrongs he himself had helped to commit.

We had not threatened him or induced him to testify. He was beyond threat, beyond inducement. He was near a terrible death. Irving Kantor simply did not want to die without doing this final act for his country.

This, then, was the corroboration we had for Rigo. There were some diaries—which the defense would no doubt claim were as false as the testimony of their owner. We did have the admissions by Gordon that he did receive money from Rigo. But, beyond that, what did we have? A dying man who, although he could show a mechanism for the generation of cash, never spoke with the mayor or the other public officials and could go no higher in the Boiardo organization than Joseph Biancone. And, finally, a handful of businessmen who had been solicited for money by Biancone, and occasionally by La Morte—the public works director—but who could not lay a verbal glove on either Mayor Addonizio or “Tony Boy” Boiardo. Only Rigo had testimonial evidence against Boiardo and Addonizio. These were the proofs to be selected in an order that was not designed either to begin strong or to end strong but to make Rigo credible on direct and as invulnerable as possible to the heavy cross-examination that was sure to follow his direct testimony.

The question was, should we put Rigo on first, at the outset of the case, to tell his almost unbelievable tale of conversations with “Tony Boy,” who claimed to be the real boss of the City of Newark, and Mayor Addonizio, whom “Tony Boy” had named “The Pope”? Or should we attempt to finish with him, as our last witness? What would be the best order of proofs, given the cross-examination, which would surely suggest that the Constrad checks Rigo had cashed for months had been used *not* to generate cash for the public officials but to fund Rigo's own fantastically high living? Should Kantor go on before Rigo, or should we reserve him to salvage the situation after Rigo was cross-examined? The same questions welled forth in respect to the other businessmen who had paid off. I struggled with these questions for days before deciding.

In the end, I put Irving Kantor on as my first witness. Why? To begin with, I believed him to be uncross-examinable. He was that witness who could help us the most, while hurting us the least.

What could he do to help us? Although his testimony did not touch either Boiardo or Addonizio directly, the Kantor testimony put the courtroom awash in cash. On just one project, the Southside Sewer Interception System, 10 million had been paid by the city to the contractors and nearly one million—10 percent—had been washed through Kantor's account and given back.[3] This, I felt, would protect Rigo from juror disbelief, *during his direct testimony as well as his cross-examination*, when he took the stand *after* Kantor and claimed to have kicked back 10 percent on all of his dealings with the city. Kantor, on direct, would prepare the way for Rigo on direct and protect Rigo on cross.

On cross-examination, Kantor could not be touched. He was a dying man. He had no motive to lie. When I announced him as our first witness, I also sought and obtained permission to convene the court in the hospital's largest room. The judge and the jury were brought to Kantor's bedside. And by that time the poor man was so weak that he could no longer speak intelligibly. The only person who could understand him was his wife, Jane Kantor.

And so Jane Kantor, sitting by her husband's bedside, was sworn as interpreter, and the first witness in the case was Irving Kantor, whose strangled words from his bed, as translated by his wife, cushioned and protected Paul Rigo before Rigo was called to testify—even though Kantor had never heard of Rigo and could not directly implicate the people Rigo would accuse.

We put on the handful of businessmen next, and, of course, agent De Amicus of the FBI with his chart, and then the stage was set for our star witness, indeed our *only* witness against the two leading defendants.

THE COUNSEL FOR THE DEFENDANTS

By the time of trial seven defendants remained in the case. First, there was the Boiardo group: Boiardo, represented by Thomas Wadden; Joseph Biancone, represented by Thomas Dyson; and Ralph Vicaro, represented by Patrick Wall.

Wadden, Dyson, and Wall were former law partners of Edward Bennett Williams. Wadden had formed a law firm with Williams known first as Williams, Wadden and Stein and later as Williams and Wadden. Wadden was a ferocious adversary and one of the most feared defense attorneys. Dyson and Wall were extremely experienced and able trial lawyers. Pat Wall I had known years before in New York, immediately after he finished a term as Justice Sarafite's law secretary and began trying cases for the defense when I had been a young assistant DA. Pat Wall was and still is a highly respected trial lawyer.

Bernard Hellring represented Hugh Addonizio. I have written of him extensively elsewhere. Such was the respect I had for him that, years after the trial, I appointed him to defend an

East German accused of hijacking a Polish plane to West Berlin when I presided over the trial as the United States Judge for Berlin.[4] And when I left the federal bench 17 years after the Addonizio trial, I became his law partner until I withdrew to start my own firm.

James Callaghan, city councilman, was represented by Joseph Hayden. We have met this fine attorney earlier; he represented Peter Weber and opened against me in that case.[5]

Anthony La Morte, the director of public works, selected Jules Feinberg as his attorney. An able trial lawyer, Feinberg later became a state judge.

The last defendant was Phillip Gordon, corporation counsel of the City of Newark. He had John Noonan, a thoroughly experienced advocate, by his side.

THE RIGO DIRECT EXAMINATION

And thus we come to the last illustration of the principles of direct examination, the direct of Paul Rigo. It consumed nearly five full days. And while it is not reasonable to reproduce all of it, significant portions are analyzed to demonstrate the principles of direct examination that we have identified.

When Rigo was called to the stand, the first task was to immunize him. This could not be done in the presence of the jury, so they were excused from the room. In those days we had no limited use immunity, called testimonial immunity. All we could convey was transactional immunity, which not only made the witness immune from the *use* of his words against him, but also gave him total immunity from prosecution for whatever crimes he testified about.

DIRECT EXAMINATION BY MR. STERN:

Q: What is your name, sir?

A: Paul W. Rigo.

Q: Where do you reside, Mr. Rigo?

A: Oldwick, New Jersey.

Q: What is your business or occupation?

A: Engineer.

Q: Mr. Rigo, did there come a time when you personally gave cash, money in cash form, to the defendant Addonizio and Boiardo?

A: I refuse to answer that question, Mr. Stern, on the ground that it may tend to incriminate me.

Inasmuch as I had to pick one question to get the refusal to testify and then the judge's order to proceed and hence the immunity, I thought I might as well pick a killer of a question. And so I laid it on the key defendants. The judge, Judge Barlow, then ordered Rigo to answer, and conveyed complete immunity to the witness:

THE COURT: . . . Mr. Rigo, you are directed to answer the question put to you by Mr. Stern. I will, on the basis of this application made to me pursuant to the provisions of 18 United States Code, Section 2514-2516, 1(c), which are the statutes, part of the Omnibus Crime Control and Safe Streets Act of 1968, pursuant to that, I will confer upon you immunity from prosecution with respect to all answers you give, both with respect to your direct testimony, all responsive answers you give, both with respect to your direct testimony and your cross-examination.

THE WITNESS: Thank you, your Honor.

THE COURT: May we have the jury?
Will you step down, so you can be resworn in front of the jury?

(The jury entered the courtroom.)

THE COURT: Your next witness, Mr. Stern.

MR. STERN: United States calls Paul Rigo.

I decided that the first order of business was to tell the jurors what had just occurred in their absence. And so I told them, right through the witness:

DIRECT EXAMINATION BY MR. STERN:

Q: Now, Mr. Rigo, during the recess which we just had, you were granted immunity from prosecution, isn't that so?

A: Yes, sir.

Q: And the judge advised you that provided that your answers were responsive to questions asked, you could not and would not be prosecuted, based on the answers given to such questions.

A: Yes, sir.

Q: This was done in open court just a few minutes ago, is that a fact?

A: Yes, sir.

And now the task was to introduce the witness to the jury properly—in other words, as a human being with a history and a background (*see* page 31 *et seq. supra*).

Q: Where do you reside?

A: Oldwick, New Jersey.

Q: And what is your business or occupation?

A: I am an engineer.

Q: Have you had any formal academic training?

A: Yes, sir. I went through Manhattan College to the point of about approximately three years of training and then had to leave it because of the birth of a daughter. Since then I have taken other courses, but that is the extent of it.

Q: Now, then, prior to entering Manhattan College, did you have any military service?

A: Yes, sir, I did.

Q: When? What period of time did you have such service?

A: From 1943 until the early part of 1946, sir.

Q: And which area did you serve in?

A: I spent two years overseas in the Pacific areas.

Q: After becoming separated from military service, was it then that you attended Manhattan College?

A: Yes.

The last question "loops" back to the witness's earlier testimony that he attended Manhattan College. The next will loop again, reminding us that he had to leave school because of the birth of his child. This is a conversation between us, as much as an interrogation by me.

Q: And after three years when you left, due to the birth of your child, did you continue to take courses at night?

A: Yes, sir, whenever I could. I was working for contractors. It was sometimes difficult.

Q: And what sort of work were you doing in the daytime?

A: I was an engineer for a construction company, sir.

Q: Which company first employed you?

A: George M. Brewster & Son.

Q: Is that a firm here in New Jersey?

A: Bogota, New Jersey.

Q: Now, can you recall approximately how long you continued to work for the Brewster firm?

A: Well, approximately a year and a half to two years, I believe.

Q: What, if anything, did you do after that?

A: I then went to work for the Joseph Miele Construction Company of Maplewood, New Jersey.

Q: In what capacity did you work for them?

A: As an engineer, sir.

In this way the man was being introduced to the jurors, who well understood that it was *essential* to them to know the kind of a man they were dealing with. After all, he was our *only* witness to *all* of the substantive counts in the indictment—and our *only* witness against the mayor and "Tony Boy" Boiardo. And so I took him through every job he had ever held as an engineer until he finally entered public service.

Q: Who made this job offer to you, was it a private firm?

A: No, sir, the state of New Jersey.

Q: If I understand you correctly then, about 1959 you became an employee of the state of New Jersey?

A: Yes, sir.

Q: What were your duties as division engineer?

A: To do the engineering and supervise the construction. May I correct that, sir. There were consultants employed on that job to do the overall engineering. We did the minor things that had to be done in conjunction with the construction.

Rigo's experience in working for the state was then developed, not in boring detail, but with enough substance to put a framework on his background. And then we were ready for the moment when he decided to go out on his own and to form the corporation "Constrad," the vehicle that ultimately got the city work and made the payoffs to the defendants.

Q: Did you continue past 1963 or the beginning of 1964 to be an employee of the state of New Jersey?

A: Yes, sir, on an on-call basis.

Q: Can you tell us why it was that you stopped your full-time work with the state of New Jersey and became an employee on, as you put it, an on-call basis?

A: Yes, sir, we were employed down there to build a construction staff, to get the reservoirs built, the project built. The state did not have sufficient people to handle it and all of us were on a temporary basis so that as the work was phased out, as one reservoir was completed, we cut back on our staff, as the second one and so on. By the time we got to the '63–'64 area, it was time to start looking ahead to what was next and one of the reasons why I went there in the first place was because of these people that we would have, we had built a very excellent staff and some of these people were going to come with me to form another company, to form a company to do engineering work.

Q: Did you in the year 1963 form such a company?

A: Yes, sir.

Q: What was the name of the company that you formed?

A: Constrad, Inc.

Now we were ready to lay the first cornerstone of the indictment. Constrad had been the vehicle used by Rigo to make virtually all of the payments to the defendants listed in the five dozen counts in the indictment. And those counts charged not only extortion, but an extortion that affected interstate commerce. So we *had* to prove that payments exacted from Constrad would affect interstate commerce due to the nature of that corporation's business. There was no help for it. It was a jurisdictional requirement for being in federal court. It *had* to be done.

> Q: I show you this document which has been marked Government Exhibit 299 for identification—withdrawn.
>
> Your Honor, at this point, I offer into evidence a certified and exemplified copy of a certificate of incorporation of Constrad, Inc., marked Government Exhibit 299 for identification.
>
> THE COURT: Any objection, gentlemen?
>
> MR. NOONAN: No objection.
>
> THE COURT: It may be marked and received.
>
> [Exhibit G-299, consisting of Certificate of Incorporation of Constrad, Inc., received and marked for identification.]

The certificate could come directly into evidence as a public document. And so, when I began to offer it by having Rigo identify it with the usual jargon, "I show you what has been marked Government Exhibit 299 for identification. . ." and intended to continue by having Rigo identify it, I stopped myself. It was unnecessary. So I just put it into evidence. But now the pertinent part had to be read to the jury. But who should read it, Rigo or I? I did it. Even then I knew better than to have a witness do it (*see* pages 175, 176 *supra*). So I not only read it to Rigo; I put the interstate commerce part into the form of a question and then hammered it home with three more.

> Q: Let me give you a copy. Now item D of Government Exhibit 299 in evidence states: "The objects for which this corporation is formed are to provide services for construction projects, for their administration, inspection, supervision and allied services and such other business as may be conveniently operated therewith. The corporation shall also have power to conduct its business in all its branches, have one or more offices and ultimately to hold, purchase, mortgage and convey real and

personal property in any state, territory, or colony of the United States and in any foreign country or place." That document recites under item D, does [it] not?

A: Yes, sir.

Q: Now, was this corporation, was Constrad formed to do business outside of the state of New Jersey?

A: Yes, sir.

Q: That was your intention at the time?

A: Yes, sir.

Q: And you put that in the certificate of incorporation?

A: Yes, sir.

The time had come to introduce into evidence—if I could get them in—some of the key documents in the case, the Rigo diaries. Those six diaries, for 1964 through 1969, were highly corroborative evidence of the testimony about to pour forth from the witness stand, for Rigo had made coded entries contemporaneous with meetings and with the payments of money over the years. These little diaries, then, would be invaluable corroboration for his testimony and would help not only to make that testimony credible on direct, but also to insulate the direct testimony from cross-examination. But the diaries had an even more essential purpose.

Each count of the indictment alleged a specific payment on a specific date. But there was no way that Rigo could independently remember each transaction. The charges were pinned to the diary entries. I had a copy of each diary for each juror. And I intended to have the jury follow along with the testimony—diary in hand. And Rigo's direct testimony was keyed to each diary entry. The prosecution simply *had* to get these entries before the jury!

But the trouble was that they were hearsay—just prior consistent statements of the witness—and not independently admissible unless they could fit into one of the exceptions to the hearsay rule. I could only think of two. One I did not want to use, and the other I feared I could not use.

I might have used "past recollection recorded",[6] but that would have forced me to make my key witness seem a moron, a man who remembered nothing except that he once remembered.[7] This I did not want to do.

The other exception to the hearsay rule was the old shop book rule, 28 U.S.C. § 1732(a).[8] This was the rule I wanted to use to put the exhibits in, in a body, and, once in evidence, to use those diaries as both aids to Rigo as he testified and footnotes to the credibility of his testimony.

But the trouble with this was that it was far from clear that these diaries qualified as books and records made and kept in the course of a regular business. Oh, there were some business entries all right. And the fact that the diaries contained records of illegal payments clearly did not disqualify them as business records. But what did hurt was that there were a great many nonbusiness entries in the diaries, perhaps too many to permit the diaries to qualify under the shop book rule. And, to top it off, others had made entries in the Rigo diaries as well. Still later, Rigo's accountant had made certain false entries in them to foil the IRS investigation. It was a mess.

Still, I simply had to use them during the testimony. And I knew that sooner or later the jurors would see them—if not on Rigo's direct then surely during his cross-examination, for the defense had had the diaries for 10 days and planned to use them too. But timing was everything. And I needed to use them on direct. So I tested the waters. I could not use the classic question, "Were these books and records made in the usual and ordinary course of business?", and, following a "yes," ask then, "And was it in the usual and ordinary course of your business to make and to keep such records?" So I got as close to that as I could, and hoped for the best.

Q: Now then, did you between the years of 1964 and 1969 and through 1969, conduct the business of Constrad, Inc.?

A: Yes, sir.

Q: I show you these diaries. They are marked Government Exhibits 44, 45, 46, 47, 48, 49 for identification and I ask you if you can identify them?

A: Yes, sir.

Q: What are those little books?

A: These are the diaries that I kept in connection with my business.

Q: Did you keep them in connection with the running of your business?

A: Yes, sir.

Q: And make entries in them in connection therewith?

A: Yes, sir.

MR. STERN: I offer them into evidence.

MR. FEINBERG: May we see them?

THE COURT: Let the defense see them, please, Mr. Stern.

MR. STERN: Who wants them?

MR. FEINBERG: I do.

MR. STERN: I think you will find they are the same as the copies we gave you.

MR. HAYDEN: The copies are not legible.

All of that was in the presence of the jury. But then Gordon's lawyer, Jack Noonan, asked for a side bar, and when we were hunched over by the bench outside the hearing of the jurors, the defense attorneys all went to work on me.

First there was Pat Wall, who spoke for Vicaro, and was, in my view, the finest legal mind on the defense team.

> MR. WALL: I object to the introduction of these diaries at this time on the ground that there has yet been no showing that these are anything other than either prior consistent statements, if that is what they are, or past recollection recorded, or anyone of the so-called exceptions to the hearsay rule upon which foundation would first have to be made. . . .

And he threw a barrage of objections at the exhibits, complaining, among other things, that the five years of diaries, copies of which he had for 10 days, might contain prejudicial material and he did not want these hundreds of pages to come into evidence *en masse*. By this time the judge was a little confused. He remembered the words of Hayden in open court just before we came to side bar.

> THE COURT: They weren't legible?
>
> MR. WALL: I think Mr. Hayden said that. I didn't have too much of a problem in reading what was in them, although I confess to you that we have so many documents that I haven't read every single page of this . . . my point is I am in no position to say no objection when I haven't read every single page.
>
> MR. STERN: I think on a question of competency, shop book rule, they can come in ultimately. I can't stand up here and make an offer of proof about all of these.
>
> THE COURT: How can Mr. Stern stand here and go through all his diaries and indicate what questions he is going to ask concerning what entries?
>
> MR. WALL: I wasn't asking for that. First of all, if Mr. Stern is going to try to get this in under the Business Records Act, I can tell your Honor that

this evening I am going to have in the mail special delivery xerox of a number of cases, and I do want to be heard with respect to whether or not these particular books can possibly qualify as a business record.

Wall began to press for an overnight recess. I did not want one. Neither did the judge.[9] We had a sequestered jury and we were on my case. I was fearful that early recesses sending jurors back to their confinement with nothing to do would be held against the prosecution. But then Pat began to do something even more dangerous from my point of view. He wanted to force me to use the entries as past recollections recorded. This would be lethal to me, as Rigo would have had to profess no recollection about the transactions in order to put the entries into evidence.

MR. WALL: My point is this: I do not believe that these can qualify as business records. I would like to argue that to you tomorrow. If they do not qualify as business records, then, as I am sure Mr. Stern knows, there is a way of getting them into evidence, and a proper way; not the whole diary. If a man has a blank recollection as to a certain date that he can testify under oath that he recorded the event when it was fresh in his mind almost contemporaneously with it, and he knew it was accurate when he did it, then it comes in as past recollection recorded.

THE COURT: To use it to refresh his recollection.[10]

MR. STERN: He may be right that there may be, if you rule against me, a way I could get this entry in. But why am I forced to argue past recollections recorded when I can get these in under the shop book rule? There is going to be a issue in this trial as to who wrote what in this diary. Ultimately I believe that these diaries are going to be used so

> much by both sides that this whole thing is going to become pretty obviated.

Pat Wall made a candid response, and with his candor I lost my effort to keep the trial going.

> MR. WALL: All I am asking, your Honor, is for the chance to take a look at the law and argue it to you tomorrow. I think Mr. Stern is basically correct, we are going to be using entries in these diaries. But one of my reasons is that I am fearful of not objecting to something significant, the significance of which I don't yet know and may quite frankly not know tomorrow.

Judge Barlow was obviously impressed. Fair-minded judges like fair-minded lawyers. And Wall's candor won him what he wished.[11]

> THE COURT: In view of the time, I think I will send the jury home and hear that argument tomorrow morning. I would like to see copies of these things myself. I have no idea what the entries are. You gentlemen have had that opportunity, I haven't.

I did not spend a happy evening. I feared the court's ruling, for if we were to be deprived of the use of the Rigo diaries during his direct examination, then vital—perhaps the most vital—corroborative and protective evidence would be lost.

The argument the next morning was heated. Back and forth it went in a seesaw effort to sway the mind of Judge Barlow. And then Tom Wadden strode into the argument and dealt the shrewdest blow of all in preventing my use of the Rigo diaries.

> MR. WADDEN: Judge, if your Honor is going to rule they fall under the shop book rule, I certainly would request that we have a voir dire of this witness, particularly, in fact, because of the fact that we have a pretty good reason to believe that Mr. Rigo

> likewise participated, as Mr. Fallon did, in making a lot of entries at one time. And if this is true, we have a right to show it on a voir dire before it ever gets to the jury. If we do establish it then, I certainly don't think your Honor would let it in under the shop book rule.
>
> Mr. Rigo is trying to cover his tracks, your Honor.
>
> THE COURT: I don't know about that, but, Mr. Stern, the foundation was quite skimpy in terms of Mr. Rigo's testimony yesterday.

I was heading straight for disaster. My offer of the diaries into evidence had brought down upon me the legitimate defense demand for a voir dire of the witness *on all six years* of diary entries right now, on the nose of my direct. It was a brooding Armageddon for the prosecution!

But at least I hoped to keep all this cross-examination within bounds—in the presence of the jury—because if the defense could get those jurors out of the room, they could turn the voir dire on the diaries into a discovery deposition of Paul Rigo.[12]

> THE COURT: . . . from my reading of the transcripts and the reading of the notes it was a very, very sketchy foundation for the introduction of this evidence as a shop book. Suppose we get to that now, and after I hear that we can hear, if necessary, further argument.
>
> MR. STERN: You want this in the presence or the absence of the jury?
>
> THE COURT: You want—I think in the presence of the jury, it should be.

I breathed a sigh of relief, albeit a small one. Judge Barlow, predictably, wanted to hear this cross on the diary just once. Ergo, he wanted it to be in the presence of the jury now, not in their absence now and then yet again in their presence during cross-examination in chief days later.[13] But now Jack Noonan waded in to help his colleagues.

> MR. NOONAN: Sir, I believe Mr. Wadden asked for a voir dire examination, and I think it should be outside the presence of the jury. If it is going to be admissible, we will go through it again. If it is inadmissible, it is not before the jury and any prejudice or harm which might thereby be done to the defendants will have been obviated.

But the judge, bless his heart, still resisted. He *knew* he only wanted to hear a potential voir dire by seven defense attorneys just once, not twice. And I was happy indeed to second his motion.

> THE COURT: Let's get back to the problem at hand. Why not conduct this voir dire, this laying of the foundation in voir dire, if they want to cross-examine on that basis before the jury? Why would we do it twice? It is either going to be admissible or not admissible. Why go through all of it once and then bring the witness back and go through it again?
>
> MR. STERN: That is agreeable to me, your Honor.

But the defense continued to pound away. "How does any of that prejudice any of the defendants?" The hard pressed judge swung around the room.

And then Noonan waded in again.

> MR. NOONAN: Perhaps I am mistaken but I thought the purpose of voir dire, which is a competency hearing, was to preclude just what we are going to do, if we do it in front of the jury if it is not admissible.

And then the tide began to turn and Judge George Barlow reversed himself. He knew it was not in his personal interest to do so. But he also came to believe that fairness required him to permit the defense attorneys to interrogate Rigo about six years of diary entries outside of the presence of the jury. And George Barlow was a fair-minded person. I did not and could not know it then, but in less than three and one-half years I was destined to be his colleague on the federal bench in New Jersey. And it was my great honor to serve with him until his untimely death, for he was a truly great judge.

But on that day in June of 1970 he dealt my case a nearly lethal blow when he reversed himself.

> THE COURT: I take it on the voir dire there may be certain reference to certain entries and if the jury hears them they are in and perhaps in that sense it is prejudicial.
>
> MR. STERN: As far as laying a foundation, I am confident that I can lay a foundation without referring to any entries, bringing before the jury any particular entry.
>
> THE COURT: I know you can do that, Mr. Stern, but on cross-examination on the voir dire they may wish to question the witness as to a particular entry in terms of the time it was made and if that is so, if they refer to a particular entry, then I suppose that evidence is before the jury to the prejudice of the defendants, if later I determine that that evidence is not admissible under the shop book rule.
>
> So I suppose we will have to conduct—I will reverse myself. We will have to conduct the examination, the foundation laying and the cross-examination based on that foundation directed to that foundation first—in the first instance without the presence of the jury.

Was the judge right in the ruling, or was he wrong? Who can say? This is one of those great areas of discretion confided to trial judges. Rare indeed is the appellate court willing to reverse because of or even review such procedural niceties as *when* the voir dire is conducted, that is, if it is to be at the outset of the direct or later, and whether the *initial* voir dire is conducted in the presence or the absence of the jurors—*provided* that a fair chance to voir dire is given and that ultimately no *unduly* prejudicial material is heard by the jurors. Yet such matters are life and death to trial lawyers in the pit, where timing can be everything.

I was staggered by the rulings. I feared that the witness and hence the case would not survive my blunder in having offered these diaries into evidence, thereby opening the floodgates for the defense. I had only one recourse. I *had* to withdraw the offer, for I thought that I saw another way, using another doctrine of evidence (suggested by the judge the day before) to accomplish all that I had hoped to do. The doctrine of "past recollection refreshed" was what I intended to use to get the maximum use of the diaries—both to authenticate the direct as to dates and to immunize it from cross-examination—without having to run the gauntlet of a voir dire by offering the six years of diaries into evidence. But, first, I had to undo the imminent danger of this massive Armageddon at the outset of the direct. And so I decided to withdraw the offer of the diaries into evidence. If I needed a specific entry, I would offer *that* entry.

> MR. STERN: Now, I know it is improper for counsel to ask the court questions, but I just for my own guidance, if you see fit to answer, if in the interest of saving time I withdraw my offer of the exhibits as a whole, and seek through the witness on direct examination to qualify any specific entry as such an entry, would that be consistent with your Honor's earlier statement that specific entries may come in as business records?
>
> THE COURT: I don't follow that, Mr. Stern. I don't know what you mean.
>
> MR. STERN: In other words, rather than trying to go through a voir dire now out of the presence of

> the jury on six years' worth of diaries, and then, of course, of having to go through substantially the same procedure in front of the jury when they are back in, if, in the interest of time I withdraw my offer of the diaries as a whole, all six years of them, and then as we begin the examination, if at any point there is a specific entry which I feel qualifies under the Business Record Act, whether I make that offer at that time consistent with your Honor's earlier thinking that there may be specific entries and documents which can qualify.

But Wadden wasn't having any of that and vigorously objected. He wanted his voir dire very badly. And I wanted very badly to pull back from the abyss my premature evidentiary offer had almost plunged me into. By now I wanted to withdraw the offer of evidence even more desperately than I had initially desired to make it.

> MR. STERN: There is no voir dire at this point if I withdraw my offer.
>
> THE COURT: If you withdraw your offer, there is never a voir dire, I suppose.

And the judge ruled that I could withdraw the offer and we would reserve voir dire for the time I offered any specific entry from one of the diaries. So I then withdrew the offer. But this infuriated Wadden, who launched a personal attack against me.

> MR. STERN: I will withdraw my offer.
>
> MR. WADDEN: Your Honor, I want the court to protect me from Mr. Stern now.
>
> THE COURT: I don't think you need much protection from Mr. Stern, Mr. Wadden. You strike me as being entirely capable of protecting yourself.
>
> MR. WADDEN: What worries me is when Mr. Stern withdraws his offers, you have laid the ground rules, as I understand them, but Mr. Stern

> sometimes doesn't understand what your Honor says. I don't want him getting up with his diary after the fellow says "I had a luncheon," and taking the diary up, as he does, and walking up to the witness when the diary is not in evidence.
>
> THE COURT: I am sure Mr. Stern is not going to do that. Mr. Stern knows exactly what I have just said.
>
> MR. WADDEN: I thank you, Judge. I hope he does now.

I have no doubt that Tom Wadden was and is a very fine trial lawyer. Indeed I know it well, having tried this case against him for weeks. But, in my view, that sort of exchange is pointless. It usually does me no good with judges when I try to attack other lawyers in that way. Indeed, it often drives the judge to protect the lawyer under assault—particularly if the ages and experience of the two lawyers are as disparate as then between Wadden and me.[14] And, finally, the sort of attack that is calculated to intimidate often has the opposite effect. It gives the other person something to "hang up in his locker room." It stiffens his resolve. In this instance it gave me the idea of how to use the diaries as much as I pleased, *without putting a single entry directly into evidence and thus totally avoiding any voir dire during my direct examination of Paul Rigo*.

> MR. STERN: I understand the rules of evidence very well, your Honor, and I also understand that a counsel may use anything whatsoever to refresh a witness's recollection.
>
> THE COURT: That is quite correct.
>
> MR. WADDEN: If he needs refreshing. Mr. Stern likes to refresh before there is any need to refresh.
>
> THE COURT: If he needs refreshing, yes. You can use anything, just about anything, to refresh a witness's recollection.

Now, there is nothing written in the Federal Rules of Evidence on past recollection refreshed. It is really a matter of the common law of the trial courts—a matter of tradition—that when a witness needs to use something to refresh his recollection he may use it. The thing so used may be anything. An old shoe—or a new one. It need not itself be legal evidence or even evidential. It does not matter because the item used to refresh the witness's recollection does not itself come into evidence. It is not presented to the jurors. The *only* evidence is the witness's now revived recollection. The adverse lawyer may see it, and the judge as well, of course. But it does not go to the jurors and may not be considered by them unless offered by the cross-examiner to impeach the refreshed recollection, which is the only "evidence." At any rate, I was finally able to conduct the direct examination of Paul Rigo.

Trial lawyers sometimes forget or misplace the perspective of the jurors. We get so caught up with what we do in their absence that we forget where we were when we were last before them. Rigo had been interrupted the afternoon before, and many hours of argument and a night had intervened. The last the jurors had heard from Rigo the day before was his pedigree. But I had made another mistake. In taking his history I had failed to elicit an unfavorable fact: that in the past he had misrepresented having a college degree. It was *essential* to bring this fact out on direct, even though it was "impeachment," for it was sure to be used on cross.[15] So I had to redo some of what had been done in order to undo my mistake.

> THE COURT: Good morning, ladies and gentlemen. All right, Mr. Stern, when you are ready, sir.
>
> MR. STERN: Thank you, your Honor.
>
> DIRECT EXAMINATION CONTINUED BY MR. STERN:
>
> Q: Mr. Rigo, I think you have told us yesterday that you left Manhattan College before obtaining your degree, is that so?

A: That is correct, sir.

Q: I think you have outlined to us, the jobs on which you had worked as an engineer?

A: Yes, sir.

Q: Prior to the time that you formed a corporation known as Constrad, is that so?

A: Yes, sir.

Q: Now then in obtaining this work that you have described to us, did you from time to time represent that you did have a degree from Manhattan College?

A: Yes I did, sir.

Q: Why did you do that?

A: Well, when I first started working, I had to get a job, so I backed up my age a year. I was rather young and I represented the fact that I had my degree, backed up my experience in accordance with those dates and this is on a number of applications that I made.

Q: Irrespective of that, Mr. Rigo, are the facts as you stated them to be yesterday and today?

A: Yes, sir.

Q: This is the truth now?

A: Yes.

In my judgment, this sort of peccadillo by way of character failing is best brought out at the spot in the chronology when it comfortably fits into the story itself—unlike the business about Conti's *major* character failings, and, as we shall see, Rigo's, which are best made part of the end game.[16] But it was time to move him along, into his newly formed business and then into business and, then, into his first meeting with the conspirators.

> Q: At the time you first formed Constrad, according to that document in April of 1963, was Constrad actually doing any work in 1963?
>
> A: No, sir.
>
> Q: Did there come a time in September of 1964 that Constrad did begin to do some work?
>
> A: Yes, sir, Dr. Capen and I started doing some work on a Perth Amboy contract which was taken under a firm that we formed called Capen-Rigo Associates, Constrad supplying the people.
>
> THE COURT: Keep your voice up, please, sir.

After a few minutes of additional background, it was time to meet Mayor Addonizio—and to employ the stratagem of using the Rigo diaries to "refresh" Rigo's memory and thereby to achieve their full value without the curse of the voir dire intrusion. But what must be emphasized is that I had *not* spoken to Rigo between the time the judge ruled that I could use the diaries that way and the time Rigo resumed the stand. *Nor had Rigo heard the dialogue*, for he had been excluded from the room. The point is that because of the *way* Rigo had been prepared—not by specific questions and answers, but rather in themes—it did not matter! I had a working partner on the stand—not a trained performer with memorized lines. Watch as we are able to deliver our message by improvisation within a clearly defined libretto.

And so when it was time for Rigo and Addonizio to have their initial meeting, which took place at the Inner Circle, a famous political dinner put on by reporters who cover government and politics in New York City, and I wanted Rigo to talk about that, I just led him to it.

> Q: Now, did there come a time, Mr. Rigo, in the year 1964 when you attended an Inner Circle dinner?
>
> A: Yes, sir.

Q: As you sit there now, can you tell us just from the top of your head what the date of that dinner was?

A: May 2nd.

That was not the answer I expected. I expected him to say he could not remember, and then use the diary to "refresh" his memory. But his answer surprised me—as one can see from the next words from my mouth—particularly as he got the date wrong. But not to worry. It was easily correctable.

Q: You can. Do you remember where the dinner was held?

A: At the Hilton Hotel in New York.

I knew that focusing him on the hotel would get him to recall that there were two dinners and he had the date wrong.

Q: Did you go to that dinner?

A: Yes, I did. Mr. Stern, I may be in error on that date. There were two dates set up for that dinner, and one was cancelled, the reason being the death of Mayor Wagner's wife. I am sorry, I am not sufficiently to clear to be positive of that May date.

And that was all I needed to hear. It was time for the first diary, and for the doctrine of past recollection refreshed. To use that doctrine, certain formula words have to be intoned. So I incanted them. And that got the defense attorneys on their feet.

Q: I show you this document, Government Exhibit 44 for identification, and ask you whether or not, using that document, you can refresh your recollection?

MR. FEINBERG: I think we are approaching the point that we were before we started. I think, your Honor—again we may be confronted with the same legal argument, and we ask the same thing that we asked before.

> THE COURT: I think not. I think I made it clear. If that is an objection, it is overruled.

The judge ruled consistently with his earlier indication, and I was on my way. And in open court I explained to Rigo—whom I had not spoken to at all—that I was using a legal form with this incantation. But that got me involved with Wadden again.

> Q: Excuse me, I have to use a certain form. Does that document, Government Exhibit 44, refresh your recollection?
>
> MR. WADDEN: It is not Government Exhibit 44, it is not in evidence.

Wadden was wrong. I had never said "in evidence," and earlier I had said "for identification," but so what? I did not want to nail Wadden. I was after his client "Tony Boy" Boiardo. So I apologized to him and got on with it.

> MR. STERN: Excuse me, I apologize to Mr. Wadden.
>
> Q: Government Exhibit 44 for identification, does that refresh your recollection?
>
> A: Yes, sir.
>
> Q: Can you now tell us the date on which you attended the Inner Circle diner?
>
> A: Yes, sir, it was May 2nd. The first date was in March.
>
> Q: Now, do you recall any of the people who were seated at your table?
>
> A: Yes, sir.
>
> Q: Who was seated at the table?
>
> A: There was Mayor Addonizio, Senator Grossi, Mr. Tonti[17] and some other gentleman whom I didn't know, plus my host.

MR. NOONAN: We are having a little trouble on this side.

THE WITNESS: I am sorry, I will try to speak louder.

MR. WADDEN: Give him some water, Mr. Stern.

MR. STERN: Mr. Wadden is being helpful again. Would you admonish him not to be helpful?

THE COURT: All right, gentlemen, let's move along.

MR. FEINBERG: Did I hear him say his host?

THE COURT: His host.

MR. STERN: Mr. Wadden would like to know who your host was. I heard him.
Do you remember who your host was?

THE WITNESS: Yes, Mr. Hayden.

The witness nailed Hayden, one of the defense attorneys. I hadn't planned to bring it out. But I got mad at Wadden, who was deviling me again. So Hayden got wounded and Wadden—who hadn't asked to know—got blamed for it in the hurly burly of the moment. But at least we obtained the introduction between Rigo and the mayor and a social conversation with him—which was introduced by a controlling question.

Q: Now, then, did you have a conversation with Mayor Addonizio that evening?

A: Yes, we spoke. He was very warm, very friendly, very pleasant. I can't recall any specifics of the conversation.

And that having been done, it was quite easy to leave the subject by "looping" into another.

Q: Now, after having had dinner with Mayor Addonizio that evening, did there come a time when you had a conversation with Mr. Ralph Cestone?

A: Yes.

We spent a few minutes developing the relationships between Cestone—another contractor, and one who had already testified—and Rigo.[18] Then it was time to introduce the South Side Sewer Interception Project, on which both Cestone and Rigo had performed services and kicked back. It was the South Side project that was dissected on the large chart the FBI agent had introduced *before* Rigo took the stand. It was that chart which graphically portrayed for the jurors the funds going from the City of Newark, to the prime contractor, through the subcontractors, and into Kantor Supply. And the jury had already heard Irving Kantor testify *before* Rigo took the stand. The stage had therefore been carefully set for Paul Rigo's testimony: one of the most incredible stories of greed, graft, and corruption ever presented in court; a story of an underground alliance between mobsters and politicians never before, to my knowledge, documented in an American courtroom. It was a true story. But that would not matter a fig if the jurors did not believe it. And if Rigo had testified *before* the important pieces of corroboration of his story had been heard, rather than after, then, or so I believed, the chances that the jury would believe him would be diminished. I did not want to have to resuscitate Rigo with this material after cross. Those jurors had to be prepared to believe him before he testified. And, or so I hoped, by now they were. It was time for the South Side Sewer project.

> Q: Now then, do you recall when it was or approximately when it was that the City of Newark awarded the contract on the South Side project to the contractor?
>
> A: I think it was in January of '65.
>
> Q: Do you recall at the time of that award whether it was awarded to a joint venture or to a single contractor?

A: Mr. Stern, I am not absolutely sure of this. To the best of my recollection, it was awarded to a single firm but I think a joint venture was then formed and actually did the work. I am not positive about that.

Q: Do you remember the name of the contractor to whom the project was originally awarded?

A: C. Salvatore & Sons.

Q: Do you remember—withdrawn. Once the project was actually awarded, did you play any role in the project?

A: Yes, sir.

Q: What role was that?

A: We manned the project to provide the supervision to provide the resident engineering services.

Q: Do you remember the name of the contractor or contracting group that was performing the contract?

A: There was the Catt Corporation, Salvatore, Mal Bros. and Malanka. I think that is the four.

Q: Were they a joint venture at the time?

A: Yes, sir.

Q: Do you recall the name of the joint venture?

A: I think it was still C. Salvatore & Sons.[19]

Q: Now then, can you fix the point in time at which you actually physically began to do anything in reference to the South Side project?

A: Just approximately, sir. I can't give you an actual date.

MR. FEINBERG: I can't hear that answer.

THE WITNESS: I said approximately. I can't give you an exact date.

Jules Feinberg had inadvertently emphasized my point, and made my use of the diary easier. Indeed, this portion of the testimony was aimed at his client, who was about to enter the stage.

Q: I show you this document which has been marked Government Exhibit 45 for identification and ask you to look at it and I ask you whether or not that document refreshes your recollection.

A: Yes, sir.

Q: May I have that back. Now based on your refreshed recollection, do you recall when it was that you first physically began to do something on the South Side project?

A: Yes, sir, I flew to Newark on February 11 and I met Joe Catenaci and Phil Salvatore at their office. It was in the airport motel.

Q: Do you recall the purpose of going to meet these gentlemen that day?

A: Yes, sir, I wanted to go over the job. I toured the job with Mr. Catenaci. They were in the process of getting set up for the work, and then returned home.

Q: Now, did there come a time, Mr. Rigo, when you met the defendant, Anthony La Morte?

A: Yes, sir.

Q: Can you recall the exact date when you first met him?

A: No, sir, I can't.

And of course we know what comes next. Good old Government 45, the diary for 1965, along with the doctrine of past recollection refreshed.

> Q: I show you Government Exhibit 45 for identification and ask you whether or not that document refreshes your recollection?
>
> A: Yes, sir.
>
> Q: Can you tell us what date it was that you met for the first time the defendant La Morte?
>
> A: February 18, sir.
>
> Q: What, if anything, did you do on February the 18th?
>
> A: I had gone to the City Hall to get more plans and specifications, and on the way out I was introduced to Mr. La Morte who was in the hallway.
>
> Q: That was the first time that you ever met him?
>
> A: Yes, sir.
>
> Q: Can you recall when it was that you met him again?
>
> A: Not exactly, sir.
>
> Q: Using that document, Government Exhibit 45, if necessary to refresh your recollection, can you tell when it was that you met him again?

It was once too often for defense counsel. They demanded a side bar conference. They could not object to refreshing the witness's recollection—the judge had already repeatedly ruled on that—but they wanted to stop me from identifying "for the record" what it was that I was using to refresh his recollection. It was Jack Noonan who had called for the side bar. But it was Wadden that waded in.

> MR. WADDEN: You don't have to make a record of what you are giving a man to refresh his memory.
>
> MR. STERN: Absolutely you do.

THE COURT: I think you certainly do, Mr. Wadden, particularly in this case where there may be some violent and vigorous objection to you using these documents at all. Clearly he has to make, at least the first time, and if you don't want to—but the record has to be clear as to what document this witness is refreshing his recollection.

We struggled over the point, which was an important one to both sides—because by identifying *what* it was that was refreshing the recollection, the diaries were authenticating the testimony without their contents going into evidence. It got hot at side bar. Wadden accused me of creating the loss of memory, referring back to my first use of the diary to refresh Rigo's recollection, But that wasn't true. And he knew it. I had not coached Rigo after the judge's ruling. I had no need to. In any event, I had had no chance to.

MR. WADDEN: Did you notice the cue? The first time he came up with the right date and he had to go back and he forgot it so he had to have him read the document.

THE COURT: I don't regard that as a cue.

MR. STERN: For Mr. Wadden's peace of mind, I have had no contact directly or indirectly with Mr. Rigo since your Honor's ruling. That is the absolute truth.

MR. WADDEN: I am sure you haven't because I am watching you.

MR. STERN: Nor my agents, to my knowledge.

THE COURT: All right, the objection is overruled.

(Whereupon the following was had in open court.)

Q: The judge said you may answer the question.

Notice the first question after the side bar ended. “The judge said you may answer the question.” Why did I do that? Because we had been at side bar for some time. The defense had brought us there. The jurors had no way of knowing whether or not that side bar had been occasioned by my having done something improper. This was my way of telling them that I had not cheated and that any complaint had been groundless.

It frequently happens that experienced lawyers after a side bar loudly say, “Thank you, your Honor,” as they leave the bench—although they may well *not* have prevailed at the side bar itself. In my view, this sort of thing is dirty pool. Yet it does happen. When it does, you may want to consider resuming your direct examination, “The judge has overruled his objection. Do you have the question in mind, or do you want to have it repeated?”

Notice also the way the direct examination is presented, piece by piece. Each defendant is introduced to the witness. The witness comes to know him. Nothing happens suddenly, or abruptly. The jurors are not to be jarred with Charlie Chaplin-like motions across their horizons. A direct examination with a friendly witness is the time of power for a trial lawyer. He must use that power to make full, complete, and correct presentations.

And so Rigo, who has just met Public Works Director La Morte, must become closer to him. He must call him by his nickname, “Sonny.” When was it that he and La Morte met, Rigo is asked. And with his diary in his hand, Rigo answers:

> A: On February 26.
>
> Q: Did you have a conversation with him on February 26.
>
> A: Yes, sir.
>
> THE COURT: What year is this we are talking about?
>
> THE WITNESS: 1965.

Q: Can you tell us where that conversation took place?

A: It took place at the trailer on the Newark—on the South Side Project.

Q: Whose trailer?

A: The office trailer.

Q: Whose trailer was it?

A: It was provided by the contractor.

Q: Can you tell us the substance of that conversation?

A: It was mostly just a general conversation about how things were going and how the job was progressing, how things were getting set up; told me to call him Sonny, that everybody did.

Q: Sonny?

A: That was the extent of the conversation, as I remember it.

I was now ready to set up the most important piece of testimony Rigo had to give: his initial meeting with "Tony Boy" Boiardo, which had been arranged by his new friend "Sonny" La Morte. It was the most important testimony, first, because only Rigo had any evidence against this mob boss and, second, the initial conversation between Rigo and Boiardo was the glue that held together the conspiracy count charging a joint enterprise between the gangsters and the politicians. But Rigo could not fix the exact date for the meeting. He had no diary entry. All he knew was that it had been on a Sunday, after he had sent his first invoice into the city for payment, but before he had received the city's check. The voucher and check had to go into evidence first. Then we would be ready.

Q: That was February 26 you say. Now I show you Government Exhibits 50 and 58 for identification and I ask you whether you can identify these documents?

A: Yes, sir.

Q: What are those documents?

A: 58 is the service and expense order, the voucher for the services of Charles H. Capon Associates on the South Side job, the month of February.

Government 50 is a check from the City of Newark to Charles H. Capon Associates for the work performed.

MR. STERN: I offer these in evidence.

Just two questions and two answers and the exhibits glided into evidence with no difficulty.

Then I read the documents to the jury. I had the right to do that as they were in evidence, and I needed to have the jury hear the date of the invoice and the date of the bill.

Q: Now, Government Exhibit 58 is a voucher or a bill dated March the 12, 1965. It is a bill from Capon—Mr. Charles H. Capon Associates to the City of Newark for work done. Government Exhibit 50 in evidence is a check and the date of the check is March 26, 1965. It is in the amount of $6,273.51 and it is made payable to Charles H. Capon Associates.

Now, we were ready. Although no one on the jury knew it at the moment, we now had the date of Rigo's first encounter with Boiardo bracketed.

Q: Mr. Rigo, did there come a time when you had another conversation with the defendant La Morte?

A: Yes, sir; I had, of course, continuing conversations with him on the project.

Rigo had failed to pick up the change of topic. So I showed him where he was to go next.

Q: Did there come a time when you had a telephone conversation with him?

A: Yes, sir.

Q: Where were you when you had it?

A: At my home.

Q: Did he call you or did you call him?

A: He called me.

Q: Can you pinpoint the time when that conversation took place?

A: Only within range, Mr. Stern.

Q: Within what range?

A: It was between the time that we submitted our bill and the time we got our first check.

Q: Between what period—

A: This means that it was between March 8 and March 26, and it was on a Sunday.

Q: Do you recall that it was on a Sunday?

A: Yes, sir.

Q: A Sunday between March 8 and March 26?

A: Yes, sir.

Q: Do you have a way of knowing that, yes or no; do you have a way of knowing that it was a Sunday between March 8 and March 26?

A: Yes, sir.

I always enjoyed leaving the future cross-examiner the problem of deciding whether to ask the witness for "the way" he has to know. Not that I was bluffing. The courtroom is not the place for that. But sometimes "the way" was not admissible (if I asked) and often it was a matter of such trivia that I did not wish to get bogged down in it—but had no objection if the cross-examiner decided to get swallowed up later. And with that we went to the heart of the conspiracy.

Q: Will you give us the substance of the telephone conversation which you had with the defendant La Morte?

A: Yes, sir. He called on a Sunday morning and told me to come up to his house right away, that it was very important. He wanted to take me to meet the real boss in Newark.

Q: Is that what he told you on the telephone?

A: Yes, sir.

Q: Did you make any reply?

A: Yes, sir, I told him I couldn't come up immediately, that I had some things to do with the children, but that I would come up as soon as possible. He gave me directions of how to get there to come to his house at 332 Ridge Street, and as soon as possible I did.

Q: When you did go to the defendant La Morte's house at 332 Ridge Street—

MR. FEINBERG: I object. That is not what he said.

MR. STERN: I believe he said 332 Ridge Street. Would you read the question?

(Record read.)

MR. FEINBERG: I withdraw that objection but I ask that he fix the date, your Honor.

MR. STERN: He said it was between two dates on a Sunday.

THE COURT: March 8 and March 26, on a Sunday.

MR. FEINBERG: Your Honor, he has the diary. He has been looking at it to refresh his recollection. I ask that he try to fix the date.

THE COURT: I take it, Mr. Feinberg, that that is as close as he can fix it.

Is that so, Mr. Rigo?

THE WITNESS: Yes, your Honor.

THE COURT: Is that so, yes or no, is that as close as you can fix it?

THE WITNESS: Yes, sir.

MR. FEINBERG: All right.

Q: What, if anything, occurred when you went to defendant La Morte's house at 332 Ridge Street?

A: He was ready and waiting for me. He came out of his house immediately and directed me on down Ridge Street.

Q: Whose car did you go in?

A: Mine.

Q: Who drove?

A: I did.

Q: Did you have a conversation with him?

A: Yes. I asked him what it was all about and he said, "This is the most important meeting you will have in Newark. I am going to take you to the man who really runs this town," words to that effect.

Q: Did you ask him who it was?

A: Yes, I did. He said, "You will see. We are almost there."

Q: Where, if any place, did you go?

In retrospect I am none too proud of the "if any place." But I was even then aware that I was having problems with Rigo. He was getting too comfortable on the stand. His conversations with the defendant La Morte were too expansive. And even to my ear the quotation marks that were to appear in the record were all too clear. I was getting uncomfortable and had a gnawing fear that the jury soon would as well.

> A: We went down a rather dingy little office on Franklin Avenue. It was the office of Valentine Electric Company.
>
> Q: Was there a sign outside?
>
> A: I think it was in the window. I am not sure.
>
> Q: Did there come a time when you went inside the premises?
>
> A: Yes, we did.
>
> Q: What happened when you went in?
>
> A: There were two or three people present. One man was seated behind a desk and he, La Morte, introduced me to him as Tony.
>
> Q: What happened after the introduction?
>
> A: He took me into a back room behind a desk.
>
> Q: Who took you into a back room?
>
> A: Tony.
>
> Q: Did La Morte go with you?
>
> A: No, he didn't. He remained outside.
>
> Q: What occurred when you got into the back room?
>
> A: He told me, he said, "This job you have down there on the South Side," he said, "that was set up by Johnny Sepede and me, and Johnny Sepede and I had an understanding and that understanding is that you pay 10 percent of what you get on that job."

To the eye this testimony reads beautifully. But it did not sound well. I was becoming progressively unhappier with Rigo's testimony. And to my dismay I began to see some trouble in the jury box.

It was nothing overt, just subtle signs. But standing where I was, at the end of the box just slightly to the rear of the shoulders of the last jurors, I could see all of the jurors from the corner of my eye. And I could see a slight shifting of some of them in their seats. I knew what it was. The testimony about the conversation sounded too pat. I tried to take steps.

> Q: Are you giving us the exact words which this man Tony said to you?
>
> A: No, sir.
>
> Q: Can you remember all the exact words that he said?
>
> A: No, sir.
>
> Q: Do you remember the substance of the conversation?
>
> A: Yes, sir.
>
> Q: Was that in substance that he said to you?
>
> A: That was part of it.
>
> Q: What else did he say?
>
> A: Well, he said 10 percent. I said, "I can't pay you 10 percent." He said, "You will pay 10 percent and you will pay it in cash."
>
> I said, "We can't pay you 10 percent." I said, "What are we getting for paying you 10 percent?" He said, "There is a lot of mouths to feed in City Hall," he said. "You pay me the 10 percent." He said, "I take care of the mayor. I take care of the council. I take of anybody else that has to be taken care of down there."

It was getting worse. You feel things in a courtroom. And the feeling in the room was terrible. The trouble was that I could not see what to do about it. Rigo was gushing out stuff which sounded like he had a photographic memory. He had become as much an advocate as a witness. I again reached for a fire extinguisher, for I was becoming desperate.

> Q: Once again, Mr. Rigo, are you giving us the exact words which this man Tony said to you?
>
> A: No, sir.
>
> Q: Are you giving us the substance of the conversation?
>
> A: Yes, sir.

Even these palliatives were of little value. There was nothing I could put my finger on directly, but I knew it was no good. The atmosphere in the courtroom was all wrong. And there seemed to be nothing I could do to reverse it.

Perhaps it would help to have a physical confrontation in the courtroom. I was willing to try anything.

> Q: Mr. Rigo, before you go on with the conversation between yourself and this man whom you identified as Tony, I want to ask you whether or not you see this man in court.
>
> A: Yes, sir, I do.
>
> Q: Will you point him out, please?
>
> A: Tony Boiardo.
>
> (Mr. Boiardo stood up.)
>
> Q: Indicating the defendant Boiardo?
>
> THE COURT: Yes.

But it really did not help. And the reason why it did not will be discerned in the next question and answer—one little question by me, followed by a Vesuvian eruption from Rigo.

> Q: Did you immediately agree to pay 10 percent?
>
> A: No, sir, the 10 percent itself was somewhat staggering. The idea of cash was even worse, so I argued. I bargained, tried to get it down to 5 percent.

> I was told, "No, it's going to be 10 percent. Everybody in Newark pays 10 percent or they don't work in Newark and they don't get paid in Newark." He said, "Look what happened to Killam. He didn't get paid or he didn't pay. He is not in Newark and he is going to sweat a long time before he gets what is owed him."
>
> I went back to the cash idea. I asked if there were not some way that I could make this by check. He told me no, but he said, "We may be able to help you on that." He said, "We have a plumbing supply company that will give you vouchers. It will only cost you 15 percent."
>
> I told him I had an engineering company; I couldn't use that. If I got 10 percent, I would have to use my other company, Constrad.
>
> He said he didn't care how I got the cash, that was what it was going to be.

It was everlasting. Endless. Eternal. The man on the stand had been transformed from a frightened soul who had to repeatedly be admonished to keep his voice up into a singer of songs. It was at this moment that I came to *know* that those who advise to let witnesses tell their own story are completely, totally, absolutely *wrong*![20]

In my panic I even reached for Irving Kantor—the bedridden man whose honesty could simply not be touched, who documented one million in cash coming out of this very project.

> Q: In the course of that conversation do you recall whether or not the word "Kantor" was used?
>
> A: Not to my recollection.

I had not asked him that in preparation, so I did not know what his answer would be. Nor did I care. In my desperation over the turn of events, I simply wanted to have the jury recall Irving Kantor. To make the question not leading, I had given an alternative, "whether or not."

I certainly did not want to ask Rigo any additional questions about that conversation. But I had to. Boiardo had told Rigo that Rigo was about to be paid by the city, and that was key. It showed that the man had a direct pipeline into City Hall. So, in I went:

> Q: What, if anything, occurred at that point?
>
> A: Well, it wound up with him telling me that I was going to get paid pretty soon and that somebody would be in touch with me. I think that was the substance of the conversation.
>
> Q: Was the defendant La Morte actually present during that conversation?
>
> A: No, sir, he was not. He was outside.
>
> Q: What happened after you concluded that conversation with the defendant Boiardo in that room?
>
> A: He opened the door and let me out of the room and motioned La Morte to come in, closed the door. They were in there a few minutes. They both came out. Telephone rang. It was for Boiardo. He hung up and he said, "I have to get out of here. That was my wife. The spaghetti is on."

That last comment by Rigo was entirely gratuitous: "The spaghetti is on." He had never told me that before. It was almost a joke by the witness. But it was simply awful. I was avid to get Rigo out of the room and away from Boiardo before the entire case went down the drain. I wanted him out. So I took him out. My next question "transitioned" Rigo physically away.

> Q: Mr. Rigo, after that conversation did you go someplace?
>
> A: I drove La Morte back to his house.
>
> Q: Did you have any conversation with him on the way back in reference to your discussion with the defendant Boiardo?

A: Yes, I did. I asked him who this man Tony was.

Q: Had you heard of him before?

A: No, sir. He told me in essence, he told me, "Don't you know? That's Tony Boy Boiardo. Don't you know Tony Boy Boiardo? Don't you know the Boot?"
I said, "No."
I said, "Who are they?"
He said, "They are"—

Q: Well, all right.

THE COURT: That's enough.[21]

We soon had a brief recess. For me it was a welcome respite. I began to think how to change the momentum in the room. How could we get that jury back in the saddle with us? But as hard as I tried I could not see the way. Nonetheless, the jury did come back into the room and I did have to get the testimony underway again.

Rigo testified that shortly after the Boiardo meeting he began to be paid by the city. As he received each check, he generated 10 percent in cash and gave it over to a Boiardo man. On these early transactions Rigo could not account for the method or the checks he had used to make the payments. Nor could he pinpoint the dates of most of these first three kickbacks because he had not begun to make systematic entries in his diary. And none of this was helpful to me in trying to change the atmosphere in the courtroom. In addition, during this phase of the direct I had to introduce the second project that Rigo had been retained by the city to work on.

Shortly after the first payments began on the South Side Sewer project, Newark had a water emergency. A new project came into existence, the "Southerly Extension Project." It was designed to extend the city's water pipe system to the south and hook it into the Elizabethtown Water Company. Rigo had been present at a key meeting with Addonizio and La Morte in the mayor's office where they had discussed which manufacturer's pipe to use and recalled that Boiardo had made the decision.

It was a more restrained Rigo who gave that testimony. And, for my part, I did all I could to ameliorate the climate in the room by constant reminders that the witness was not pretending to give the exact words of anyone at the meeting. But I felt that it was all too little, too late. And I was still mentally thrashing about to find some device to restore the full credibility of the prosecution's star witness—and thereby the prosecution's case.

At the conclusion of the meeting in his office, Mayor Addonizio had given permission for La Morte to travel with Rigo to Portland, Oregon, to attend the American Water Works Convention. It was to speed the Southerly Extension Project. It also gave me a fortuitous opportunity to corroborate Rigo, for he had paid for La Morte's trip as well as his own, and I had the documentation.

> Q: Do you recall how you went to Portland, Oregon?
>
> A: Yes, sir.
>
> Q: How did you go?
>
> A: We flew out. We left by small plane from Newark Airport. That again was on a Sunday. We went over to Kennedy and then took a plane, large plane, out to the coast.
>
> Q: Do you recall whether or not anybody went with you?
>
> A: Yes, sir, I took my son along. He was about 12 then and he had been heckling me somewhat. He wanted to get a ride on a jet, so I thought this was as good time as any.
>
> Q: Do you recall who paid for the trip?
>
> A: Yes, sir, we did.
>
> Q: When you say "we," who paid?

A: Constrad.

Q: Do you recall whether or not you rented a hotel room?

A: Yes, sir, we did, or I did.

Q: When you say we or I, who are you indicating?

A: I am indicating the company, sir.

Q: Constrad?

A: Yes, sir.

Q: Do you recall who paid for the defendant La Morte's trip?

A: Constrad.

Q: I show you these documents, Government Exhibit 247a and 247, and I ask you if you can identify them.

A: 247 is a Constrad check to Hunterdon Travel, Inc., in the amount of $1,104.65.
247a is a bill from Hunterdon Travel, Inc., for three United Airline tickets from Newark to Portland, to Chicago, to Newark, $1,104.65.

This gave me a first-class opportunity to buttress not only the testimony of Rigo, but the authenticity and reliability of his diary—Government 45—as well.

Q: Can you tell us, Mr. Rigo, exactly the day when you and the defendant La Morte and your son left for Portland, Oregon?

A: It was the Sunday after the meeting at City Hall.

Q: Using Government Exhibit 45 to refresh your recollection, if necessary, can you tell us the exact date?

A: Yes, sir, Sunday the 27th of June.

Q: How do you know that?

A: I made an entry in my diary.

MR. STERN: At this point, if your Honor please, I will offer into evidence Government Exhibit 247 and 247a.

MR. FEINBERG: May I please have a side bar at this time, if your Honor please?

Jules Feinberg, La Morte's lawyer, was not a happy man at this moment. He very much wanted to prevent admission of these documents, proving that Constrad had paid for La Morte's trip and corroborating the Rigo testimony.

(The following occurred at side bar:)

MR. FEINBERG: Your Honor, my objection to the introduction of this testimony and testimony along this line is its relevancy to the conspiracy indictment.

THE COURT: And your response to that?

MR. STERN: Is I believe I am entitled to introduce documentation to corroborate the witness when he says he took a trip with the defendant La Morte, and I represent to the court they had a very meaningful conversation on the flight.

THE COURT: With that representation, I will admit them. The objection is overruled.

(The following occurred in open court;)

(Exhibits G-247 and G-247a received and marked in evidence.)

MR. STERN: Does your Honor want to continue on? Any way you want to do it.

THE COURT: Maybe it is a good time to break now, gentlemen, for lunch. All right. The jury may step down first, please.

(The jury left the courtroom.)

I needed a recess. I had to figure out something to turn the tide in the courtroom back to where it had been before Rigo launched his speech about his first conversation with Boiardo, culminating in that terrible "the spaghetti is on" finale. I needed something dramatic. But what?

We were in real danger of losing the case, with the eyes of just about everyone on us. Just four days before Rigo took the stand, the Newark voters cast their ballots in the runoff election for mayor. In spite of the fact that Addonizio was under federal indictment, he had received enough votes to force a run-off election with Ken Gibson. The final decision was held in the middle of the trial.

We on the prosecution team held our breaths the night of the election. An Addonizio victory would have brought thousands of his supporters to the courtroom the next morning. Even the sequestered jurors—insulated as they were from all the electioneering—would have known of an Addonizio victory. But it was Gibson who won that night. And the streets of Newark erupted with racial fury and violence.

This time it was the white citizens of the city who were gushing into the streets, reacting to the realization that they were about to be governed by a black mayor. And the mostly white police department was emotionally attuned to the rioters. Indeed, expressions like "kill the niggers" could be heard crackling over police radios. Television camera crews were chased through the streets.

The next morning the courthouse in Trenton—for the trial had been moved out of Newark at its inception—was quiet and peaceful. No demonstrators or supporters were at hand to cheer the defeated mayor. Such are the ways of politics. The mayor was defeated, probably because of the federal case, and now he was on his own. But the result in the polling places in Newark would be brought into disrepute if the Trenton jury voted the other way. It was not a case that the prosecution cared to lose.

So that was the problem, a too talkative witness. And those were the stakes. And over lunch I believed I had come up with a solution.

A few weeks after his return from Portland, Rigo had been taken to Boiardo's home for a meeting. They had had another dramatic conversation at Boiardo's house. It was imperative that the jury credit it.

I decided to issue a direct challenge to Boiardo and to his lawyer, Tom Wadden. If Rigo could do it, I would ask Rigo to draw the inside of Boiardo's home for the jury. Then no one could deny Rigo had been there—unless, of course, Rigo could not draw it correctly.

Over sandwiches I asked Rigo if he could do it. He was confident that he could. I gulped hard, long after finishing lunch. The stakes were very high. But in my judgment the alternative to not doing the demonstration was chaos.

But first we had to dispose of the Portland trip when court was reconvened.

> THE COURT: All right, Mr. Stern.
>
> Q: I believe, Mr. Rigo, we were at the point where you told us that according to your recollection as refreshed by your diary, you recall leaving on January 27 for Portland—June 27, is that correct?
>
> A: Yes, that is correct.
>
> Q: I think you have told us that you had your boy with you and you had Mr. La Morte with you and that you paid for Mr. La Morte's ticket, is that correct?
>
> A: That is correct, sir.

After a break, this sort of leading to recapitulate the end of testimony just before break is quite usual. Almost all judges will permit at least some leading to "pick up the thread." It is really just repeating the last of the testimony before the interruption.

MR. STERN: With your Honor's permission, I want to pass out Government Exhibits 247 and 247a, which are in evidence, to the jury.

THE COURT: Yes, sir.

(Exhibits G-247 and G-247a were passed to the jury.)

MR. STERN: Your Honor, may I inquire of the jury through the court whether anybody is missing one of the documents?

THE COURT: Does everyone have both?

Q: Did I leave the originals with you, Mr. Rigo?

A: Yes.

Q: Government Exhibit 247a is made up of the bill from the Hunterdon Travel Service, Hunterdon Travel, Inc., to Constrad, is that correct?

A: Yes, sir.

Q: For three United Airline tickets from Newark to Portland and then Chicago back to Newark?

A: Yes, sir.

Q: For Paul Rigo. Is that you?

A: Yes, sir.

Q: John Rigo; who's that?

A: My son.

Q: And A. La Morte, who is that?

A: Mr. La Morte.

Q: With that bill there appear three ticket stubs, am I correct?

A: Yes, sir.

Q: One in the name of Paul Rigo, one John Rigo and one Mr. Anthony La Morte, is that correct?

A: That is correct, sir.

Q: Next to John Rigo is a bracket, 12, close bracket. Do you see that?

A: Yes.

Q: What does that reflect?

A: I guess it reflects his age.

Q: Was that his age at the time?

A: Yes, sir.

Q: Government Exhibit 247 is a check drawn on the account of Constrad to Hunterdon Travel, Inc., is it not?

A: Yes, sir.

Q: Is that the check which you used to pay for yourself and Mr. La Morte's ticket and your son's ticket?

A: Yes, it is.

It was my intention to introduce conversations between Rigo and La Morte during this lengthy flight. To validate those conversations, I had to show that the two men had privacy. Keeping tight control on Rigo, this was easily done, even though the witness obscured the point initially.

Q: Now, looking at Government Exhibit 247a, those tickets, can you tell us what class of flight you took?

A: It was a first-class flight with the exception of the ride from Chicago to Newark—that is the second-class flight, Mr. Stern.

Rigo blended in the second class leg *on the return*. But it was the flight *to Portland* that had the conversation I wanted. So I clarified it:

Q: Whatever it is, try to keep your voice up. That indicates, does it not, that you flew first-class over to Portland and then on the way back you were downgraded a little bit, is that correct?

A: It is a first-class flight to Portland, first-class flight from Portland back to Chicago, and then second-class from Chicago to Newark.

Q: Do you recall when you flew with the defendant La Morte where you and he and your son were seated in the airplane?

A: Mr. La Morte and I sat together and my son sat on the other side of the plane.

Q: Do you recall whether or not this was a night flight?

A: Yes, sir, it was.

Q: Looking at those tickets, can you tell approximately what time you and the defendant La Morte left?

A: It was 11 P.M.

Q: Eleven o'clock at night?

A: Right.

Q: Do you recall approximately how long a flight it was?

A: I seem to remember we got into Portland around six o'clock in the morning their time. It was a considerable flight.

Q: Did you fly a considerable period of the night?

A: Yes, we did. It made several stops on the way out. I think Cleveland, Chicago, Seattle, and then Portland.

Q: As you and Mr. La Morte sat on the airplane together—withdrawn.

When you sit in first class, how many seats are there abreast?

A: Two.

Q: Was there anybody sitting next to you or the defendant La Morte?

A: No, we were seated together.

Q: Just two seats. As you flew that flight, do you recall whether or not you had a conversation with the defendant La Morte.

A: Mr. Stern, on the long flight we chatted on and off all the way out in between catnaps.

I then took the conversations that I wanted. I had the men check into a hotel, proved that Rigo paid the bill, had them do their business in Portland, and brought them home. And then approached the moment of confrontation.

Rigo was working on two jobs, the sewer and the water projects, but was being paid only on the one, the sewer job. He could no longer afford to make his kickbacks. So he began to get pressure. He tried unsuccessfully to see Boiardo at Valentine Electric. Then he went to see Mayor Addonizio. But his problem remained unsolved. Finally, he asked La Morte to arrange a meeting with Boiardo. La Morte did so, and Rigo waited in the street for La Morte to pick him up and convey him to Boiardo's home.

Q: What, if anything, did you do after you got that call from the defendant La Morte?

A: I waited outside at the appointed hour. He came along with another car. It wasn't his and a driver and I got in.

Q: Were you taken somewhere?

A: Yes, sir.

Q: Where were you taken?

A: To Mr. Boiardo's house.

Q: What community was that in?

A: In Essex Fells.

Q: Can you describe to us what you saw as you approached this house?

A: It is a very nice residential community, winding roads. We got down the end of the road. The road curves around to the right and there is a winding driveway up to Mr. Boiardo's house. The house is situated on a rather steep slope.

Q: Did there come a time that you entered Mr. Boiardo's house?

A: Yes, sir.

Q: After you entered Mr. Boiardo's house, did there come a time when you had a conversation?

A: Yes, sir.

Q: Do you think you could sketch for us the approach you took up to his house and so much of the inside of his house as you saw that evening.

A: Yes, sir, I think so.

There it was, I was going to have the sketch *before*, not after, the conversation. Why? Because I wanted the corroboration to inspire belief before I needed to invoke belief. And Tom Wadden, who knew exactly what I was about, was up on his feet for a side bar.

MR. STERN: With the court's indulgence, may I have the easel and crayon set up?

THE COURT: Yes, sir.

MR. WADDEN: May we approach the bench.

MR. STERN: May I have it done in the meantime.

THE COURT: Let's have the conference first.

(The following occurred at side bar.)

THE COURT: What is the objection, gentlemen?

MR. WADDEN: The objection is, your Honor, that Mr. Stern wants to have him do it with, what's his name, the Boot sitting on his horse.

Wadden was referring to the elder Boiardo's house, which was quite famous. It had statutes of horses and jockeys outside the gates of its palatial grounds. Inside those grounds it was well known that men had died. There had been a large exposé in the Sunday *New York Times* magazine section, with a picture of the statues of the horses on the *cover* of the magazine. But that was not Tony Boy's house. It was his father's. Wadden simply had the wrong house. And I told him so.

MR. STERN: You have the wrong house. That is in Livingston.

THE COURT: Give me an offer of proof.

MR. WADDEN: Is there a need for this?

MR. STERN: If he can draw part of the inside of the defendant's house, that is corroborative of the fact he was there. . . .

MR. WADDEN: Have him describe it. You don't have to go into theatrics.

MR. STERN: I like to try my own case.

THE COURT: Perfectly all right. Are you going to introduce some proofs concerning the inside of the house other than that or just let it lie there.

MR. STERN: Sure. If Mr. Rigo is wrong, Mr. Wadden under appropriate circumstances can introduce proof he is wrong, but the best evidence that we can have of his good faith is that he was willing to say, "I was there, and will give you a sketch of so much of the house as I remember." That is why Mr. Wadden doesn't want it.

MR. WADDEN: It is a lot of nonsense like putting in checks having nothing to do with the case and now wanting a drawing. I don't see why he can't describe it.

THE COURT: On the basis it is corroborative of the fact he was there, it is entirely admissible on that basis.

Well, I had my wish, and now Rigo had to deliver. I guess he did, because no witness was ever called to refute what happened next.

MR. STERN: With the court's permission, may the witness get off the stand and do this sketch?

THE COURT: Yes, Mr. Stern.

THE WITNESS: I am no artist. Pease excuse—

MR. FEINBERG: I can't hear.

THE COURT: He said he was no artist.

THE WITNESS: The road is on the base down here and curves. The house sits up on a slope in somewhat this fashion, as I remember it. This down here I don't know.

There is a winding driveway which curves up, comes into a parking lot, as I recall this is the garage area in here. There is a walkway which you walk along along the back of the house, maybe 20 feet or so to a door about here, back in here there is a pool, very nice good size pool, well lit, with a cabana back here. We went in this door, just an ordinary back door and there is a long hallway which juts into a T, here into another room off this way. We came in here, just inside this door on the left there is a bar done in dark wood. There is an entrance way of some kind on the far side of the room which leads to the rest of the house. I was never there. This room itself, as I recall, just opposite the bar is like a conversation area here with a couch, some chairs. Along here I seem to recall—I am not positive—that there is a rail along in there. That is basically this sketch.

Q: Is that your best recollection of what you saw that night?

A: Yes, sir, very pleasant one.

MR. STERN: May we have it marked for the time being?

THE COURT: It may be marked for identification.

(Exhibit G-247-B marked for identification.)

THE WITNESS: I could do maybe a better job on that room.

I had just marked the exhibit for identification when Rigo *had* to make a joke. I had just wagered the case to restore his credibility after the spaghetti dinner business, when he had to throw out that he—presumably as an engineer—could have done a better job on "Tony Boy's" room. I was furious with him and let it show. "Please," I began my next question, virtually telling him to cut it out.

Nonetheless, the stratagem *had worked*. The jury was now sitting back. They were relaxed. They even smiled at Rigo's witticism. The curse had been lifted.

Q: Please. When you got inside the defendant Boiardo's home, did you have a conversation with him in reference to the problem as you have described it?

A: Yes, sir.

Q: Would you tell us what that conversation was?

> A: In substance he was somewhat angry with me. He said that we hadn't been making our payments, didn't know, couldn't understand why we were having any money difficulties.
>
> I explained this to him. This was in essence the whole gist of the whole conversation. He made some reference, as I remember to the job itself, and said that if the contractors who are presently on the South Side Interceptor Sewerage didn't get the Southerly Extension, that I might have to pick that money up, too.
>
> I told him in essence that if we didn't get a contract on that Southerly Extension job, I wasn't going to be able to pay 10 percent because we had more money eaten up in interest again and everything else, and we wouldn't have any money left.
>
> He told me, "You pay your 10 percent or I'll break both your legs."
>
> Q: If I understand you correctly, Mr. Rigo—

Now I was ready to go back over the conversation, calling for details, and so forth. But Tom Wadden was on his feet. And he stopped me cold.

> MR. WADDEN: Your Honor, may he just ask questions and give answers?
>
> THE COURT: Don't go over it again, Mr. Stern.
>
> MR. STERN: I have to have a frame of reference.
>
> THE COURT: You may have a point of reference but just don't go through the same question.

I had to be content with just one time—that time. But I did put the Rigo drawing of Boiardo's house into evidence. And it went in without objection. It was therefore in the jury room with the other exhibits in evidence during the jurors' deliberations—and at the time of their verdict. It was a constant reminder of Rigo's testimony.

There is no substitute for the painstaking analysis of a trial record. It is the moral equivalent of a surgeon in an amphitheater dissecting the techniques of another surgeon. And the more critically the transcript is examined—with the reader asking himself, "How could I improve on that question?" or "How could I have avoided that blunder?"—the more the reader makes his own muscles in his own profession.

In any event, I was satisfied that the Rigo drawing of the interior of the Boiardo house had moved the pendulum back to where it had been before the Rigo testimony about his initial meeting with the gangster. But, right or wrong about that, I simply had to get on with it. Count I, the conspiracy count, had been established, or it hadn't been and never would be. My next task was to prove each one of the next 63 counts in the indictment—the counts that alleged specific payments of money on specific dates. And when I refer to "proof," I do not mean merely introducing enough material on direct examination so that it could be "argued" later that it was proven. By proof I mean proof then and there. I mean arguing and proving then and there that each successive count is true. Let me illustrate the point.

Shortly after his meeting with Boiardo, Rigo received his contract on the Southerly Extension job. And then the city began to pay him. That is, the city checks were paid to Capen-Rigo. They amounted to nearly $300,000. Based on what Boiardo had told him, Rigo needed to raise $30,000 in cash to kick back 10 percent. So he transferred $100,000 from Capen-Rigo to Constrad and then issued checks out of Constrad to raise the cash. Now, that is not an easy transaction to translate into admissible testimony—particularly testimony that can be understood then and there rather than in final argument. And yet, it can be done.

> Q: I show you these Government Exhibits 55, 56, 57, 58, 59 and 60 and I ask you if you can identify them.
>
> A: Yes, sir.

Q: What are those checks?

A: 55 through 59 are checks for the Southerly Extension work and 60 is the check for the Southerly—South Side Interceptor Sewer.

Q: For all those exhibits, one is for the South Side and the remainder are for the Southerly Extension, is that correct?

A: Yes.

Q: For the benefit of the jury, Mr. Rigo, are those checks of different color?

A: Yes, sir, the Southerly Extension—the South Side checks are yellow and these are green.

Q: And they also have different markings on the face of them, is that right?

A: Yes, one of them is a water capital account and the other just says capital account.

MR. STERN: I offer these checks in evidence.

THE COURT: Any objection?

MR. STERN: I will show them to counsel as soon as I get them out of the folder.

MR. HELLRING: No objection, your Honor.

THE COURT: They may be marked in evidence.

(Exhibits G-55, G-56, G-57, G-58, G-59 and G-60 received and marked in evidence.)

Q: Now, Mr. Rigo, these checks are dated between September the 1st and the last check is dated September the 10th, 1965, isn't that correct?

A: Yes, sir.

Q: So that by September the 10th you had received on or approximately September the 10th you had received the last of those checks, isn't that so?

A: Yes, sir.

Q: You have already told us, I believe, that in reference to Government Exhibits 51, 52, 53 and 54 you had made no 10 percent payment on these because you simply didn't have the funds available, is that so?

A: That's correct.

Q: Do you know approximately how much the total of all these checks, Government Exhibits 51, 52, 53 and 54 which you testified to earlier, and Government 56, 55, 57, 58, 59 and 60 are? Do you know what the approximate total of all those checks are?

A: Approximately $300,000.

Q: How, then, based on your understanding of your conversations with the defendant Boiardo, how much money did you understand was due pursuant to that conversation?

A: $30,000.

Q: I don't think anyone can hear you.

A: $30,000.

The first prong was established. And the testimony "looped" into the Boiardo conversation of days earlier. Now for the cash. We had to get the cash together before the next step could be taken.

Q: After you submitted your bills to the city calling for the payment of those checks, did you do anything in reference to raising $30,000.00 in cash?

A: Yes, I did.

Q: What, if anything, did you do?

A: Issued a series of checks, some real, some fictitious which we cashed and got some 35 or $36,000.00 cash together, I believe.

Q: I show you these checks which have been marked Government Exhibits 63, 66, 67, 68, 69, 70, 71, 72, 240 and 306 for identification and ask you if you can identify these checks? And also Government Exhibit 73 for identification.

Q: Can you identify those checks?

A: Yes, sir, these and the green checks are the checks I used to raise cash with. This other check is a check which I drew from the Capen-Rigo account, I believe, over to Constrad.

THE COURT: Keep your voice up.
You say this other check.

THE WITNESS: This other check is a transfer of funds to the account of a $100,000 to the Constrad account.

Q: Which number is that.

A: This is Government 63.

Q: You say Government 63 is a check by which you transferred a $100,000 into Constrad?

A: Yes, sir.

Q: From where did you transfer it?

A: This was from Capen-Rigo.

Q: Which company had received these checks which have just gone into evidence from the City of Newark?

A: For the Southerly Extension was the Capen-Rigo project.

Q: After receiving those checks, you drew a $100,000 check from Capen-Rigo and made it payable to Constrad, is that right?

A: Yes, sir.

This repetition was deliberate—and calculated to make it as likely as it could be made that the jurors would be able to understand the testimony as it went in—and not have to rely on summation weeks later to explain what the testimony meant to the case. But, of course, Tom Wadden was not pleased.

> Q: What did you do after you deposited a $100,000 in Constrad?
>
> A: I developed these checks from Constrad to raise cash.
>
> Q: Is that the way you raised the cash?
>
> MR. WADDEN: He just said it was the way he raised cash.
>
> MR. STERN: Why is he afraid to hear it again?
>
> MR. FEINBERG: Now, your Honor—
>
> THE COURT: Gentlemen, gentlemen, he answered it, Mr. Stern. Don't go into it again.
>
> MR. STERN: I offer these checks in evidence.
>
> THE COURT: Any objection, gentlemen?
> Do you want to see them?
>
> MR. FEINBERG: I want to see them, yes, sir.
>
> THE COURT: Suppose we take a brief recess.

Well, you can't win them all. I lost the objection. Or did I? In any event, I found the recess more troubling because it broke up the explanation of a most difficult transaction. When that happens, you try to go back at least one or two steps to pick up the thread.

> DIRECT EXAMINATION (CONTINUED) BY MR. STERN:
>
> (Government Exhibits 63, 66, 67, 68, 69, 70, 71, 72, 240, 306 and 73 previously marked for identification, received and marked into evidence.)

Q: Now, Mr. Rigo, while those checks are marked, I think you have told us already that Constrad would supply the labor on the South Side job, is that correct?

A: That's correct, sir.

Q: Was Constrad involved in any way with the southerly extension project?

A: Supplying labor there, too.

Q: I believe you also told us that as of September the 10th, or September the 11th, between both the South Side job and the water job, the southerly extension job, you had received almost $300,000 in payment from the city, is that correct?

A: Well, we had—we received more than that, sir.

Q: Without making a payment back?

A: Yes, sir.

Q: Now, then, Government 63 in evidence is a check dated September the 1st, 1965, payable to the order of Constrad in the amount of $100,000, isn't that so?

A: Yes, sir.

Q: Whose account was that check drawn on?

A: I believe this was drawn on Capen and Rigo account.

Q: Can you tell us by looking at the check, was it deposited to the account of Constrad?

A: Yes, sir.

Q: I believe you have told us that by utilizing these remaining checks, Government 66, 67, 68, 69, 306, 71, 27, 240 and 73 you were able to obtain approximately $36,000 in cash, is that so?

A: Yes, sir.

Q: Can you by looking at the back stamps on those checks tell us by what date you had collected the $36,000 in cash?

A: By September 17th.

Q: What was the last date reflecting the withdrawal of cash that you see?

A: September 17.

Q: According to those checks now in evidence then by September 17, you had collected $36,000 in cash.

A: Yes, sir.

I had a *very* good reason to pound and pound on the date of September 17th. Now for the advocacy. I intended to tell the jury then and there that we were proving Count II of the indictment. I had no intention of waiting for summation two or three weeks later. I wanted them to understand at the moment.

Q: Now, Mr. Rigo, count two of this indictment charges that on September 17th, the defendants received $30,000 of Constrad money. Can you tell us whether or not you made any payments on September the 17th?

A: Yes, sir, I did.

MR. HAYDEN: If your Honor please, may the full year be added that is referred to.

MR. STERN: 1965.

A: Yes, sir, I did.

Q: Who did you pay the money to?

A: Ralph Vicaro.

Q: Do you see Ralph Vicaro here in the court?

A: Yes, he is seated between Mr. Biancone and Mr. Boiardo.

Q: Point him out.

MR. STERN: Indicating for the record, the defendant Vicaro.

Count II down! Only 62 more to go! The point, of course, is that direct examination *is* an *argument* every bit as much as it is the introduction of evidence. And I had no intention of putting in testimony and exhibits, wholesale, without the jury understanding—*as they came in*—that the counts were being proven by these exhibits before their eyes. I had no intention of waiting for summation to recapitulate all 64 counts, one by one.

It is well to pause for a moment and to interrupt the cascade of Rigo direct examination with a reference to a trial practice work by one of the most prestigious organizations in the law, and to judge whether the advice in this work as to how to conduct direct examination (which reflects the received wisdom) makes any sense based on the empirical evidence we are in the process of dissecting.

> The first rule of direct examination is that the witness should usually testify in the narrative form (citing C. McCormick, Evidence, § 5 (2d ed 1972). This means that the witness's testimony should sound as though he is simply telling the story with as little help or guidance from counsel as possible. Narrative testimony is much easier for the witness because it corresponds to the way he speaks in normal conversation. We all are familiar with the fact that interruptions in the story often distract the story teller and make him lose his thread. It is much easier for the fact-finder to listen to and follow a narrative. In addition, narration by a witness sounds less contrived, and the story sounds like it is the witness's story and not the lawyer's.[22]

And here is some additional advice which reflects the orthodox teachings: "Closed questions inhibit narrative testimony and should generally be avoided. Open questions call for narrative testimony and should usually be used on direct."[23]

Of course, I do not subscribe to this theory of examination of advocacy today, nor did I 25 years ago. Nor have I ever seen a truly effective *advocate* who did. Sometimes, it is true, the examiner must use a witness narrative. And when he has no other choice, then, of course, he does. But we often get into difficulties when we do—as I did with Rigo in the first Boiardo meeting. When that happens, the testimony loses its credibility. But even when that sort of misfortune does not befall the examiner, narrative testimony is simply not as memorable or as clear as short answers given under control, which can achieve small and sometimes repetitive steps in the march to a verdict. If there is any doubt about that, then only recall Buckner's direct of Kresel to be reassured.

My next question to Rigo did call for a brief *narrative*. But it was the last for a time. For then it was time to use questions to hammer the defendants.

> Q: Can you tell us the circumstances which led up to your paying this $30,000 in cash to the defendant Vicaro?
>
> A: Yes, sir. Before or shortly after we started getting the checks, the checks started to be issued on the southerly extension job, I was asked to go to Valentine Electric by Mr. Boiardo. I met him there in his office and he introduced me to Ralph Vicaro. He told me that henceforth I would make any payments, or if I wanted to contact him, I should do it through Mr. Vicaro.
>
> Q: Did he give you some means by which you could contact Mr. Vicaro?
>
> A: He told me to call Valentine when I had gotten my money together.

Now to use a transition question to provide the back and the fill for smoothness.

Q: When you did get your money together, did there come a time when you did call Valentine Electric?

A: Yes, sir, I did.

Q: Do you recall who it was that you spoke to?

A: I think it was Mr. Boiardo. I am not positive.

Q: Do you remember anything of the substance of that conversation?

A: No, only that Ralph would call me.

Q: He indicated that to you?

A: Yes, sir.

Looping back and forth from question to answer and back to another question and then to transition.

Q: Did there come a time when you did receive a phone call from Mr. Vicaro?

A: Yes, sir.

Q: During that phone conversation with Mr. Vicaro, did you receive any instructions?

A: Yes, sir. We arranged a meeting place.

Q: Where did you arrange to meet with him?

A: In front of the apartment at 555 Mt. Prospect Avenue.

Q: That was where your apartment was?

A: Yes, sir.

Q: Did you keep the meeting?

A: Yes, sir, I did.

Q: Did you have anything with you?

A: Yes, sir, I did.

Q: What did you have with you?

A: $30,000.

Q: Where did you have it with you?

A: In a bag, brown paper bag.

Tongue and groove. Nothing herky-jerky. No script. And the examiner is as much a part of the examination as the witness is.

Q: Did you see the defendant Vicaro?

A: Yes, sir. He pulled up to the curb, told me to get in the car. We rode around the block and I left the money on the seat beside him. He gave me a telephone number to call him, to call him between two and five in the afternoon at any time in the future. It was a Humboldt number.

Q: Do you have any recollection as you sit there now of exactly the number?

A: No, sir, I don't.

Q: I show you Government Exhibit 45 for identification and I ask you if it refreshes your recollection.

A: Yes, sir. It is Humboldt 3-9007. I wrote it in my diary, and he dropped me off in front of the apartment and that was that.

The diary authenticated the testimony, and vice versa. Sometimes I succeeded. Sometimes I failed.

Q: Have you subsequently had an occasion to dial that number?

A: Yes, sir.

Q: Did you discover the nature of the premises where that telephone number was located by dialing that number?

> A: No, sir, not by dialing the number, but somewhere along the line I found out that it was a club of some kind. It was a pay phone.
>
> Q: Now, you have told us that you made this payment to the defendant Vicaro on September 17, 1965, is that right?
>
> A: That is correct, sir.
>
> Q: Do you have a way of knowing that it was September 17, 1965?
>
> A: I noted it in my diary.
>
> MR. WALL: Excuse me, your Honor. I thought we had covered this. This is an impermissible comment. The diary is not in evidence.

I got cracked with another objection. This time it was Pat Wall. And this time I failed. And it hurt because I not only lost the point, but I lost it in the presence of the jury.

> MR. STERN: Your Honor pleases, even though the diary is not in evidence, I think the witness must be permitted to say why he knows something to be a fact. The entry itself will not come in until your Honor permits it to come in.
>
> THE COURT: I think that type of question should be avoided, Mr. Stern. He can refresh his recollection. You can ask if he has a way of knowing it, but I don't think the next step should be taken.
>
> MR. STERN: I will abide by your Honor's ruling.
>
> MR. WALL: Thank you, your Honor.

I then began the second task, one that would abide throughout the examination. Not only would I have to prove each count of the indictment *during* the direct examination, with the use of the checks to generate cash and the diary to refresh Rigo's recollection, but I also had to *simultaneously* prove that Rigo did not use the cash for any other purpose.

This was essential! Rigo was a high liver, a profligate spender, a prince of excess. I wanted to prove on direct—not on redirect *after* cross—that even as he *had* used the cash to pay the defendants, he *had not* used the cash to finance his own excesses.

> Q: Now, then, after you paid the $30,000.00 to the defendant Vicaro, you still had some cash left over, is that so?
>
> A: Yes, sir, I did.
>
> Q: Did there come a time in the same month of September that you took a trip?
>
> A: Yes, I did.
>
> Q: Do you know as you sit there now, the exact date when you left on that trip?
>
> A: September 21.
>
> Q: How do you know?
>
> A: I got married that day.
>
> Q: And you left. Where did you go on your trip, Mr. Rigo?
>
> A: To Jamaica.
>
> Q: Do you remember approximately how long you stayed down there?

The stage was set, prop by prop. And now to remove them, one by one. This honeymoon trip was a journey we were destined to take again.

> A: About 10 days.
>
> Q: I can't hear you.
>
> A: I think about 10 days.
>
> Q: Did you stay at a hotel down there?
>
> A: Yes, we did.

Q: What hotel did you stay at?

A: Plantation Inn at Ochorios.

Q: Did you fly down there?

A: Yes, we did.

Q: Fly back?

A: Yes.

Q: Did you make certain purchases while you were down there?

A: Yes.

Q: Did you use any part of either the 6 or the $36,000.00 either to go down there to pay for your hotel room or to pay for any of your purchases?

A: No, sir.

Q: How did you pay for your air fare?

A: By check.

Q: How did you pay for your hotel?

A: By check.

Q: How did you pay for your purchases?

A: By check.

Q: I show you these documents Government Exhibits 250-A, 250, 252, 251 253, 254, 255 and 256 and I ask you if you can identify them?

A: Yes, sir.

Q: What are those documents?

A: Checks for the hotel and certain purchases in Jamaica, and the travel.

Q: Let us to through them item by item. Will you call off the number and identify it?

Wadden wanted none of this. He tried various ways to stop it. Finally he claimed it was irrelevant. And this fight in front of the jury I was fortunate enough to win.

MR. WADDEN: Your Honor, they haven't been offered in evidence yet.

MR. STERN: I have to identify them for the record first, Judge.

THE COURT: Identify them first and then they will be offered.

THE WITNESS: G-50 is a check to the Hunterdon Travel Bureau for $648.00. G50-A is a bill from the Hunterdon Travel for $648.00.

MR. WADDEN: They might as well be in evidence if you are going to read the face of them.

THE COURT: Just identify them by check date, to whom it is made payable and I think that is sufficient.

THE WITNESS: Check dated 29 September to Plantation Inn. Check dated 25 September to Caribbean Camera Center, 28 September Swiss Shop, 22 September Caribbean Camera Center, 25 September Hindu Bazaar, 25 September La Marquis.

MR. STERN: I offer these documents in evidence.

THE COURT: Any objection, gentlemen?

MR. WADDEN: I fail to understand how this gentleman taking a honeymoon trip has anything to do with the facts in this case and I object to the materiality.

MR. STERN: It shows he paid by check, although he had $36,000.00 cash.

THE COURT: Yes, I will permit them unless there is some other objection. If that is an objection based on relevancy, that is overruled. Any other objection?

MR. WADDEN: No, your Honor.

THE COURT: Any other objection? They may be marked in evidence.

(Exhibits G250-A, G-250, G-251, G-252, G-253, G-254, G-255 and G-256 received and marked in evidence.)

THE COURT: I think this might be a good point to stop.

But I did not believe it was a good place. Not at all. I had not finished hammering nails into the point. So . . .

MR. STERN: I have only one or two questions.

THE COURT: All right, quickly, if you will.

Q: By means of these checks which you have identified earlier, Government 63, 66, 67, 68, 69, 306, 71, 27, 70, 73 and 240, you raised $36,000.00 in cash by September 17, is that a fact.

A: Yes.

MR. FEINBERG: He already testified to that.

THE COURT: Are we going over that?

MR. STERN: This is a difficult area.

THE COURT: I will permit it. Objection overruled.

Q: You raised $36,000.00 in cash, correct?

A: That is correct.

Q: And four days later when you took your honeymoon you paid all of your expenses by check, is that so?

A: That's correct.

MR. STERN: I would like to hand these exhibits out among the jury.

MR. WADDEN: Can't that wait until tomorrow, Judge?

MR. STERN: We have a sequestered jury.

THE COURT: Let us start tomorrow at that point. I think we ought to adjourn now. You may step down.

(Jury excused.)

There is no more popular work today in law schools on the subject of trial advocacy than Professor Mauet's *Fundamentals of Trial Techniques*. In it he writes:

> *USE OPEN ENDED QUESTIONS*
>
> Effective direct examinations are best achieved by using open-ended questions which elicit descriptive responses. This serves two functions. First, such questions let the witness tell the story and reveal the important evidence himself. Secondly, they minimize the presence of the lawyer. Remember that during direct examinations the witness should be the center of attention. Your questions should merely guide the witness from one area to another as he testifies, and break up the testimony into digestible capsules.[24]

I do not know where this "orthodoxy" originated—except, as we have seen, it has been around since the 19th century. I do believe I know why we trial lawyers *want* to believe in it. Most of us are afraid of asking questions. Why? Because we are afraid of the embarrassment of successful objections. We believe it best for the case to ask few questions because we believe it is best for *us* not to have to run the gauntlet of objection too often. We know we will lose more the more we run. The judge, who is busy trying to keep things even, will see to that. And so, because we are afraid to advocate, we make advocates of our witnesses and our clients. We train them to be their own spokesmen. And we tell ourselves that this is better for them.

The truth is that objections are won and lost by the hundreds in every case—by both sides—and in the hundreds of thousands in the career of any busy trial lawyer. It is not a momentous event, in and of itself. To be sure, it hurts when your evidence is excluded or the adversary's comes in over your objections. But that is true because it hurts the *case*. But no juror expects any advocate to prevail on every trial objection. The fear of objections is simply no valid reason to make witnesses into advocates or even into story tellers.

This advice to make storytellers of witnesses is not merely a modern fallacy. It is as old as the courtroom fear of advocates itself. And it is not confined to trial lawyers on this side of the Atlantic. Our English colleagues have been raised in the same "let the witness tell his own story" tradition that we have been. Here is Irving Goldstein, in 1936, quoting from a work of an English authority some two dozen years earlier:

> ". . . In the first place then he . . . [the witness] is agitated, confused and bewildered. Now put to examine him an agitated confused and bewildered young advocate, and you have got the worst of all elements together for the production of what is wanted, namely, evidence. . . .
>
> Now the best thing the advocate can do under these circumstances is to remember that the witness has something to tell, and that but for him, the advocate, would probably tell it very well, 'in his own way.' The fewer interruptions therefore the better; and the fewer questions the less questions will be needed. Watching should be the chief work; especially to see that the story be not confused with extraneous and irrelevant matter. . . .
>
> While a witness is telling a story in a natural manner (indeed he will generally do *if* left to himself with due attention to the order of time), counsel

> suddenly breaks in with some such observation as this: 'One moment. What was said when you spoke to the defendant?'
>
> The thread of the story is immediately broken; the witness's mind is carried back like a wounded soldier to the rear, and it is some time before he can be brought to the front again. Nor is this all. The judge is angry (if a judge can be), and the mind of the jury is prevented from following the course of the narrative."[25]

It may be seen that our English friends espouse this same "hands off" policy of examination as we do. Frankly, with their self-imposed prohibitions against a barrister speaking with his own witnesses before their testimony, such may be all that they can do.[26] Nonetheless, I think this above advice is plainly and demonstrably wrong. How in the name of heaven could the jury possibly have followed Rigo if he had been permitted to "tell his own story"—even assuming that he had one to tell? Indeed, the times when I got into trouble with him were precisely the moments when he had seized the reins and galloped off.

Of course I drew objections from my adversaries. And they were not objecting because I was hurting *myself* by asking lots of questions rather than encouraging narratives. And, of course, sometimes the objections were sustained—even as sometimes they were overruled. But that is as nothing if it is necessary to suffer an occasional blow to make the testimony clear, memorable, credible, and invulnerable to cross-examination.

We had broken for an overnight recess after the second day of Rigo's direct with the rendition of how Rigo had used checks—not any part of the $36,000 in cash—to pay for his honeymoon trip. As the court reconvened the next morning I wanted to be sure that the jury remembered. I wanted to burn it into their minds for the future that we had proven Count II beyond *all* doubt. I not only wanted them to hear the verbal testimony again, I was determined to engage their eyes as well as their ears (vividness); to use physical pieces of evidence not only to corroborate Rigo but to invoke frequency and vividness.[27]

> THE COURT: Good morning, ladies and gentlemen. Whenever you are ready, Mr. Stern.
>
> MR. STERN: With your Honor's permission, may I pass to the jury Government Exhibits in evidence 63, 240, 73, 70, 72, 71, 306, 69, 68, 76 and 66?
>
> THE COURT: Yes.
>
> MR. STERN: I withdraw that request. With your Honor's permission, may I circulate among the jury the checks, the actual checks?
>
> THE COURT: Yes.
>
> MR. STERN: I am now handing Government Exhibit 63 in evidence to the jury.
>
> DIRECT EXAMINATION (CONTINUED) BY MR. STERN:
>
> Q: Now, Mr. Rigo, Government Exhibit 63 is a check in the amount of $100,000 which was deposited into the account of Constrad, is that correct.
>
> A: Yes, sir.
>
> Q: For what purpose was that check deposited in the account of Constrad?
>
> A: For the purpose of paying Constrad back for the expenditures it had and had incurred.
>
> Q: And what kind of expenditures?
>
> A: Payroll of people involved on the work, the equipment and so forth. Constrad actually paid all these bills for work and the payroll.

Whew! First question of the day, and the man who, according to the authorities was supposed to "tell his own story" had forgotten his story. He simply forgot to say that the $100,000 had been used by Constrad to generate the $36,000 in cash payments. He was usually nervous at the first moments each day. So I did what I *had* to do—I led him. And I drew an objection.

> Q: Was it also to provide Constrad with money to make the cash payments?
>
> MR. FEINBERG: I object.
>
> THE COURT: That is leading. Rephrase that, please, Mr. Stern.

So I rephrased it. And, of course, I then got the correct answer.[28]

> Q: Was there any other purpose in putting $100,000 in Constrad?
>
> A: Yes. I had to put the money into Constrad from Capen and Rigo to be able to draw it out from Constrad to get the cash I needed.

I needed that predicate for what I intended next: to demonstrate how Rigo had taken $36,000 out of Constrad after Constrad had received the $100,000 check.

> Q: You told us yesterday that you used a series of checks in the period of early September in order to raise the check for the first payment, is that so, for the payment on September the 17th, is that so?
>
> A: Yes, sir.
>
> Q: And you told us that some of these checks were fictitious, is that so?
>
> A: That is correct, sir.
>
> Q: I show you Government Exhibit 240 in evidence which is one of the checks which you identified yesterday as having used to raise cash. It is a check made payable to a Mr. C.H. Capen. I ask you to look at that check and look at the endorsement of it, and I ask you whether or not Mr. Capen endorsed that check.

A: No, sir, he did not.

Q: Who did?

A: I did.

Q: That is your endorsement of his name?

A: Yes, sir.

Q: Did you obtain cash for that check?

A: Yes, sir.

Although the defendants had been given copies of all of these checks before the trial, they insisted on demanding to see the originals each time I presented one to a witness. While this was their right, in a technical sense, it caused me problems because I had to constantly interrupt the presentation of the testimony while passing the original checks and documents to and from each one of seven separate counsel. There were times when I was virtually running around the room. There were even occasions when an adversary asked to see a check which I had already passed to him on an earlier occasion. This was just such an instance.

MR. HAYDEN: May I see this check.

MR. STERN: It was shown to you yesterday.

THE COURT: You may look at it again.

MR. HAYDEN: I don't think you have to comment when I ask the court if I may do something.

MR. STERN: It is very tedious.

THE COURT: He may, of course, see this exhibit at any time, Mr. Stern.

MR. STERN: May I pass it to the jury?

THE COURT: Yes.[29]

The jury, of course, saw very well what was going on. Indeed, on one occasion, as I trotted up to Rigo to show him an exhibit I had just circled the room with, I thought I heard one of the six alternates say, "Don't let them get you down, kid."

It was time to do it again.

> Q: I also show you the check which is Government Exhibit 67 in evidence. It is dated September 2 in the amount of $5,365.00 made payable to a J. Franklyn Picken, endorsed J. Franklyn Picken, and apparently endorsed for cash, and I ask you if this is one of the checks which you used to raise the $36,000 which you say you got by September 16th, 1965.
>
> A: Yes, sir, it is.
>
> Q: Did you ever know a Mr. J. Franklyn Picken?
>
> A: Yes, I did.
>
> Q: Did he sign that check?
>
> A: No, sir, he did not.
>
> Q: Who endorsed that check?
>
> A: I did.
>
> Q: For what purpose?
>
> A: Obtaining cash.
>
> MR. STERN: May I pass this out, too?
>
> THE COURT: Yes, Mr. Stern.

Now I asked the long question just one more time—as they say—to make sure that every juror had it. And then I hammered the $36,000 home in staccato.

> Q: Now, Mr. Rigo, I show you the remainder of these checks, Government's Exhibit 71, 306, 69, 68, 72, 73, 70 and 66 in evidence. These are checks which you identified yesterday as having been used by you to raise the remaining portion of the $36,000 in cash, and I ask you whether you can identify the payees of those checks.

A: Yes, sir, 66 is Charles E. Robinson.

Q: Who is Mr. Robinson?

A: He is my partner in Constrad.

Q: Did Mr. Robinson endorse that for cash?

A: Yes, sir.

Q: The next one.

A: 70 is myself.

Q: Did you endorse that for cash?

A: Yes, sir.

Q: 72.

A: 72 is Leslie H. Farley.

Q: Who is Mr. Farley?

A: One of our employees.

Q: Did he endorse that for cash?

A: Yes, sir.

Q: What did he do with the cash when he got it?

A: Gave it back to me.

Q: What did Mr. Robinson do with the cash when he got it?

A: He gave it to me.

Q: Please continue.

A: 68 is to me.

Q: Did you endorse it for cash?

A: Yes sir.

Q: 69.

A: 69 is Bernard Benada.

Q: Who is Mr. Benada?

A: Another employee.

Q: An employee of Constrad?

A: Yes, sir.

Q: Did he endorse his check for cash?

A: Yes, sir.

Q: Did he give it back to you?

A: Yes, sir.

Q: 306.

A: 306 is L.D. VanSwerengen.

Q: Do you know Mr. VanSwerengen? Do you know a Mr. L.D. VanSwerengen?

A: No, sir, I don't know a Mr. L.D. VanSwerengen.

Q: What is the endorsement on the back of the check?

A: L.D. VanSwerengen.

Q: Who put that endorsement there?

A: My present wife.

Q: For what purpose did Mrs. Rigo put that endorsement on?

A: To obtain cash.

Q: For whom?

A: For me.

Q: Please continue.

A: 71 is Thomas Vanderhofen.

Q: Who is Mr. Vanderhofen?

A: Another employee.

Q: Did he endorse it?

A: Yes, sir.

Q: Did he himself give the cash back to you?

A: Yes, sir.

Q: For what purpose did you collect this cash?

A: To make a payoff.

MR. STERN: With your Honor's permission may I pass these checks out among the jury?

THE COURT: Yes, Mr. Stern.

So much for the generation of cash. It had been proven. No one could doubt it. And now for the honeymoon trip. It was *essential* to *prove*, and to prove *then and there*, that Rigo had not used any of this cash on his honeymoon. Why?

It was vital to demonstrate before cross-examination that Rigo had not personally used the cash in order to defuse cross on the subject. Of course, I could have waited for redirect. But that would have been foolish. I knew that redirect would not take place for *at least* another week.[30]

But the most compelling reason to prove that he did not use any of this cash on his honeymoon trip—as alluring as that would have been—was that if he forsook that sort of opportunity he *must* have a more pressing need for the cash than his own personal needs. And so we proceeded to *prove* it, in detail.

Q: Now then, Mr. Rigo, by those checks all cashed, the last on September 17, 1965, you obtained $36,000 in cash, is that so?

A: Yes, sir.

Q: And you have told us that four days later you left on your honeymoon, is that right?

A: Yes, sir.

Q: By the way, the Mrs. Rigo to whom you are referring is your second wife, is that so?

A: That is correct, sir.

Q: I believe you have told us that four days after September 17, on the 21st, you flew down on your honeymoon and you paid for that flight by check, is that so?

A: Yes, sir.

Q: You have identified 250-A as the bill you received from the travel service and—

MR. FEINBERG: I offer an objection. Haven't we gone over this yesterday?

MR. STERN: It was at the close. I was about to do this yesterday.

THE COURT: I don't think we finally got to this ultimate step, Mr. Feinberg.

MR. FEINBERG: All right, sir.

Q: Government 250 in evidence, which was the Constrad check which paid for those tickets, is that correct?

A: Yes, sir.

MR. STERN:With your Honor's permission, may I show them?

(Shown to the jury.)

Q: I believe you told us that you stayed in the Plantation Inn, is that right?

A: Yes, sir.

Q: You identified Government Exhibit 252 in evidence, a check, your personal check dated September 29 in the amount of $425 as the check you used to pay your hotel bill, is that so?

A: Yes, sir.

MR. STERN: May I pass that out, your Honor?

THE COURT: Yes, Mr. Stern.

We were still early enough in the game so that I wanted every juror to personally see and handle the pieces of paper that demonstrated that Rigo had not used the cash on the trip.

Q: You told us that you made some purchases while you were down in Jamaica, is that so?

A: That is correct, sir.

Q: You identified a check to the Swiss Shop as one of the checks you used to purchase something, is that correct?

A: That is correct, sir.

Q: What did you purchase at the Swiss Shop?

A: A number of things, Mr. Stern. I can't recall them all.

Q: You identified this check to the Swiss Shop in the amount of $972 as one of the checks you used, is that correct?

A: Yes, sir.

MR. FEINBERG: May we know the number of that?

MR. STERN: Government Exhibit 253 in evidence.
May I pass this out to the jury?

Q: I believe you identified these other checks, Government Exhibits 253, 255, 256 and 251, all drawn on your personal account as checks used by you to make various purchases while you were on your honeymoon in Jamaica, is that so?

A: Yes, sir.

Q: These are dated September 22, September 25, September 25 and September 25. May I pass them out to the jury, your Honor?

THE COURT: Yes, you may.

> These checks are all in evidence, ladies and gentlemen. You will have a future opportunity to examine them.

And now we were ready to make the point. And so we did—plainly, clearly, and as pointedly as we could. With all respect to the fine people in the jury box, I was simply *not* going to let them figure it out for themselves.

> Q: Mr. Rigo, why didn't you use any part of the $36,000 which you had collected by September 17, 1965, either for your airplane ticket, your hotel bill or the purchases you made on your honeymoon?
>
> A: Because I knew I would be needing more cash when I got back.

For some, this may be too detailed. But I did not and do not think so. We were asking the jury to trust us in returning a remarkable verdict under Count I, a verdict that the chief executive of New Jersey's largest city had entered into a conspiracy with the mob to extort money from everyone doing business with the city. We simply had to earn their trust in this way.

When I selected the jury, I did not exercise a single peremptory challenge. I did not challenge Italian veniremen—although Addonizio was of course an American of Italian ancestry and Boiardo brought the whiff of the Mafia into the courtroom—and even though certain groups had accused Fred Lacey and me of anti-Italian bias after the *DeCarlo* case and the Addonizio indictment. But we were not only indifferent to the ancestry of the people we prosecuted, we refused to use stereotypes in selecting the jurors. As a result, an Italian American sat on that jury—from beginning to end. And after some six weeks of trial that jury convicted the five remaining defendants of all 64 counts in less than five hours of deliberation.[31] They must have raced through the verdict form, which had 320 guilty and 320 not guilty boxes to check off (64 guilty and 64 not guilty for each of five defendants), plus eating their dinner in the jury room.[32]

Of course, we had a lot of evidence. But it does no good to have evidence if that evidence is not presented in a clear, memorable, persuasive way. And while we had a lot of evidence of payoffs in general, we had no evidence against any lead defendant except Biancone—*no* evidence against Addonizio, Boiardo, Vicaro, or La Morte—except for the testimony of Paul Rigo. And, in addition to having no testimony beside Rigo's, *none* of the physical evidence—except for Rigo's diaries—mentioned any of these lead defendants. We used the checks and other physical evidence to earn credibility where we could corroborate Rigo. We hoped the credibility would spill over to the places—and those were the key areas—where there was no corroboration.

It is now time to explode another myth. Most writers in our field advocate the chronological approach to direct examination. That is, they suggest that the testimony be given in chronological order. In advice reminiscent of that given on how to open, their works advocate the "story telling" approach. And stories are "told," of course, event by event in chronological order. Here, for example, is what Professor Mauet writes:[33]

> *ORGANIZE LOGICALLY*
>
> Once you have determined what the key elements of the direct examination will be, you must organize these points in a logical order. Usually, but not always,[34] this will result in a chronological presentation of the testimony. Experience has shown that jurors, like other people, are best able to comprehend a series of events or other information if they are presented in the same chronological order as they really occurred. Jurors are used to hearing *stories* presented chronologically, so they will be more likely to grasp and retain evidence at trial if a *story* is presented that way. (Emphasis added.)

And here is what Professor Tanford writes:

> *ORGANIZATION*
>
> It has long been the collective opinion of trial lawyers that most direct examinations should be organized chronologically. This keeps the witnesses from becoming confused, makes their testimony easy for the jury to follow, and allows you to use simple non leading questions such as "what happened next?" knowing that all events will be covered.[35]

This advice, obviously, welcomes narratives from witnesses, and puts onto the shoulders of those in the witness box the burden of getting the "story" or the "events"—as Tanford puts it—to the jury.

It is no wonder that writers who view the giving of direct testimony as the equivalent of telling "a *story*" counsel the chronological approach. But no one who views the direct examination as an *argument* would counsel a straight chronological presentation or the continued use of open questions like "What happened next?" so the witness can tell his own "story" and all the events will be "covered."

Interestingly enough, many of the same writers inveigh against "argument" on opening—and counsel that openings should be organized chronologically. But no one who views a presentation as an argument—whether it is a presentation of an opening or the presentation of direct testimony—would make a straight chronological organization. Why? Because the whole purpose of the argument is to persuade, and "the organization of what you have to say is as persuasive as what you have to say." (*See* Volume I, pages 199–209.)

Some scholars in the field suggest to begin the direct examination with the background information on a witness—even though this is *not* an important topic—because it breaks the ice for the witness and puts the witness at ease, and also because it is chronologically correct. See, for example, Professor Tanford:

> *BACKGROUND INFORMATION*
>
> Despite the potential advantages of beginning a direct examination on an important topic, most trial practitioners begin by asking witnesses about their backgrounds—age, address, occupation, family, and so forth. The most commonly stated reason for starting with neutral biographical questions is that they present familiar topics that are easy for witnesses to talk about, thereby helping them over their initial nervousness.[48] Starting with background information also is consistent with a strictly chronological presentation, and it helps the jurors get to know something about a witness before they are asked to accept that person's testimony.[49] This traditional approach seems equally as defensible as starting with an important issue.[36]

I believe that the basis for this advice is not merely wrong, but that rather it is simply beside the point. The background of witnesses, *who* the witness is, is central to *all* that the witness will say. In any case in which the reliability of that witness's testimony will be at issue, the material is essential. It is during these early moments of the testimony that the tribunal will ask itself, "Do I like this witness, or don't I?"

For example, the true advocate does not begin the direct examination of the witness with "background information" because it is either chronologically first or because it puts the witness at ease (although it does do that). We begin there because this is the *most* important point about the witness.[37]

Turn back for a moment to the way Edward Bennett Williams organized both his openings for his clients *and* their presentation to the jury on direct examination. The directs always began with an *extensive* development of their backgrounds. Why? Because that is one of the most critical issues for the jurors who must judge the man before them. And that is true for judges, too. For, as we have seen, Williams opened for Walter Jones before Judge Whipple, and presented Jones on direct examination before the judge in the same manner that he opened and presented his clients on direct examination to the juries.

LESSON: Even as points of proofs are grouped together in openings to make arguments, points of proofs are grouped together to make arguments on direct examination.

I tried to organize the Rigo testimony as an argument. That is, once I began to make a point, I followed it through, even though this meant I had to skip over chronological events that intervened, and which I would have to return to later. Why? Because those intervening events—while important for *other* purposes—would have distracted the tribunal from the *point* I was trying to make through the witness to the jurors.

MAXIM: When you enter a point, close it. Allow nothing to interfere or to intervene.

Let me demonstrate what I mean. Shortly before August 4th Rigo met Boiardo at Boiardo's house. He was threatened and told to pay off 10 percent. Then the contract came on August 4th and the city checks came between September 1st and 10th. These points, the Boiardo meeting and the receipt of the contract and the checks, *had* to be grouped together, even though many other important events had intervened. Then Rigo began to generate cash. By September 17th he had collected $36,000 in cash. These checks and activities *had* to be placed immediately next to the receipt of the city contract and the city checks weeks before. Why? Because the $30,000 payoff of September 17th had to be clustered as closely as possible to the Boiardo meeting some six weeks before. *But, of course, many other events relevant to the case had occurred in those six weeks, between August 4th and September 17th. Nevertheless, I did not let them intrude or even mention them because this grouping must not be disturbed.* Why? Because this was not a chronological story that Rigo and I were telling. We were making an argument.

Then, on September 21st, four days after the payoff, Rigo went on his honeymoon trip. That trip, too, *had* to be placed in close proximity to the previous chain of events, to prove that the payoff cash was not used. Again, nothing must be allowed to intrude between the extortion demand of Boiardo, the receipt of the held-back city contract and city money, the raising of the cash, the payoff to Boiardo's man Vicaro, and the honeymoon trip all paid for by check.

Were there other events of significance to the case interspersed between these events? Absolutely! And they were critical events to the case.

While in Boiardo's house, Rigo had discussed other contractors on the water job. Still later all the bids on the jobs were thrown out to avoid one man, Ralph Cestone. But Cestone received the contract anyway. Then, in a later meeting—but one before September 17th—Rigo was ordered by Boiardo to collect $100,000 from Cestone. And while all these events occurred between the first Boiardo meeting in early August and the honeymoon trip of September 21st, none of them were permitted to intrude. If they had been recounted before the point was closed, that point could never have been made—at least not until summation.

Of course, once the honeymoon was done, and the initial point had been made, Rigo and I had no difficulty in returning to the events in Boiardo's house for the initial meeting in order to group the next points together. In other words, we went back to the August meeting and grouped the other pre-September 21st events together. How was this done? By the use of a simple transition question.

> Q: I want to take you back for a minute. You have told us you received, finally received your contract for the Southerly Extension on August 4, 1965, is that so?
>
> A: Yes, sir.
>
> Q: You have told us about a conversation you had with Mr. Boiardo prior to receipt of that contract; do you recall it?
>
> A: Yes, sir.

Q: Now then, under the terms of your contract, your contract of August 4 on the Southerly Extension, did you have any duties in reference to the bids of contractors who were desirous to construct that line?

A: Yes, sir, we had to be there to receive the bids.

Q: Do you recall that the first bids were taken the month of August?

A: Yes, sir.

Q: Were you there at the first bidding?

A: Yes, sir.

Q: Do you recall who entered bids on that project?

A: I don't think I recall them all, sir, but there was the joint venture from the South Side Sewer. There was Verona Construction Company, Cestone's corporation, and several others.

Q: Do you recall what happened when the bids were opened?

A: Yes, there was a pre-qualification packet attached to that. Cestone's was not filled out. There evolved an argument over the thing, and we rejected all of the bids on that technicality.

All of that was fine. It *was* in the record. It *could* be argued later. But I believed that the jury could not understand it in the moment. So . . .

Q: First of all, when the bids were opened, who was found to be low bidder?

A: Cestone.

Q: Now, when the bids were opened and Cestone was found to be low bidder, you said, "We threw it out on a technicality." Who threw it out on a technicality?

A: I guess it would have been Mr. La Morte, myself—

MR. FEINBERG: I didn't hear that.

THE WITNESS: Mr. La Morte, myself and, I think, Mr. Biunno was down there, too, as I remember.

MR. HAYDEN: What was the other name?

Q: Did you have a reason for throwing out Mr. Cestone's bid on this technicality in the middle of the water shortage which you indicated?

A: I had a personal one.

Notice the blending of the points. Disqualification. Technicality. In the midst of an emergency.

Q: What was that reason?

A: Frankly, Mr. Stern, I didn't want to be involved in picking up any cash. If Mr. Cestone got the bid, from what Mr. Boiardo said before, it seemed that I would.

And so we were right back in time. Right back in Boiardo's house. Right back to Rigo's first meeting with the mobster. But no one was confused—except Pat Wall, who wanted a date. So we got it bracketed for him, in the same way we had done earlier.

Q: Which conversation are you referring to now?

A: Back at his house, I believe.

MR. WALL: Fix the date on this.

MR. STERN: He testified that was between July 7 and August 4, I believe.

MR. WALL: The bid I am talking about.

MR. STERN: There is a document in evidence.

Q: Do you recall the exact date when the first bids took place on the Southerly Extension and events which you just discussed happened?

A: No, sir. I can't recall the exact date right now.

Q: Can you give us an approximate area of time?

A: About the last—the third week of August, as I recall.

Q: Did there come a time when the project was rebid again?

A: A week later.

Q: Was he awarded the contract?

A: Yes, sir, he was.

Q: Now, can you place the period of time when Mr. Cestone was awarded the contract to do the Southerly Extension work?

A: No, sir.

Q: Well, do you recall whether it was before or after your honeymoon?

A: It was before it.

And so it was time to re-orient the jurors to the fact that we were back in time before September 21st.

Q: You told us you left on your honeymoon September 21st.

A: Yes, sir.

MR. STERN: May I have Exhibit 61 in evidence, please.

Q: In any case, Mr. Rigo, you do recall that the contract was finally awarded to Cestone before you left on your honeymoon?

A: Yes, sir.

It may be seen that these events *had* to be carved out of the earlier grouping of facts. They would have not only obscured the earlier point about the collecting of cash used only for the payoff and none for the trip, but the testimony about the cash and the trip would have also obscured the point we were about to make now.

> Q: After the contract was awarded to Mr. Cestone and before you left on your honeymoon, did anything occur in reference to Mr. Cestone's contact?
>
> A: Yes, sir. I can't recall the exact date but I think it was possibly Valentine Electric—I don't know.
>
> MR. FEINBERG: It's difficult to hear.
>
> THE COURT: Yes. Keep your voice up again.
>
> THE WITNESS: I am sorry, your Honor. I can't recall the exact date of this, Mr. Stern. It occurred sometime in that period, and I don't remember exactly how, and I think it was up at Valentine. I'm not sure, and Mr. Boiardo informed me I would have to collect $100,000 from Mr. Cestone as his payment for his work, and that that amount would take him up to the point of the amount that he had bid. After that, it would be another negotiation.

It was time to blend a new point in, and not because it chronologically belonged there—for it did not. I believed that the Rigo diaries would eventually come into evidence. They would certainly, at the least, be extensively inquired into during cross-examination. But they were written in Rigo's private code. It was now time to familiarize the jurors with the code names of the defendants as they appeared in the Rigo diaries with amounts next to their names.

> Q: Did Mr. Boiardo refer to Mr. Cestone by any other name?
>
> A: Yes, sir, he did.

Q: What name did he refer to him by?

A: Chestnuts.

Q: Chestnuts?

A: Chestnuts.

Three Chestnuts. Just in case the jurors did not hear the answer the first time.

Q: Did Mr. Boiardo have nicknames for any other people?

A: Yes, sir. He had quite a few.

Q: Do you remember some of them?

A: The mayor was the Pope. Mr. Schiff was Swifty Morgan. Mr. Malanga was Two-Ton. I can't recall them all.

Q: And Mr. Cestone was Chestnuts?

A: Chestnuts.

Just one more time. And for an excellent reason. It was now time to introduce Rigo the extortioner of Cestone (Chestnuts)—the unwilling extortioner, that is. And this, too, was prehoneymoon stuff.

Q: Now, when Mr. Boiardo told you that you would have to collect $100,000 from Mr. Cestone did you agree to do it?

A: I argued about it a bit, but I didn't have much choice. I was told to do it.

Q: You did agree to do it

A: Yes, sir, I agreed to do it.

Q: Did you agree to do it because you wanted to?

A: No, sir.

Q: Now, when you did get back from your honeymoon did you do anything to implement the conversation which you had with the defendant Boiardo before you left on your honeymoon?

A: Yes, sir, I did, but I believe I had a conversation with Mr. Cestone before I left on my honeymoon.

It must be obvious that this point—or argument—could never have been made if Rigo and I had adopted a "chronological" or a "story telling" approach. Each group of events between August 4th and the end of September, although intertwined chronologically, had to be separated out into separate lines of examination.

It was now time to introduce the conversation between Cestone and Rigo, wherein Rigo implemented Boiardo's orders and put the demand to Cestone. The record shows that I let Rigo do that one all by himself. Why? I frankly no longer recall. Perhaps I sought to change the pace. Perhaps I was just fatigued. Perhaps in the moment my muscles failed me and I needed help from the witness. In any event, the record reveals the following:

Q: Do you recall any of the details of that conversation?

A: I outlined the demand for $100,000. He was, of course, quite angry. I can't recall the details. He had—he was very angry at first. He outlined some of the difficulties that he had had with the Boiardo group before he—on the Southside Interceptor Sewer, and expressed to me—I think his—well, in essence what was he paying a $100,000 for, you know, and then after a while he calmed down and said, in essence, that he didn't mind paying the hundred thousand dollars, but he hated to pay it to them, but he supposed it was the best thing to do in order to avoid any trouble.

Q: Did he finally agree to pay the money?

A: Yes, sir.

It was now time to establish the Cestone payoffs charged in the next counts of the indictment. Cestone had already testified. The checks he had used to make the payoff he had given through Rigo, had been put into evidence, through Cestone. I called for them at this point.

> MR. STERN: May I have Exhibits 760, 761 and 762 in evidence?
>
> Q: Mr. Rigo, I show you these three checks which are in evidence, Government's Exhibits 760, 761 and 762. They are all drawn on Allstate Associates, Inc. They are all dated October 4th, all three of them, and they total approximately $30,000, and I ask you if you have ever seen those checks before.
>
> A: Yes, sir, I have.
>
> Q: Where have you seen them before?
>
> A: I deposited these checks to the Constrad account.
>
> Q: Can you tell from the rear of them, the reverse side of the checks, on what date you deposited them to the Constrad account?
>
> A: October 5th.
>
> Q: All three are deposited on October 5th, isn't that so?
>
> A: Yes, sir.

At last we are irrevocably in the posthoneymoon period. Or so I thought. I hoped not to have to mention that blessed topic again. While I did not know it then, I was wrong. For earlier—during Rigo's account of his payment for his honeymoon expenses by check—out of the corner of my eye I had seen the jurors unhappy when they examined the checks Rigo had identified as having been used to pay for the famous honeymoon. I had seen one juror nudge another and point to something. I could not see what it was that had attracted their attention, but I had mentioned it to Fred Lacey sitting next to me as I had continued the inquiry of Rigo and moved it beyond this topic. But once we got the checks back from the jurors, Fred had raced upstairs to where we had a small factory of assistant United States attorneys and federal agents working over documents. He was determined to get to the bottom of the unhappiness in the jury box, if he could.

After a time, Fred returned. By that time I was knee deep in the Cestone payments. Fred whispered to me that I had forgotten to put in two additional checks to fully account for one of the travel agent bills for Rigo's honeymoon. He handed them to me. I bit my lip in frustration as I realized my error. Thank goodness I had been standing at the end of the jury box and had been able to see the jurors and their reaction at the periphery of my vision. But before I went back again to straighten out the honeymoon, I had to complete the Cestone payoff. For having entered that point, I had to close it.

> Q: Now, then, I show you Government's Exhibit 241 and 242 for identification and I ask you if you can identify them.
>
> A: Yes, sir.
>
> Q: What are those two checks?
>
> A: Exhibit 241 is a check to me for $15,000. Exhibit 242 is a check to Charles E. Robinson for $5,000.
>
> Q: What are the dates of those checks?
>
> A: The 5th of October.
>
> Q: The same day the other checks were deposited?
>
> A: Yes, sir.
>
> Q: And are those checks drawn on the Constrad account?
>
> A: Yes, sir.

Q: And were they endorsed for cash?

A: Yes, sir.

MR. STERN: I will offer them in evidence, if your Honor please.

THE COURT: Is there any objection, gentlemen?

MR. FEINBERG: May I see them?

MR. STERN: Certainly.

We had a side bar. But the two checks came in.

Q: Now that Government Exhibits 241 and 242 are in evidence, these two checks dated October 5, 1965 in the amount of $20,000, can you tell us from the rear of those checks when it was that you collected this $20,000 in cash?

A: On October 5, sir.

Q: Is that the same date that you deposited the three Cestone checks?

A: Yes, sir.

Q: Now then, do you recall exactly what you did on October 5?

A: Not exactly, sir.

Q: I show you this document, Government Exhibit 45 and I ask you if it refreshes your recollection.

A: Yes, sir, it does.

Q: What did you do on October 5?

A: I made a $20,000 payment to Ralph Vicaro.

Q: On whose behalf?

A: Mr. Cestone's.

Now to establish the basis of his ability to identify the date. But I had to be careful. The defendants had gotten the judge to rule that while I could bring out that Rigo had a way of knowing, I could not bring out that he had made a diary entry.

> Q: Do you have a way of knowing that you paid the money October 5?
>
> A: Yes, sir, I made an entry—

No good. Rigo should just have said "yes." But he went further. And that got everyone involved.

> THE COURT: No. Do you have a way of knowing?
>
> THE WITNESS: Yes.
>
> MR. NOONAN: Of course, your Honor, I hate to do it but may we see you at side bar.
>
> MR. STERN: I tried to stop that.
>
> THE COURT: Yes, gentlemen, I will see you at side bar.

And off we went again. It may be seen that courtroom procedures are not calculated to expose the truth with alacrity. All the more reason, then, for clear advocacy. Witnesses just cannot do the job, at least not alone. And so we had a lengthy side bar. But, eventually, the side bar ended.

> Q: Mr. Rigo, please just answer this question yes or no. Do you have a way of knowing—
>
> A: Yes.
>
> Q: Let me ask it first.
>
> A: I am sorry, sir.
>
> Q: That on October 5, the same day that you deposited the check from Cestone, the same day that you received the $20,000 in cash, you made a payment to Ralph Vicaro?
>
> A: Yes, sir.

MR. NOONAN: I object to the form of the question.

THE COURT: Overruled.

MR. STERN: May I pass these checks out?

THE COURT: Yes, Mr. Stern.

Then it was time for another $20,000 payment, two weeks later.

Q: My question to you is do you recall the next date when you made a payment on behalf of Mr. Cestone?

A: No, sir, I don't.

Q: Will you take a look at Government 45 for identification before you and see if that refreshes your recollection.

A: Yes, sir, I do. It does.

Q: When was the date when you made the next payment?

A: On October 14, sir.

Q: Please answer this only yes or no. Do you have a way of knowing that you made the next payment on October 14?

MR. NOONAN: I renew my objection made at side bar to the form of the question.

THE COURT: Overruled. You may answer yes or no.

THE WITNESS: Yes.

Q: Do you have a way of knowing how much money you paid on October 14?

A: Yes.

Q: How much did you pay?

A: $20,000.

Q: Do you recall how you raised the cash for that payment?

A: I had $6,000 left over, Mr. Stern, and I believe at this time I raised some cash through a political campaign in New York.

MR. FEINBERG: I am sorry.

THE COURT: He raised cash through a political campaign in New York.

Rigo detailed the way he gave $30,000 in checks for ads for Abe Beame's campaign for mayor of New York City, and received back $15,000 in cash. And the cash went to Vicaro on October 14th.[38]

There is little point in detailing the next three or four payments that went in. The prosecution went step by step, but never without making sure that the jury understood that we were proving our case right then and there. For example:

Q: Count five of the indictment before this court alleges that on January 4 a payment was made of $7,000. Do you know to whom you made the payment?

A: Yes, sir.

Q: Do you have a way of knowing who you paid this payment to?

A: Yes, sir.

Q: Who did you make this payment to?

A: Ralph Vicaro.

Q: Do you recall where you paid him the $7,000?

A: I can't tell you the name of the place, Mr. Stern, but it is a little diner on Franklin Avenue by Heller Parkway in Newark.

And so it went. When I wanted to change topics, I did so with transition questions. When I wanted to correct an earlier error, like the honeymoon payment, I transitioned backwards.

By now, Fred Lacey had me straightened out, so I interrupted myself to get straight with the jury.

Q: Mr. Rigo, I am going to interrupt this line of questioning for a minute.

Mr. Rigo, earlier this morning we passed out to the jury a series of checks reflecting a trip you took to Singapore, is that correct?

A: Yes, sir.

Q: In that series of checks and bills was a bill from Hunterdon Travel, Inc. for your air fare and other charges, is that so?

A: Yes, sir.

Q: And that was Government Exhibit 257a in evidence, am I correct?

A: Yes, sir.

Q: What was the amount of that bill?

A: $4,052.83.

Q: We passed out to the jury a Constrad check number 257 in evidence in the amount of only $1,052.83, isn't that so?

A: Yes, sir.

Q: Now, did you pay the remaining part of that bill by cash or by check?

A: By check.

Q: I show you these two checks and I ask you if you can identify them?

A: Yes, sir.

Q: Are those the two checks that were used to pay the remaining portion of that bill?

A: Yes, sir.

MR. STERN: I would like to mark these Government Exhibits 257b and 257c and I offer them in evidence, your Honor.

(Government Exhibits 257b and 257c received and marked in evidence.)

It was as easy as that—or as difficult. The framing of the questions was not difficult. And the testimony rolled on and on, like the Mississippi. But the order and the organization of the proofs were something else. Sometimes we did a payment. Sometimes a vacation trip. If it was a payment, then the back-up checks went in, the cash came out, and the diary was invoked to fix the date and the payee of the cash.

If it was a vacation, the plans were laid. The checks that were used to pay for the trip were introduced. And the reason for the exercise was made clear to the jury.

Whether the testimony concerned a payoff or a vacation, the examination was not a matter of checking off a list of questions, or a narration by the witness. It was an argument by the examiner. For example:

Q: Did there come a time, Mr. Rigo, after October the 20th that you took a trip?

A: Yes, sir, there did.

Q: Do you recall the exact date that you left?

A: No, sir, I don't.

Q: Directing your attention to Government Exhibit 45 for identification—

MR. FEINBERG: If your Honor please, I offer my objection because I am anticipating Mr. Stern's question in view of his preliminary foundation. Mr. Rigo has had a diary in front of him. He has been observed reading it, and the pages are open directly in front of him. He just put them down time and time again, and this farce of saying he can't remember, and then referring to it, your Honor, is purely for the sake of the jury.

THE COURT: The objection is overruled.

Q: Will you please look at Government Exhibit 45 for identification. Can you tell us when you left on the trip?

A: On October 22nd.

Q: 1965?

A: Yes, sir.

Q: Do you recall where you went?

A: Yes, sir.

Q: Where did you go?

A: First to San Francisco, then to Hong Kong, then to Singapore, back to Honolulu, and back to New York.

Q: And this was two days after you had withdrawn $37,000 from the bank, is that so?

A: That is correct, sir.

Q: How did you pay for your air fare on this trip?

A: By check, sir.

Q: How did you pay your hotel bills?

A: By check, as I remember.

Q: How did you pay for the purchases you made during the trip?

A: By check.

Q: Did you use any part of the $37,000 for any of your trip expenses?

A: No, sir.

Q: Did you have to cash any checks while you were on the trip?

A: Yes, sir, I think I did.

Q: I show you these documents, Government's Exhibits 257, 257a, 258, 258a, 259 and 259a, and 323, and I ask you if you can identify them.

A: Yes, sir.

Q: What are those documents?

A: They are checks I used in connection with the trip, sir, and bills from travel agencies, hotels.

MR. STERN: I offer them in evidence.

THE COURT: Do you wish to see them, gentlemen?

(Defense counsel indicate an affirmative response.)

MR. FEINBERG: No objection—there is a continuing objection, but it is to the admission of this type of evidence, as to the relevancy.

THE COURT: Objection overruled.
Maybe this would be a good time to take a break.

MR. STERN: I would just like to pass them out while it is still fresh in the jury's mind.

MR. NOONAN: I can't hear you, Mr. Stern.

MR. STERN: I was suggesting that I would like the jury to see them while the testimony is still fresh in their minds. Then I have no objection to taking a break.

THE COURT: All right.

Q: Mr. Rigo, why is it that you wrote one of those checks to cash during that trip in the amount of $500.00?

A: I needed some cash.

Q: But you just drew out $37,000 in cash two days before.

MR. WADDEN: This is not cross-examination.

THE COURT: Yes. That sounds a little argumentative for direct examination.

Maybe it was, and maybe it wasn't. That is a purely subjective decision. All the objection did, however, was to allow me to do it over again. The point is that you win some and lose some but you do not give up.

Q: Why did you need cash on October 22nd? Why did you need cash for your trip on October 22nd when you had drawn 37,000 out in cash two days before?

A: I had already given that 37 away, sir.

Q: To whom?

A: Ralph Vicaro.

THE COURT: All right. The jury has examined those various documents. We will take a brief recess now, ladies and gentlemen. Kindly step down.

(The jury left the room.)

Shortly after this testimony, and the proof of another payment or two—one directly to Mr. Boiardo, I decided that now was the appropriate time to begin two other tasks. The first was to bring out additional material harmful to the witness: the fact that he had used Constrad checks to pay for purely personal trips and thereby to obtain unlawful tax deductions.

This *had* to be brought out because the defense would *certainly* do it if we did not. And this was highly critical material. Why? Because the tax cheating was on a wholesale basis and the grant of immunity Rigo had received had forgiven his *criminal* liability for massive tax cheating. To top it off, the IRS and not the FBI had been the primary investigating agency. This tax cheating and *criminal* forgiveness, then, went right to the heart of Rigo's credibility.

In my judgment, this was the proper time to *begin* to enter this subject—not because of chronology, and not because of clarity or comprehensibility, but because this was the most appropriate time in the presentation to *begin* to make the argument about the tax violations. But that argument would not conclude until the end game. And, of course, I knew very well even before day one of the direct examination just how I wanted to conclude, even though that would be many days in the future.

And so, two and a half days into the direct—that is, about halfway through—I launched into the task of identifying the IRS violation, preparing for the end game, and for the conclusion of the direct.

Let us examine the transition from a payment to this task, which was not at all discomforted by objections.

> Q: Then count six of this indictment charges that on January, or on or about January 19, 1966, a payment was made of the funds of Constrad. Is this the payment you are referring to?
>
> A: Yes, sir.
>
> Q: Do you remember where it was that you paid this money to the defendant Boiardo?
>
> A: I am not honestly sure, sir. It could have been at Valentine. It may have been at that little diner. It was in that area, I think.
>
> Q: Do you have any way of refreshing your recollection as to exactly where it was?
>
> A: No, sir, I do not.
>
> Q: Do you have a way of knowing where you were three days later on January 20?
>
> A: Yes, sir.

Q: Where were you three days later on January 20, 1966?

A: Chicago.

MR. WALL: That's not three days later.

MR. STERN: Three days after you received the cash you say you were there?

MR. WALL: I apologize.

THE WITNESS: The next day I was in Chicago, sir, and I was there over the weekend.

Q: The next day after you made the payment but three days after you received the cash, is that correct?

A: Yes, sir.

Q: Now then, did you fly to Chicago?

A: Yes, sir.

Q: How did you pay for your ticket?

A: By check.

As I entered the area of his next trip, taking Rigo from Chicago to Martinique, I am certain that my adversaries had no clue to my purpose. It sounded like a mere repetition of what I had been about for days.

Q: Did you stay at a hotel in Chicago?

A: Yes, sir.

Q: How did you pay for your room?

A: By check.

Q: From Chicago, do you know where you went?

A: Back to New York, sir.

Q: From there did you continue on someplace?

A: Yes, sir, to Martinique.

Q: To Martinique?

A: Yes, sir.

Q: How did you pay for your tickets?

A: By check.

Q: I show you these documents Government Exhibits 260, 260a, 261, 261a, 262, 262a and 262b and I ask you whether or not you can identify them.

A: Yes, sir, they are the bills and checks associated with this trip.

MR. STERN: I offer them in evidence, your Honor.

There were no objections. And now we were ready to begin the next argument, the one about cheating on taxes. Watch the next question after the exhibits were received and passed among the jurors. It changes topic by leading without leading, using alternatives in a question.

MR. STERN: May I pass these out to the jury, your Honor?

THE COURT: Yes.

Q: Now, Mr. Rigo, this trip, was it a business trip or a pleasure trip?

A: Pleasure trip.

And because we were making a point, *not* telling a chronological or any other kind of "story," I did not hesitate to drop back months into the past to his honeymoon trip—guiding him back using the same techniques—and then forward again to Singapore.

Q: Of course your honeymoon, the one you told us about earlier on September 21 of, I believe, 1965, was that a business trip or a pleasure trip?

A: Pleasure trip, sir.

Q: And then the trip you took to Singapore, was that a business trip or a pleasure trip, sir?

A: Pleasure trip.

And now to bring the point up to date and to close it.

Q: Now these trips, the air fare for these trips, how were they paid?

A: By Constrad.

Q: By your company, is that right?

A: Yes, sir.

Q: Who was it within your company who arranged to make the payments for these flights, for these trips?

A: The checks were made out by the accountant, I presume.

THE COURT: Louder, please.

THE WITNESS: The checks were made out by the accountant, I presume. I am sorry.

Q: Now the bills from Hunterdon that the jury is now looking at indicate that you went to Martinique with your partner, Dr. Capen, do they not?

A: Yes, sir, they do.

Q: Did you in fact go to Martinique with Dr. Capen?

A: No, I did not.

Q: Do you remember who you went with?

A: My wife.

Q: Do you know why the bills reflect that you went with Dr. Capen?

A: Undoubtedly to avoid—

MR. HAYDEN: I couldn't hear that.

THE COURT: Keep your voice up.

THE WITNESS: Undoubtedly to avoid taxes.

The point was made. But did the jury grasp it? That could not be left to chance. Then Julius Feinberg did what I did not dare to. He said he could not hear the answer.

MR. FEINBERG: I didn't get that.

THE COURT: "Undoubtedly to avoid taxes."

Very good indeed! But in our business we can afford to take no chances in key points. So . . .

Q: You mean you charged these off as business expenses to avoid paying taxes?

MR. FEINBERG: I object to the leading question.

THE COURT: Yes. That is leading, Mr. Stern.

All you have to do is reframe the question. OK, let's do it again.

Q: Why were these trips which were pleasure trips made to look as though they were business trips?

A: So that they could be counted as a business expense, and not charged to me personally.

The objection, although sustained, had not hurt. It had helped. It helped because the examiner was not afraid to rephrase the question again.

A word about this exchange, and a few we have seen earlier. There may be some who raise a concern about the ethical implications of all of this. And it is well to do so.

Where do the ethics lie here? Well, to begin with, what were the motivations of the examiner and those of the objector? Who was interested in making testimony clear and memorable to the jury, and who was attempting to keep information from them? What was the purpose of the questions? Was it to make the testimony obscure, or to be sure that it was clear? What was the purpose of the objection? Was the purpose of the objection to prevent misinterpretation, or was it to prevent clarity and understanding? Was the objection really to prevent the examiner from putting words in the mouth of the witness, or had the witness already testified to everything in the question? Indeed, as one reviews the exchange, can it be fairly said that the question was not leading at all, given the prior answers?[39]

Well, the point *was* made. Rigo had been cheating, making pleasure trips look like deductible business expenses. And the final thrust had to be made right into Rigo himself.

> Q: Were you aware of the fact at the time that this was being done?
>
> A: At some time, sir, not at the time.
>
> Q: I can't understand it myself.
>
> A: At some time, but not generally at the time.

It may be seen that Rigo himself was not happy to "fess up." But, for his sake as well as mine, I could not let him get away with it. And so I had to nail him before the cross-examiners did. I had to prove he was knowingly cheating on his taxes. And once I did that, I just got on with the next *job*.

> Q: You became aware that this was being done, isn't that so?
>
> A: Yes.
>
> Q: And it continued after you became aware of it, did it not?
>
> A: Yes, sir, it did.
>
> Q: Now, Mr. Rigo, can you tell us the next date on which you made any payment of cash to any of the defendants?
>
> A: No, sir, I can't.

Q: Will you look at Government Exhibit 46 for identification and see if it refreshes your recollection?

It may be well to pause and note the confluence between my theories about direct examination, with their lessons and their maxims, and the transcript of a case that was tried nearly a quarter of a century before this work was written—and some decades before these theories, lessons, and maxims were formulated. The truth is that the theories evolved over many years. They were not formed until long after the Addonizio trial. Indeed, it was this trial experience along with others—it was the mistakes I made in not timing the offer of exhibits, along with other blunders—that brought me to the lessons and the maxims throughout this work.

Nonetheless, I am certain that there are those who will opine that the direct examiner was given undue latitude by the judge, and that this sort of examination could not be done before a stricter judge. Still others will say that the direct examiner was able to examine in this way only because his adversaries were not vigorous enough. There are those who will proclaim that tougher foes would have stopped the direct examination in this form.

But nothing could be further from the truth. The counsel for the defendants were all very experienced. Let us direct our attention to Joe Hayden. Rigo had just testified that he made a payment of $20,000 to Vicaro on the 10th of February, 1966.

Q: Do you have a way of knowing that it was the 10th of February?

A: Yes, I do.

Q: Do you know who you paid it to?

A: Yes, I do.

Q: Who did you pay it to?

A: Ralph Vicaro.

Q: How much did you pay?

A: $20,000.

Q: In what form?

A: Cash.

Q: Do you have a way of knowing on whose behalf you paid the $20,000 to the defendant Vicaro?

A: Yes, I do.

Q: Who did you pay the $20,000 on behalf of?

A: $10,000 on behalf of Constrad and $10,000 on behalf of Cestone.

MR. STERN: May I have Government's Exhibit 763 in evidence?

Things were indeed complicated for me with Rigo making his own payments while collecting Cestone's. I needed a document. But Hayden was on his feet.

MR. HAYDEN: If your Honor please, may I respectfully request that after the witness has refreshed his recollection from this exhibit that he not sit there and continue to read it? I think that should be put down.

THE COURT: Yes, put it down after each occasion, if you will, Mr. Witness.

That only made my job tougher. If anyone doubts Joe Hayden's ability, they have only to refer to the appendix of Volume I to read in toto his able and strong opening against me in *United States v. Weber*. Joe Hayden was a formidable foe. My very next question about exhibit 763 got me sandwiched between Jack Noonan, one of the leading defense attorneys at the time, and Julius Feinberg, who finished his career as a state court judge.

Q: I show you this exhibit, Government's Exhibit No. 763 in evidence, an Allstate Associates check, that is Mr. Cestone's company, payable to Constrad in the amount of $9,960, and I ask you if you have ever seen it before.

MR. FEINBERG: I object to the form of the question. I object also to Mr. Stern's testifying that Allstate is one of Cestone's companies. There is no testimony from this witness that it was.

MR. STERN: It was the uncontroverted testimony of Ralph Cestone who sat there and told us all he did under oath. This is a frivolous objection, your Honor.

MR. NOONAN: I object to this on behalf of Mr. Feinberg, your Honor.

THE COURT: Whatever another witness has said the jury will recall that. You didn't have to add that on examination of this witness.

MR. FEINBERG: Thank you, your Honor.

THE COURT: If this witness knows, you may ask him that question if you wish.

MR. STERN: Yes.

Q: Do you know who owes [sic] that company or who is one of the principals in that company, Allstate?

A: Yes, sir, Ralph Cestone.

Q: Have you ever seen that check before?

A: Yes, sir, I have.

Q: When have you seen it before?

A: When it came into—

MR. NOONAN: I am sorry, Mr. Rigo.

THE WITNESS: I am awfully sorry.

THE COURT: Keep your voice up, Mr. Rigo.

MR. NOONAN: What was that?

THE WITNESS: I will try.

Q: Please keep your voice up so Mr. Gordon's attorney can hear you.[40]

MR. NOONAN: I am Mr. Noonan, not Mr. Gordon's attorney.

THE COURT: Respectfully, Mr. Noonan, who is Mr. Gordon's attorney.

MR. STERN: I am sorry.
Mr. Noonan, who is Mr. Gordon's attorney.[41]

As for Wadden and Hellring, the former not only had once formed a law firm with Edward Bennett Williams, but had made a specialty of driving prosecutors from their own courtrooms. Wadden has been described in these words in Evan Thomas's biography of Edward Bennett Williams:

> Wadden, in particular, was a brilliant trial lawyer, a shrewd gamesman with uncanny instincts. He was a master at obfuscation and stalling, essential qualities while defending outrageously guilty mobsters. Using schoolyard tricks, he had a special knack for rattling prosecutors: He would shoot paper planes over their heads when the judge wasn't looking. He purposefully mispronounced a prosecutor's name until the prosecutor jumped to his feet demanding, "Your Honor, direct Mr. Wadden to get my name right!" Defending a mobster named Tony Giacalone on trial for bribing a policeman, Wadden was assaulted by an exasperated prosecutor in the hallway. Wadden, who'd been baiting his opponent for days, was all wounded innocence before the judge ("Your Honor, I can't imagine what I've done . . ."). Handsome and warm, Wadden was so endearing to jurors that one sent him cookies, prompting the prosecutor to demand a mistrial, or at least equal cookies.[42]

Hellring's achievements I have described elsewhere.[43] Tom Dyson and Pat Wall had also been with Williams and upon leaving him enjoyed national trial practices. It was a constant struggle in the courtroom, one that I would be flattered to hear another say was a struggle among equals.

Shortly after the last interchange, however, the struggle took on a new dimension. As I labored another time to use the diaries to refresh recollection, the defense suddenly shifted ground. They had, they said, no objection to putting the diaries into evidence.

> Q: Mr. Rigo, can you tell by these checks when it was that you received the $20,000 in cash?
>
> A: February 10th, sir.
>
> Q: Now, you have told us you have an independent way of knowing that you paid $20,000 in cash to the defendant Vicaro, is that right?
>
> A: That is correct, sir.
>
> Q: Do you recall where you paid that money to the defendant Vicaro?
>
> A: Outside 555 Mt. Prospect Avenue.
>
> Q: Whose address is that?
>
> A: The apartment we had in Newark.
>
> Q: Mr. Rigo, can you recall the date when you made another payment to any one of the defendants in cash?
>
> A: No, sir, I can't.

So I reached for my trusty "recollection refresher," the current edition of the Rigo diaries. And then Tom Dyson was on his feet with an announcement that would transform the shape of the direct examination.

> MR. DYSON: May I interrupt, your Honor? Apparently Mr. Rigo is making continuous reference

> to diaries, and the questioning is going along through those books. I have conferred with the other defense counsel, and we have no objection if Mr. Stern sees fit to introduce these books into evidence.

I was stunned. I could hardly believe my ears. For days I had been hopscotching around the testimony, using "refreshed recollections," picking up a diary for the question and then putting it down again after the answer. It was difficult to believe that this was all to be ended.

> MR. STERN: The diaries?
>
> MR. DYSON: That is correct.
>
> MR. NOONAN: In the interest of saving time.
>
> MR. STERN: I will offer them, as I did on Monday, I will offer them again in evidence.
>
> THE COURT: All right, gentlemen. They may be admitted into evidence.
>
> (Government Exhibits 44, 45, 46, 47, 48 and 49 are received and marked into evidence.)

And with that, five years worth of diaries were marked into evidence. I was now where I had wanted to be nearly three days earlier. I had with me enough copies of each diary for each juror and every alternate. It had been my original intention to place the diaries into evidence and then go through each entry with Rigo as he described each payoff and each trip and, indeed, each entry that had been made in a hand other than his own. But it was now days later. More important, the jury had already heard the testimony about several years worth of transactions. Should I pick up where I had left off—or should I attempt to go back to the beginning and redo some or all of it? I was at a loss as to what to do.

> MR. STERN: May I have a few minutes recess now. I think I can make a different kind of presentation. I think we can save a lot of time.

THE COURT: Step down briefly, ladies and gentlemen. Hopefully a brief recess, a brief respite will save considerable time.

(Jury left the courtroom.)

THE COURT: Mr. Rigo may leave.
We will recess.

(Short recess.)

What would those who counsel the use of scripts do now? And what of those who advise to practice with videotape? My entire world had just changed. There was no time to rehearse the witness, or with the witness. But I was not the least concerned. Indeed, I was delighted. I was not concerned because Rigo had never been trained to follow a script of precise questions and answers. He had been taught to think in the themes of the testimony—with the details marshalled to support those themes. He was no brittle, programmed witness who might break if bent to a new wind. I had no fear for him.

And I was delighted to see an opportunity to go right back to the beginning of Rigo's direct—this time with every juror holding a personal copy of the appropriate diary—and to do, in abbreviated form, what I had originally intended to accomplish. So, with no more than a brief recess, Rigo was brought back into the room and we—he and I—went back two full years, right back to the beginning.

PAUL W. RIGO, resumed, and testified further as follows:

THE COURT: Have the jury in, please.

(Jury entered the courtroom.)

MR. STERN: May I proceed, your Honor.

THE COURT: Please do.

MR. STERN: May I pass out copies of Government Exhibit 44 now in evidence to the jury. For the record, I am handling Government Exhibit 44 in evidence to the witness.

DIRECT EXAMINATION (CONTINUED) BY MR. STERN:

Q: Mr. Rigo, I ask you to look at Government 44 in evidence. I believe you have already identified this to be your diary as of 1964, is that right?

A: Yes, sir.

Q: Now, Mr. Rigo, were you the only one that ever made any entries in this diary, Government Exhibit 44 now in evidence?

A: No, sir.

Q: Who else, if you know, made entries in this diary?

A: My first wife made some entries in this diary, I believe.

And with that I went through the 1964 diary with Rigo, redoing the significant dates. In the midst of this I realized that I had foolishly failed to provide Judge Barlow with a copy to follow along with.

MR. STERN: Your Honor, shall we provide the court with copies?

THE COURT: That may be helpful. I was sitting here trying not to look wounded, Mr. Stern.

MR. STERN: You are the last one in the courtroom I want to wound.

And when Rigo and I had finished with the diary for 1964, I had it collected from the jurors, passed out copies of the 1965 edition and went right back to it. For now I had to introduce the jury to the diary entries made by Rigo's accountant, Fallon, for I was sure that if I failed to do that job my adversaries would certainly do it for me.

MR. STERN: Now, with your Honor's permission, I would like to hand out copies of Government's

Exhibit 45 now in evidence, a diary for the year 1965.

With your Honor's permission, may the Marshal now collect Government 64, because I think it would be too bulky for the jury to try to—

THE COURT: Yes, all right.

MR. STERN: For the record, I am now handling Government Exhibit 45 in evidence to Mr. Rigo.

Q: Now, Mr. Rigo, were you the only one who wrote in that diary, Government Exhibit 45 in evidence?

A: No, sir.

Q: Do you know who else made entries in that diary?

A: I believe it was Mr. Fallon in my office.

There is no point in reproducing the testimony that Rigo gave as he re-reviewed each one of the diaries we had previously covered using the doctrine of past recollection refreshed. The point is, of course, that because Rigo had been prepared without a script, he was able to successfully meet the exigencies of a moment that neither he nor I could possibly anticipate.

And so the testimony rolled on, proving each of the allegations of the indictment, count by count. New projects were awarded to Rigo by the city. So new payments were begun by him to public officials and to mobsters. And payments had to be collected by Rigo from others working on various projects as well. And the coded entries in the diaries became the working tool by which Rigo kept track of whom he paid how much on which project, and on whose behalf. For Rigo not only had to keep track of the breakdown of each 10 percent payment on each separate project of his; he had to keep account of the collections that he made for and from other contractors.

It was thus clear that those entries in the Rigo diaries were in fact business records. They were made to enable Rigo to conduct the business of paying off the Boiardo-Addonizio ring members on behalf of himself and others.[44]

Use The Judge

During direct examination a lawyer should use every tool of argument and persuasion at hand, including the judge. By that I mean that an advocate can interrupt his own examination and request the judge to instruct the jury on a specific point that has arisen during that immediate point in the testimony.

For example, at one point during Rigo's direct testimony we *had* to establish that one of the counts in the indictment alleged a payment on an erroneous date. We had returned the indictment within a few days after the initial meeting with Rigo. Errors like these were bound to creep in. The first task was to explain to the jury—*then and there*—that there was an error, but that it was not a serious one. Rigo's diary recorded that he had made a payment on November 26th. Indeed, his diary indicated a payment on that day of $10,000. *But he could not have made it because according to the cancelled checks he did not have the cash on hand as yet.* The checks used to generate the cash had not been negotiated until four days later. All that had to be explained *before* cross-examination—explained so that the jury understood it, and explained without leading.

> Q: Will you tell us what your recollection is now?
>
> A: Yes, sir. I *had planned* to make a payment on Friday, the 26th of November.
>
> Q: Do you have a way of knowing that you *had planned* to make a payment on that day?
>
> A: Yes, sir.
>
> Q: Did you actually make a payment on the 26th of November?
>
> A: No, sir, I didn't.

Q: Do you have any recollection as to why you did not make a payment on that day?

A: No, sir, just something vague to the effect that it was Thanksgiving weekend, and I can't tell you anything more about it than that.

Q: Do you have a way of knowing how much you *had intended* to pay on November 26th?

A: Yes, sir.

Q: How much was that?

A: $10,000.

[Emphasis added.]

The stage was now set to explain away (without appearing to) an erroneous diary entry that indicated that the money *had been* paid on November 26th.

Q: Did there come a time when you did raise $10,000 in cash?

A: Yes, sir.

Q: I show you this check, Government's Exhibit 94 for identification, and I ask you if you can identify it.

A: Yes, sir.

Q: What is that check?

A: It is a check, a Constrad check, drawn to cash, for $10,000.

MR. STERN: I offer it in evidence.

MR. FEINBERG: May I see it, Mr. Stern? The copy of the exhibit that we have we can't read the amount.

THE COURT: No objection?

MR. FEINBERG: No objection.

THE COURT: It will be marked in evidence.

(Exhibit G-94 was received and marked in evidence.)

Q: Mr. Rigo, by looking at this check can you tell us when you raised the $10,000 in cash?

A: On December 1st, sir.

Q: Of what year?

A: 1965.

So far so good. Not even Rigo could pay money he did not have to give until five days after he was supposed to have given it. Now to get the payment made properly, and to show the jury that the indictment was erroneous—before the adversaries did it for us.

Q: Did you make payment from that $10,000 in cash?

A: Yes, I did.

Q: Do you remember the details of those payments?

A: No, sir. I don't remember the exact details of that payment.

Q: Do you have any way to refresh your recollection?

A: Yes, sir.

Q: As to the details of the payment?

A: No, sir, not as to the details, but I do know that I paid at least $5,000 of this by December 7th, and the balance by the end of the year.

Q: Do you have a way of knowing that you paid $5,000 of that $10,000 by December 7th?

A: Yes, sir.

Q: And the remainder by the end of the year?

A: Yes, sir.

Q: Now, Count IV of the indictment alleges that $10,000 in cash was paid out by Constrad on November 26th.

MR. HAYDEN: What year?

MR. STERN: 1965.

Q: Is that accurate?

A: No, sir.

Q: But how far wrong maximum, according to your recollection, could it be?

A: Approximately a month.

MR. STERN: May I approach the bench, your Honor?

It was now time to get a judicial blessing over the error—if I could. How? By going to side bar and asking the judge to tell the jury that such minor errors in dates did not invalidate the count. Of course, the judge need not have granted a side bar. But Judge Barlow was a judge, not an autocrat, and he readily granted such opportunities to both sides.

THE COURT: Yes.

(The following proceedings were had at side bar, out of the hearing of the jury.)

MR. STERN: Would your Honor instruct the jury at this point that on or about—that criminal acts in the indictment which are alleged in terms of "on or about November 26, 1965" need not be proved immediately on the date alleged, but it is sufficient if proven within a reasonable period of time of the date alleged in the indictment?

THE COURT: That is the law, is it not?

It was the law then, and it is the law now. But that did not mean that the judge had to give this instruction at that precise moment. And he had plenty of reasons not to, as the defense made clear in their immediate and forceful objections.

> MR. HAYDEN: I would agree to that, except that it is obvious to everybody—there is a definite argument of law that I want to present at the proper time, and I would not want the court's instruction now to create the inference that it could be a different year altogether. I know what your point is, and I don't object, but since I just asked you to specify the year it is obvious to the jury, and I want the court's instruction not to be an answer to what I just asked.
>
> MR. STERN: No. It can't be off by as much as six months.
>
> MR. HAYDEN: A reasonable time is correct, but I don't want the court to say that when I just asked about the year.

And, of course, Joe Hayden got plenty of help from his colleagues. For Pat Wall, Feinberg, and Wadden immediately jumped in with reasons of their own.

The "safe" thing for the judge to have done, surely, was to deny the instruction, or to say he would give it later in his final charge, or to demand that I draft one for him in the next recess. Any or all of that would have been unreviewable. And any of these safe judicial harbors would have ruined my ability to make a timely explanation to the jury. But Judge Barlow was a fine judge, who gave to both sides what *he* felt they were entitled to. As we stepped back from the bench, he gave an immediate instruction, and I then hammered the point home with the next question.

> THE COURT: Ladies and gentlemen, I want to instruct you now that in an indictment in which a specific criminal act is alleged as happening on a specific date the law is that it doesn't have to be proved to have occurred on that specific date if it is

established to your satisfaction that beyond a reasonable doubt it happened within a reasonable date thereafter.

BY MR. STERN:

Q: You say although you cannot fix the exact date when you paid out or paid over this money, you say you know you paid some of it by December 7th and the remainder before the end of the year, within a month of November 26th, is that so?

A: That is so, sir.

There will be those who will say that the above demonstration is an oddity, that it could not be done before this judge or that judge. Perhaps some judges will not do it, but other judges will. Later, when we explore cross-examination and study the *Manton* trial record, we will see the technique used in the bribery trial of the chief judge of the United States Court of Appeals for the Second Circuit, in 1939.[45]

But the point is that no judge will do this for you as advocate if you do not at least ask him to do so. Of course, the judge may refuse if you ask. Judicial rulings can always defeat advocacy. But the lawyer who does not know what is possible, the advocate who does not at least attempt what is possible, defeats himself.

LESSON: Use judicial instructions throughout your case to enhance and validate your arguments to the jury.

Anticipate Objections to Testimony

It is vital to anticipate and to be able to deal *immediately* with objections to the testimony of your witness. If you can deal with such matters efficiently, you not only preserve jury attention time, but make adversaries less willing to challenge you. On the other hand, if such interruptions can cause major breaks in the presentation of your testimony, they not only destroy clarity but encourage additional efforts to interrupt with additional objections. Here is a prime example of this point.

When Rigo reached his diary entry for March 21, 1966, he met with a supplier of pipe named Mack Albertson. Rigo had been instructed to collect $35,000 from this man, and they had had a conversation on March 21st. I intended to get that conversation in. I also knew that my adversaries would object. But I was ready. First, however, the stage had to be set for the jurors. Watch the leading without leading by the use of the "whether or not" questions.

> Q: Mr. Rigo, I ask you to turn to your diary for March 21, 1966, Government Exhibit 46 in evidence and the entry there is "Sick all week," is that correct?
>
> A: Yes, sir.
>
> Q: And by that entry, did you indicate that throughout that week you were ill, is that correct?
>
> A: Yes, sir.
>
> Q: You remember what you had, what illness you had?
>
> A: Pneumonia.
>
> Q: You remember whether or not you were confined to your bed?
>
> A: Yes, sir, I was.
>
> Q: Now, can you recall whether or not prior to March 21, 1966, you had occasion to have a conversation with Mr. Mack Albertson of Lock Joint—Interpace?[46]
>
> A: Yes, sir, I did.

And then the objections started to pop. And on its face the conversation between Rigo and Albertson did appear to be hearsay.

> MR. FEINBERG: Your Honor, I object to conversation, a recital of what Mr. Albertson told this witness.

THE COURT: I guess we will have to go to side bar, Mr. Stern.

MR. FEINBERG: If your Honor please, the objection made by me is as to the relation of the conversation by Mr. Rigo that he had with Mr. Albertson. Of course, I can't object to anything he did as a result of that conversation, but I object to anything Mr. Albertson told him as not within the exception to the hearsay rule.

MR. STERN: At page 1888 of the record, your Honor has already ruled on that question in connection with Mr. Albertson's testimony, and ruled that Mr. Albertson could give conversations between himself and Mr. Rigo.

THE COURT: Was that the conversation?

It may be seen that the judge had forgotten the ruling and the subsequent testimony he had earlier ordered. But this too had been anticipated, for I had the transcript with me at the bench.

MR. STERN: "Mr. Albertson, *the judge says you may tell us the conversation between yourself and Mr. Rigo.*

"Answer: Paul suggested we meet at a—this was at some bar out toward where his office was. I drove down there and sat with him and had a drink. *Paul said that he had been saddled with the chore of collecting some of this money.*

"Question: *Saddled with the chore of collecting it?*

"Answer: Yes; and that—well, then, I went through the same discussion with him about the problems that we were confronted with in trying to come up with any sums of money. He suggested that we try to work out some scheme with Ralph Cestone whereby we could get the money to him."

THE COURT: If the conversation is within that part, the objection is overruled.

(End of side bar conference.)

Q: Mr. Rigo, *the judge says you may tell us the conversation between yourself and Mr. Albertson.*

[Emphasis added.]

Notice how the question was put to Albertson after the judge had ruled permitting him to answer. Notice how the question was put to Rigo after the judge had ruled that he may answer. And notice the way Albertson's key statement had been repeated in the next question.

Certain it is that by this time the reader is drenched—if not drowned—in direct. All to the good. This is but another method of getting the experience of doing direct examination personally. These examinations do not happen by chance in the courtroom. They were not the product of a momentary existential leap, or an instinctual reflex. It was a method, deliberately and constantly applied for days, not a momentary accident. And it is method that we are studying.

The examination continued. Rigo's own payments on different contracts must be accounted for, even as his separate collections from Lock Joint (now Interpace) and Cestone had to be segregated, and all of this had to be identified from sources of cash that themselves had to be separated from his personal junketeering. It was possible to achieve this without a single written question. It would not have been possible to achieve with a written script.

This examination had been greatly slowed by the need to pause whenever the exhibits were passed among the jurors. This technique of showing copies of exhibits to jurors—as old as the struggles between the likes of Buckner and Steuer in 1931, as we have seen, and as we still see every day in our courtrooms—carries its own price. It does slow the pace of the examination. This is often a price worth paying to purchase credibility with jurors. But too much of anything is just too much. After three days of direct, I finally stopped the practice of stopping the testimony during the viewing. Why? Because I sensed that the jury had heard so much and seen so much that it was now more important to pick up the pace than to pause for the jury to handle a fourth day of checks.

Q: Do you recall whether or not you and Mr. Biunno and Mr. La Morte had an occasion to go to the Eden Roc during that trip?

A: Yes, sir, we had the yacht tied up at the Eden Roc dock and we had a cabana over at the pool. We would go over to that.

Q: Did you incur any charges at the Eden Roc?

A: Yes, sir, considerable.

Q: Did you pay them by cash or by check?

A: By check, sir.

Q: I show you Government Exhibits 271 and 271-A and ask if you can identify them.

A: Yes, sir. Eden Roc bills and a check from Constrad to the Eden Roc.

MR. STERN: I offer them in evidence. Does any counsel want to see them?

MR. WALL: Give me the numbers.

MR. STERN: 271 and 271-A.

(Exhibits G-271 and G-271-A received and marked in evidence.)

Q: According to these documents, Mr. Rigo, at the Eden Roc you incurred charges of $3,834, is that so?

A: Yes, sir.

Q: You paid it by check, is that so?

A: Yes, sir.

MR. STERN: May I circulate these documents among the jury?

THE COURT: Yes, Mr. Stern.

MR. STERN: Your Honor, may I inquire of you whether it is your desire for me to continue the questioning while the jury is looking at the documents or to wait?

THE COURT: I think you can continue the questioning, Mr. Stern. If the jury can't follow both, let me know.

From that point on, the speed of the examination could increase.[47] And we went through the life and times of Paul Rigo, working hand in hand with a Mafia leader to control New Jersey's largest city. So that, after his return from Florida, Rigo and "Tony Boy" got together to discuss La Morte's promotion in the Addonizio administration. The first task was to place the conversation in reference to the return from Florida, and its location.

Q: Now, after you returned in that first week of June did there come a time when there was a water break in the City of Newark?

A: No, sir. That was later than the first week of June.

Q: I say after you returned did there come a time when there was a water break?

A: Yes, sir.

Q: When was that?

A: On the 16th of June.

Q: Did you make an entry reflecting that?

A: Yes, sir. There is an entry in here.

Q: Is that in your handwriting?

A: I believe it is, but I don't recall when I wrote it.

Q: How about the other entries on that page, are they in your handwriting?

A: No, sir.

Q: Do you remember that there was a water break independently of anything written in your diary?

A: Yes, sir.

Q: Why do you remember?

A: It was Mrs. La Morte's birthday. We were at a birthday party and it was somewhat interrupted by this event.

Q: What did you have to do?

A: Mr. La Morte and I both had to go down to the water break. Broad Street was completely flooded.

Q: In between the time that you returned from Florida and the time of this water break did you have an occasion to see the defendant Boiardo?

A: Yes, sir, I did.

Q: Do you recall the exact date when you met him?

A: No, sir, I do not.

Q: Do you remember where it was that you met him?

A: Yes, sir.

Q: Where was it?

A: At Pal's Tavern.

Now that the place was fixed and the date was bracketed, the target was within the cross hairs and we were ready to fire our shells.

Q: Do you remember any of the conversation between yourself and either the defendant La Morte or the defendant Boiardo?

A: Yes, sir. I think after we had had lunch Mr. Boiardo drew me aside and asked me if I thought the defendant La Morte—excuse me—could handle the job of director.

Q: Director of what?

A: Director of public works of Newark. I thought he could. He indicated to me that the mayor was not of that mind. The mayor was somewhat fearful.

Q: Fearful of what?

A: Of Mr. La Morte not being able to do the job, and Mr. Boiardo indicated to me that he was going to get Mr. La Morte appointed director, but that he would expect us to be on hand if any engineering problem arose.

Q: Did you agree to it?

A: Yes, sir.

But even as we picked up the speed of the examination, Rigo and I never forgot that we had to make the testimony clear, memorable, and credible—and we never forgot as well that we were arguing to the jury as much as or more than merely introducing stuff into the record for argument later.

Q: I am going to try to see if I can't go a little faster, Mr. Rigo. The last entries in your diary for 1966, turning the page beginning December 19th. Are those entries in your hand?

A: It is possible that some of them are, Mr. Stern.

Q: Only identify the ones that you are positive of.

A: I can't be positive of them, Mr. Stern.

Q: How about the December 23rd entry?

A: Yes, that little note, "AWAY."

Q: Yes.

A: That is in my hand.

Q: Did you go away approximately that date?

A: Yes, sir.

Q: Do you recall where you went?

A: I believe I went to Nassau, sir.

Q: I show you Government's Exhibit 47 in evidence which is your diary for the year 1967. Can you tell from that diary when you returned from Nassau?

A: On the 3rd of January, sir.

Q: 1967?

A: Yes, sir.

Q: I ask you did you pay for that trip by cash or by check?

A: To the best of my recollection, by check, sir.

Leading without leading by alternatives. Now, to make a point, Rigo and I dropped back into time.

Q: You have told us, Mr. Rigo, that in the years 1965 and 1966 you had occasion to meet the defendant Vicaro in an automobile driven by him, is that so?

A: Yes, sir.

Q: And you have described to us several occasions on which you passed money to him in that automobile, is that so?

A: Yes, sir.

Q: Do you remember, sir, what kind of an automobile the defendant Vicaro was in on those occasions?

A: It was a Chevy sports coupe, sir, a Chevrolet sports coupe.

And now to go forward into a new year, transitioning as we go, and passing out documents to the jury to keep up the speed.

Q: With your Honor's permission may I hand to the jury the 1967 diary, Government Exhibit 47, and may we collect back Government's Exhibit 46?

THE COURT: Yes, you may.

Q: You have told us that you had a conversation with the defendant La Morte about his becoming the director of public works and then again a conversation with the defendant Boiardo about the defendant La Morte becoming director of public works, the first time in early June and the second sometime between early to mid-June, is that so, of 1966?

A: Yes, sir.

Q: Did the defendant La Morte become the director of public works?

A: Yes, sir, he did.

Q: Do you remember approximately when that was, roughly; was it within the year 1966?

A: Yes, sir.

Q: Was it after your conversation with him and with the defendant Boiardo to which you have testified?

A: Yes, sir.

Now that copies of the diaries had been handed to each juror, we were able to add more corroboration to the testimony.

Q: Turning to the year 1967, and Government's Exhibit 47 in evidence, I ask you to look through that exhibit and to tell us, if you can, whether anybody other than yourself made any entries in that diary for that year.

A: No, sir.

Q: Pardon me?

A: No, sir.

Q: To the best of your knowledge and belief did you make all the entries in your diary for 1967?

A: Yes, sir.

Q: Turning to the first page, there is a list of telephone numbers. You made all those entries, I take it?

A: Yes, sir.

Q: On the last page there are some additional numbers. Did you make that entry, or those entries?

A: Yes, sir.

Q: The last number is HU 3-9007, and I believe you have told us that that is the number where you used to call the defendant Vicaro at some kind of club, is that right?

A: Yes, sir.

Q: The first number, 484-7300, I believe you identified as Valentine Electric, is that so?

A: Yes, sir.

Q: What is the second number from the top?

A: I believe that is Mr. Boiardo's.

Q: Where?

A: At his home.

Q: You told us that in 1966 you had written 239-8734 and 239-8733 for Mr. Boiardo's home number, isn't that so?

A: Yes, sir.

Q: Do you know why you wrote his home number as 239-3198 in 1967?

A: I think it was changed.

Again, a direct challenge to Boiardo and to his attorney. Rigo even had Boiardo's old telephone number. How could he have that if it were all a lie? The defense counsel never answered that—unless they were willing to make the preposterous argument that we on the prosecution team had used the resources of the government to feed the information to Rigo, years later, and to collaborate with him in making *ex post facto* entries into his diary.

The End Game

It is time to describe and to analyze the "end game" of the Rigo direct examination, as we have defined that term elsewhere. Direct examination must end properly. Most particularly, it must end on the notes that provide not only great impact, but the greatest protection for the witness from cross-examination.

In the case of relatively short direct examinations, the end game is usually brief. In the case of a massive examination such as Rigo's, the process is far more lengthy. But the principles are identical.

For Rigo, the end game included affirmative and negative factors. First, we knew that the defense had an expert handwriting analyzer, Ordway Hilton. And we had to put some evidence in on that account.

Second, we had to deal with Rigo's helicopter and yacht. And now, deep into the testimony with the jury on our side—if they ever were—was the time to do that.

Third, we had some wonderful corroborative evidence, and we had to pave the way for this. We had Gordon's admissions before the grand jury that not only had he, Gordon, received the payoffs, but that he had collected money from Rigo for Councilman Guiliano. And we had Councilman Callaghan, who had been so indiscrete as to accept a check from Rigo. This check we had marked Exhibit 1 and were waiting for the moment before cross-examination to introduce into evidence.

The trick, of course, was to knit all of this into an end game without being obvious about it. Here then is the home stretch, touching all of the bases. First, the handwriting expert with a touch of the Gordon-Guiliano connection thrown in:

> Q: Now I direct your attention to your entry of February 13 and your entry of February 14 and your entry of February 15. Did you make those entries?
>
> A: Yes, sir.
>
> Q: What year did you make those entries?
>
> A: 1968, sir.
>
> Q: Did you sit down and make those entries all at one time or did you make them at various times?
>
> A: Various times.
>
> Q: Were you always using the same pen or using different pens?
>
> A: Different pens.
>
> Q: As you sit there now looking at it, can you tell at what moment you made which entry?
>
> A: No, sir.
>
> Q: Will you read the entries and explain them to the jury?
>
> A: February 13, La Morte, Bernstein, 11 shifts, 2K plus 1.
>
> February 14, NWK for Newark, AWWA 12, C plus 1, I plus a half, J a half, Joe plus a half, T plus a half, F plus a half.

February 15, La Morte, Van Riper, sewer contents meet. Newark. Schiff. P plus 1. L plus a half. F plus a half.

Q: Explain those entries to the jury.

A: Yes, sir.
2K plus 1 indicates a thousand dollars each—excuse me—a thousand dollars each to Mr. Bernstein and Mr. Frank Addonizio.

Q: Who were they at that time?

A: Two councilmen.
The C plus 1 indicates a thousand dollars to Calvin West.
The I plus a half indicates $500 to Irving Turner.
The J plus a half indicates $500 to Jim Callaghan.
The T plus a half indicates $500 to Tony Guiliano.
The P plus a half indicates $500 to Phil Gordon.
The Joe plus a half indicates $500 to Joe Melilio.

Q: Do you recall the details of exactly where it was that you gave this money to the persons that you named?

A: No, sir, not exactly.

Q: Can you recall whether or not you gave Councilman Guiliano his money directly?

A: No, sir, I never gave it to Councilman Guiliano directly.

Q: Who did you give Councilman Guiliano's money to?

A: Mr. Gordon.

Q: Was there any understanding between you and Mr. Gordon?

A: Yes, sir.

Q: What was that understanding?

A: That he would pick up Mr. Guiliano's money.

And now to use the next series of entries to review and to summarize the case—particularly against Boiardo.

Q: I direct your attention to your entry for February 15. Will you read it and explain it to the jury?

A: Yes, sir. The P plus 1 was, again, Mr. Gordon, a thousand dollars.
N plus 1 is Mr. Schiff, a thousand dollars.
The L plus a half is Mr. Bernstein, $500.
The F plus a half is Frank Addonizio, $500.

Q: Under your entry of February 13, 2K plus 1, did you have a reason for calling Mr. Bernstein and Mr. Addonizio or referring to them both as 2K?

A: Yes, sir, I did.

Q: What was that reason?

A: They were known as the Katzenjammer kids.

Q: Where had you heard that?

A: Mr. Boiardo.

Q: Was that his nickname for them?

A: Yes, sir.

Q: If I understand you correctly, Mr. Cestone was Chestnuts, according to Mr. Boiardo. Bernstein and Frank Addonizio were the Katzenjammer kids. Malanga was Two-Ton.

A: Two-Ton.

And now to argue the case that the diaries were themselves worthy of belief—and I mean *argue*.

Q: When you made these entries, Mr. Rigo, did you make them for the purpose of testifying in a case?

A: No, sir.

Q: For what purpose did you make them?

A: For my own information solely.

Q: Why did you need that information?

A: There were a number of people involved here, Mr. Stern. It would be very difficult to keep track of it without some kind of a record.

Q: Did you ever think that this diary would come into the possession of the United States when you made that entry?

MR. FEINBERG: I object to what he may be thinking.

THE COURT: No, you can rephrase that, I think, Mr. Stern.

Q: At the time you made these entries, did you ever anticipate anyone connected with law enforcement would see them?

MR. FEINBERG: I object to the anticipation.

THE COURT: No, I don't think that is objectionable, Mr. Feinberg.
You may answer, Mr. Rigo.

THE WITNESS: No, sir.

Of course, the second question was identical in spirit to the one that had just been successfully objected to. But this time it was overruled. But that was commonplace in our courts then, and it is commonplace in our courtrooms now.

The judge tries to be fair. He makes a thousand calls. He rarely calls them universally against one side. Frequently he subconsciously tries to even them out. One for you. One for the other side. Every experienced trial lawyer hates to win five objections in a row—and then have to make a really important sixth objection. The chances of prevailing are diminished by the immediate past victories.

And so very often when we ask a question on direct that is objected to by the adversary the judge says, "Please rephrase that." This is code for, "Next one for you." In my view, when you hear the judge say that, make the next question a lethal one. But we return to Rigo.

And now the time had come to explain about the boat and helicopter. The jury had heard about them both, of course. Indeed there had been mention of them for days. But Gordon, part of the end game, would be the vehicle for explaining about these accouterments of venal excess.

> Q: Can you tell us why you made that entry?
>
> A: I was going to Nassau that day with Mr. Gordon and his son.
>
> Q: Did Mr. Gordon and his son fly down with you?
>
> A: Yes, sir.
>
> Q: Who paid for Mr. Gordon and his son's trip?
>
> A: I did, sir.
>
> Q: Did Mr. Gordon ever pay you back?
>
> A: No, sir.
>
> Q: How did you pay for it, by cash or by check?
>
> A: By check, sir.
>
> Q: I show you these documents Government Exhibits 296, 294a and 294 and I ask you whether or not you can identify them.
>
> A: Government exhibit 296 is my airline ticket, sir. 294a is a bill which lists a series of flights, included on this one is the Pan Am ticket for Mr.

> and Mrs. Rigo, Phillip and Leo Gordon, Kennedy-Nassau-Miami, Kennedy. Government 294 is a check to Travel Everywhere from Constrad dated April 19, 1968 for $1842.60.

And in they went. And that provided a transition into the yacht. And the yacht into the helicopter, and the cars . . . and the jeeps. But it was essential to introduce the jury to these toys in the proper way—that is, by showing how the defendants as well as Rigo used them.

> Q: Where did you stay when you went on this trip, Mr. Rigo?
>
> A: On the boat, sir.
>
> Q: Whose boat was that?
>
> A: Mine.
>
> Q: What kind of a boat did you have?
>
> A: Sixty-five foot Wheeler.
>
> Q: Do you recall whether or not you owned that boat personally or it was owned by one of your companies?
>
> A: It was owned by Loripaul, sir.
>
> Q: Was that one of your companies?
>
> A: Yes, sir.
>
> Q: And do you recall how Loripaul paid for the boats, whether by cash or check?
>
> A: By check.
>
> Q: Now, you have mentioned this company, Loripaul, before. What was the purpose of your formation of Loripaul.
>
> A: Equipment, sir. Loripaul owned the office trailers, most of the cars, jeeps, the helicopter and the boat.

We were steaming along just fine. It was time to make more payments and to prove more counts. So we brought out how Rigo's secretary showed up at City Hall "with a bag full of money." Rigo and his man Fallon stuffed separate envelopes, and passed out the envelopes around City Hall. Counts 34 through 45 went into evidence as the men went through the building dispensing cash. But then we had an emergency.

Fred Lacey whispered in my ear and we immediately asked for a conference in the judge's chambers. Our colleagues in our office in Newark had just uncovered a plot to kill Rigo, and Fred decided to bring it to the attention of Judge Barlow. The conference in the judge's chambers both interrupted and enhanced the end game in the courtroom.

Rigo's barber, Joseph Robert Stracco, had a small shop in Chester, New Jersey. A few weeks before trial two hoodlums entered Stracco's shop and demanded to know the date of Rigo's next appointment. When Stracco refused to tell them, they stormed out.

Next day his shop was burglarized and its fixtures wantonly destroyed. Shortly thereafter, Stracco was approached in a bank by the same two men who had entered his shop, and they again demanded to know Rigo's next appointment. Again, Stracco refused to tell them.

Within a week, a car pulled up next to Stracco's as he waited for a red light. Someone—Stracco could not identify the person—fired a shot over Stracco's car, narrowly missing a school bus unloading down the street. The shooters sped off, leaving Stracco shivering behind the wheel of his car.

Shortly thereafter the two thugs who first encountered Stracco in his shop and then at the bar, entered Stracco's shop again. "Forget about it. It's all a mistake," one of them reassured him. "When we win, you're invited to Tony Boy's party."

That was all the frightened barber needed to hear. He finally passed the information to the authorities, and Fred Lacey and I found ourselves in Judge Barlow's chambers, behind closed doors, moving to revoke Boiardo's bail.

The application was granted. But the rest of the day had been consumed. So the jurors were sent back to their hotel. They, of course, did not know the reason for the delay or the outcome of the application. They did know it would be another day, a fifth day, before direct examination could conclude.

On Friday morning, June 25, 1970, we brought Rigo's direct examination to a close. First there was government's exhibit 1—the check the defendant Callaghan had taken from Rigo. I had labeled it exhibit 1 not because it was to be the first exhibit—for I intended to reserve it for the end—but because it was very important and I wanted not only to highlight it, but to put it into evidence close to the beginning of cross-examination. Its importance lay in its corroborative power of Rigo. No one could claim that Rigo had made this check up later—as they could and would in regard to his written diaries and his oral testimony. This check had to be spotlighted and introduced before cross-examination in order to protect Rigo from that cross-examination.

> Q: Now then, Mr. Rigo, I show you these two checks, Government Exhibits 1 and 201 and I ask you if you can identify them?
>
> A: Yes, sir, I can.
>
> Q: What are those checks?
>
> A: Government G-1 is a bank check, National Newark & Essex Bank, to James Callaghan in the amount of $5,000, May 23rd.
> No. 210 is a Capen-Rigo check issued to National Newark & Essex Bank for $5,000 May 23rd.
>
> MR. STERN: I offer these in evidence.
>
> MR. HAYDEN: No objection whatsoever.
>
> MR. FEINBERG: No objection.
>
> MR. E. STERN: Our continuing objection.
>
> THE COURT: Yes. Your objection is noted, Mr. Stern.

(Exhibits G-1 and G-210 received and marked in evidence.)

This Stern was Ed Stern, then a young partner of Bernard Hellring, assisting in the defense of Hugh Addonizio. Today he is a distinguished appellate judge in New Jersey.

Q: Mr. Rigo, can you tell the circumstances which led up to the issuance of these two checks, Government's Exhibit 1 in evidence and Government's Exhibit 210 in evidence?

A: Yes, sir.

Q: What were those circumstances?

A: Mr. Callaghan had come to me and said he needed money, needed $5,000. He was in a bind. He wanted to be paid ahead on the $10,000 commitment. I told him I wouldn't pay him ahead on that basis in cash.

Q: Did you have a reason?

A: Yes, sir, I did.

Q: What reason was that?

A: I wanted the check.

Now that answer was just not clear enough. So, I made it clearer.

Q: Did you feel you needed that for your records?

A: Yes, sir.

Q: Well, what if anything did the defendant Callaghan say when you told him you wouldn't give it to him in cash?

A: He said he wouldn't take a company check or personal check, and I suggested, "How about a bank check?" And he said he would accept that.

MR. STERN: May I pass these checks out among the jurors, your Honor?

THE COURT: Yes.

Q: Now, Government Exhibit 210 is your Capen-Rigo check drawn to the National Newark & Essex Bank in the amount of $5,000, drawn on May 23rd, and Government Exhibit 1 in evidence is a bank check issued by the National Newark & Essex on May 23rd to James Callaghan in the amount of $5,000, with an endorsement, and the endorsement appears on the rear. Do you recall how the defendant Callaghan received the check?

A: Yes, sir. Mr. Fallon gave it to him.

Q: Now then, at the time Mr. Callaghan received that check was he still a councilman, to the best of your knowledge and belief?

MR. HAYDEN: I will stipulate he was.

MR. STERN: All right. Thank you.

Shortly thereafter Callaghan pled guilty. And while that plea was taken in the absence of the jury—and they were never formally told about it—suddenly he was gone, just after Government Exhibit 1 was received, and after having been on trial for weeks. This, too, might help protect Rigo from the onslaught that was sure to shortly come in the form of cross-examination.

It was now time for the end of the end game: the dealing with Rigo's initial lies to the authorities and his initial contacts with Fred Lacey.

MR. STERN: Now, with the court's permission I would like to hand out Mr. Rigo's diary for the year 1969, Government's Exhibit 49 in evidence.

Q: Mr. Rigo, did there come a time either late in the year 1968 or in the year 1969 when you became aware of the fact that the Essex County Grand Jury was conducting an investigation?

A: Yes, sir.

Q: Can you pinpoint the date, the exact date when you became aware of that investigation?

A: No, sir, I cannot.

Q: Now, addressing yourself to Government's Exhibit 49 in evidence, can you pinpoint any date in that diary by which you were certainly aware of the investigation?

A: Yes, sir.

Q: What date are you indicating?

A: January 16th, sir.

Q: Which entry are you indicating?

A: "Genola 3:00 p.m. Newark."

Q: Did you make that entry in your diary?

A: Yes, sir, I did.

Q: Did you make all the entries in your diary for the year 1969?

A: Yes, sir, I believe so.

Q: Do you recall having a meeting with Mr. Genola?

A: Yes, sir, I do.

Q: Do you recall what the subject matter of the meeting was?

A: Yes, sir, I do.

Q: What was the subject matter?

A: The subject matter was basically to inform me that the Essex County Grand Jury was investigating certain financial transactions between the mayor and me.

Q: The defendant Addonizio and you?

A: Yes, sir.

Q: Thereafter, in the month of January, 1969, did you have certain conferences and meetings in reference to this grand jury investigation?

MR. E. STERN: Objection, if your Honor please. May I approach the sidebar?

THE COURT: Yes.

There were a welter of objections. But eventually we returned to our places and I was able to get to the conversation that I wanted, a telephone conference with Ralph Vicaro. And this conversation I intended to introduce word for word. No more of that "in substance" jargon.

Q: Now then, between the time of that conference on January 23 and the scheduled meeting that you had with Mr. Hellring which was cancelled on January 28, did you have a telephone conversation with any of the defendants in this case?

A: Yes, sir, I did.

Q: With which defendant?

A: Mr. Vicaro.

Q: Do you recall the substance—withdrawn. Do you recall the exact words of that conversation?

A: Almost.

Q: Will you give us what he said to you?

A: "Stay away from the Pope. Keep your mouth shut and remember you have a pretty daughter in Suffern."

Q: What did you understand this to mean?

A: I took it to be a threat against my daughter in Suffern. She attends school up there.

Q: Now then, I direct your attention, Mr. Rigo, to March 3 of 1969. You have a diary entry Acapulco. Did you go to Acapulco then?

A: Yes, sir, I did.

The stage was now set for Rigo's lies to the county grand jury and his flight to freedom to the federal authorities. He had established his reasons—good reasons—for both. But this "story" had to be taken from Rigo—piece by piece. It had to be plucked, not offered. The integrity of the witness in the eyes of the jury demanded an interrogation by me rather than a narration by him.

Q: Do you recall what occurred while you were in Acapulco?

A: Yes, sir, the Essex County Grand Jury began interviewing people in my employ.

Q: Did you become aware of what they were investigating in that regard?

A: Yes, sir.

Q: What was it that they were investigating?

A: The payments that Constrad made on behalf of Mayor Addonizio for work done on his house at the shore. We made payments to Genola.

Q: *Did you become aware they were investigating anything in addition to that?*

A: *I don't believe so at that time, sir.*

Q: *Did there come a later time when you were aware of anything in addition that they were investigating?*

A: Yes, sir, I did.

Q: What did you become aware of in that regard?

A: They were investigating certain areas of the business transactions that we had had with the City of Newark, specifically the padding of bills.

[Emphasis added.]

Rigo had forgotten to mention bill padding. But I had to have it. It was *essential* to bring this out on direct. And now was the time. The jurors would *now* be prepared to forgive Rigo this—if not now, then never. I therefore kept pressing him until he remembered. And, once he did, off we went.

Q: Had you in fact at least to some degree padded your bills with the City of Newark?

A: Yes, sir, to some degree I had.

Q: Why had you done so?

A: To attempt to get back the 10 percent. I never quite made it.

Q: Did there come a time when you yourself received a subpoena to appear before the Essex County Grand Jury.

A: Yes, sir, there did.

Q: Please answer this question just yes or no. Between the time you first received that subpoena to testify before the Essex County Grand Jury and the time that you did testify before the Essex County Grand Jury, did something happen, yes or no?

A: Yes.

Q: Can you tell us when it was that you appeared before the Essex County Grand Jury?

A: March 27, sir.

Q: You can do that because you made an entry in your diary, is that right?

A: Yes, sir.

Now to handle the lies before the county grand jury. He lied because his life was threatened. He found a bomb threat in his car. But before I dared to use this, I had to seek judicial approval. This was one of the rare instances where I made a motion in limine addressed to my own evidence. But I had to. The evidence was simply too dramatic and the danger of mistrial was simply too great for me to gamble at this stage of so important a trial. So we went to side bar.

> MR. STERN: Your Honor, I am going to ask a question now which counsel might object to. I think I should make a proffer of proof.

We had a vigorous fight, of course. But Judge Barlow ruled that the evidence was admissible. As soon as the bench conference ended, I stepped back to my place.

> Q: Mr. Rigo, after you were notified to appear before the grand jury but before you actually appeared and gave testimony on March 27th, what, if anything, occurred?
>
> A: I found a card on the seat of my car when I came down from my attorney's office.
>
> Q: What did the card say?
>
> A: "This could have been a bomb. Keep your mouth shut."
>
> Q: What did you understand this to mean?
>
> A: I took it to be a threat, sir.
>
> Q: Did you, after receiving that note, appear before the Essex County Grand Jury?
>
> A: Yes, sir, I did.
>
> Q: Did you tell them the truth?
>
> A: No, sir, I did not.
>
> Q: Did you lie to them?
>
> A: Yes, sir, I did.

Q: Did you lie to them under oath?

A: Yes, sir, I did.

Q: Why?

A: I was afraid.

The point was nailed and re-nailed. Now we were ready to change topics and move on. And so we did. I wanted to introduce a conversation Rigo had with La Morte on August 20th. But I wanted to set the stage for it. But I also wanted the jury to know that I was setting the stage. So I told them so, by going back and forth in time.

Q: Now then, I direct your attention to August 20, 1968. You have an entry in your diary.

MR. WALL: 1968 or '69?

MR. STERN: I apologize. I meant to say 1969.

THE COURT: What date 1969?

MR. STERN: August 20.

Q: The first entry in that box, La Morte, is that 8:30?

A: Yes, sir.

Q: Did you make that entry?

A: Yes, I did, sir.

Q: Did you meet the defendant La Morte on that date?

A: Yes, I did, sir.

Q: Now, Mr. Rigo, between March 27, 1969, the date you testified before the Essex County Grand Jury and August 20, 1969, what, if anything, occurred?

A: Mr. Stern, the situation was it was becoming intolerable. I was getting pressure from Boiardo's group to keep up payments, keep my mouth shut. The grand jury began bringing in their accountants, and they were subpoenaing records every couple of days. Nothing was moving in Newark. The whole situation was just plain building up to a completely intolerable situation.

Q: On October 20 when you met with the defendant La Morte, did you have a conversation?

A: Yes, sir, I did.

Q: I meant August 20. On August 20, did you have a conversation with La Morte?

A: Yes, sir, I did.

My second mistake on dates in just two pages of transcript. I am not proud of that, of course, but in my excitement I had stumbled. But so what? It was far from fatal. On the other hand, a written script would certainly have been lethal. But the stage had been set for the La Morte conversation, which the jury could now understand against the backdrop of its history, and there had been a smooth transition from March to August.

Q: Do you remember the substance of the conversation?

A: Yes, sir.

Q: What did you tell him?

A: I told him Newark could go to hell.

Q: Meaning what?

A: I was fed up. I didn't want any more of it and I wasn't going to continue under the way things were going.

Q: Did you put those very words in your diary?

A: Yes, sir, I did.

It was time to change topics. But not to tell a story. It was time to drive Rigo into the arms of the federal authorities. It was time to introduce the federal authorities, particularly the IRS. Their agents were exploring the checks Rigo had issued to the Buck Companies, which Rigo had used to generate cash. This would be the vehicle for the end of the end game. Watch how the pace increases.

> Q: Mr. Rigo, what occurred after your meeting with the defendant La Morte on August 20, 1969?
>
> A: Well, sir, shortly thereafter, two federal agents went to see my accountant, Charlie Fallon.
>
> Q: What kind of federal agents were they?
>
> A: Internal Revenue. They questioned about these book of Buck accounts. I now got into the situation where I had a three-way thing going, a three-way squeeze going, Boiardo's people on one hand; and I had the Essex County Grand Jury on the other and I had, now, the federal people in the act. I was beginning to become very desperate. I didn't know, I didn't know who to go to.
>
> Q: What did you do?
>
> A: I searched this thing out and waited, and finally I contacted one of the few people I felt I could trust, an old friend, a gentleman by the name of Foran.
>
> MR. FEINBERG: I didn't hear the name.
>
> THE COURT: A gentleman by the name of Foran.
>
> THE WITNESS: And I asked him to make an appointment for me with the United States Attorney.
>
> Q: What happened after you asked Mr. Foran to set up that appointment?

A: Two days later, sir, I got a telephone call. It was anonymous, just said, "Keep the hell away from the Federal Building."

Q: What did you do after you received that telephone call?

Now we had a momentary interruption for some objections. Notice what happens at the end of the colloquy. The same question is repeated, almost verbatim, even though the question was not written down.

MR. E. STERN: Same objection.

THE COURT: Objection overruled.

MR. DYSON: May we have a reference to time?

THE COURT: Can you give us a rough time, or an exact time, if you can?

THE WITNESS: Approximately October.

Q: What did you do after you got that phone call?

A: I got hold of Mr. Foran again and told him to cancel it, which he did. Now I was getting to the point where you are really getting worried. It seemed that everybody knows exactly what you are doing, when you are doing it. You feel your phone is tapped.

This was now story telling time. And so I let Rigo tell the story.

Q: What did you do?

A: Well, an opportunity presented itself later in the year, just after November 16th. I didn't want anybody to know what I was doing. I again contacted Mr. Foran and told him I would be going away and that I would call him when I got where I was going, and when I did, I asked him to call Washington, D.C., for me and set up an appointment with somebody that I could go to about this thing.

On the 16th I had a meeting in Newark—I think it was the 17th—this was in the attorney's office. I think it was on the 17th. For the first time, Mr. Stern, I paid for a ticket by cash.

Back to control and to a staccato presentation.

Q: Why did you pay in cash?

A: I didn't want anybody to know where I was going.

Q: Where did you go?

A: I went back to Acapulco.

Q: What did you do when you went back to Acapulco?

A: I was sick for about a week.

Q: What did you do when you recovered?

A: I called Mr. Foran. Mr. Foran then went ahead and called Washington for me.

Q: Do you know where he called in Washington?

A: Yes, sir. The first place he called was Flanagan's office.

Q: Do you know where his office was?

A: The White House Annex.

Q: What occurred then?

A: He referred Mr. Foran to Mr. Kleindienst's office. Mr. Kleindienst's office referred Mr. Foran to Mr. Wilson's office, and Mr. Foran called me back and gave Mr. Wilson's telephone number. I called Mr. Wilson from Acapulco and made an appointment with him for the 1st of December at nine o'clock.

Q: Did you keep that appointment?

A: I did.

It was time to bring Rigo into contact with Fred Lacey and me.

> Q: Do you know Mr. Wilson, the Assistant Attorney General in charge of the Criminal Division of the U.S. Department of Justice?
>
> A: Yes, sir.
>
> Q: Did there come a time after you met with Mr. Wilson that you met with various attorneys in the Department of Justice, including Mr. Lacey and myself?
>
> A: Yes, sir.

And now . . . the grand finale. How would one end the examination? Why, right on our most sensitive point. The place where the cross-examination was most likely to begin—the immunity that had been granted to Rigo.

But we had a point to make. And that was that although Rigo had been immunized against *criminal* prosecution, he was still liable for his civil taxes—and that he would have to pay, pay a lot. The point was, of course, that he was not getting off scotfree. Let us see if we were able to make the point, and to make it clearly.

> Q: Now, Mr. Rigo, you understand that you have been immunized by this court and by the United States for your testimony? You understand that?
>
> A: Yes, sir.
>
> Q: You understand that you cannot be prosecuted criminally for what you told here; you know that?
>
> A: Yes, sir.
>
> Q: And that means you cannot be prosecuted for any violations of the Internal Revenue Service Law; you understand that?
>
> A: Yes, sir.

Q: Do you also understand that you are civilly liable for every dime in tax that you owe this government?

A: Yes, sir, I do.

Q: And for every trip you took as a business deduction that wasn't, and for every deduction that you took that wasn't honest and legitimate; do you understand that you are still liable for the tax?

A: I certainly do, sir.

And on that note the direct examination of Rigo ended. There were days and days of cross-examination, of course. But before it began, I introduced Gordon's grand jury testimony admitting that he had in fact taken money for himself, and for Councilman Guiliano in indistinguishable envelopes—passing Guiliano's on to him. That testimony heard immediately before Rigo's cross-examination further buttressed and cushioned him. Of course, I might have elected to read it to the jury *after* Rigo's cross—to rehabilitate him if he needed it. But even so many years ago I believed as I believe now: save nothing; do not redeem; do not prepare for resurrection; do not save Custer after he has ridden into the Little Big Horn. Instead, "Get there firstest with the mostest."

Redirect Examination

With that philosophy in mind, it may be seen why I counsel against the need for extensive redirect examination. Indeed, in the case of Rigo, I asked *no* redirect questions even though the cross-examination consumed five full days. But that is not to say that redirect has no place in the scheme of trial lawyering.

Sometimes one must redirect. A cross-examination may reveal the unexpected. Or that examination may have created an ambiguity that *must* be clarified. There may be many reasons for a redirect. But those reasons should arise, not be planned for. In the best of all possible worlds, the direct examiner will feel no need to take another round after cross-examination has concluded.

For remember, the cross-examiner will almost always get the last word. Even after re-re-redirect, there will be re-re-re-cross.

And so the wise trial lawyer who is well ahead after cross-examination is done, goes not near the fire again, unless he fairly plainly has to. And the more dangerous the cross-examiner, the more true this particular piece of advice is.

Of course, if there is to be redirect, the examiner will be given greater latitude in the framing of his question. "Leading" will be allowed here when it might be forbidden earlier. It is for this reason that it is easier—on a craft level—to "argue" on redirect than it is to argue on direct. And we shall turn again to this subject after exploring cross-examination. The task, now, however is to learn the techniques that give you that freedom to make the correct argument initially, on direct. As for the argument to make—ah, that is the highest art of all.

ENDNOTES

1. The agents we used, primarily, were IRS agents—for in those days the FBI under J. Edgar Hoover was not responsive to such investigations. But under Commissioner Randolf Thrower the IRS was—and it remained so until late 1973, when a successor commissioner decided not to allow the IRS to be used to make bribery and extortion cases. But, by that time, the Hoover reign had ended, Watergate had begun, and the FBI became available.
2. Of course we took a terrible risk with the conspiracy count in that form. Nothing would prevent the defendants from meeting this broad trial by calling a host of businessmen to testify that they did work for the city but did *not* have to make payments. And yet, in spite of the wording of the conspiracy count, not one such witness was called by a single defendant during weeks of trial.
3. We had been unable to "break" the contractors who worked in this project, except for Gallo, who was killed in an auto accident just four months before the trial. Gallo would have confirmed everything and more—for he was one of the largest construction businessmen in the state. But he was dead at the time of the trial, so we used just Kantor, and the checks. But that was quite enough. Neither Mal Bros., nor C. Salvatore & Sons, nor C.F. Malanka & Sons came into court to deny the checks they had written to Kantor's fictitious company for nonexistent services.
4. *See Judgment in Berlin.*
5. *See* Volume I.
6. Now called 803(5) of the Federal Rules of Evidence, which were not in existence then.
7. *See* page 226 *supra.*
8. Now Federal Rule 803(6). *See* pages 226, 227 *supra.*

9. The excerpt below illustrates this battle.

> THE COURT: Can we have them marked now for identification, laying whatever foundation you want and go on to something else?
>
> MR. STERN: I can't do it. I have keyed my whole direct examination around these diaries for a number of years through intimate transactions, detailed transactions, transactions involving lots and lots of checks, lots and lots of meetings and lots and lots of conferences. I made these records available. I am sorry that Mr. Wall has not gone through them in 10 days. I mean nothing impolite by that. But surely counsel must have anticipated Mr. Rigo being on the stand. I could not anticipate that they were going to have no cross-examination of most of my witnesses. We are at the point now where unless I want to shut down the trial, or ask you to shut down the trial this afternoon, I had to put him on. I must have them in. I don't know quite how to solve Mr. Wall's problem without having the time in 10 days to read them.
>
> MR. WALL: I will ask that we adjourn and I will be prepared to argue tomorrow morning about the documents as to whether or not they are business records. Because if they are not, your Honor, then the proper way of doing this is to find out when Mr. Rigo's recollection is blank and then lay a proper foundation for these as past recollection recorded, if they can be.

10. It may be seen that the judge was wiser than all of the lawyers, or at least wiser than the prosecutor.

11. *See* Volume I, pages 29, 30.

12. *See* pages 176–180 *supra.*
13. *See* page 178 *supra.*
14. For example, a few pages earlier in the record, while arguing against a voir dire in the presence of the jury, Wadden launched this missile at me, and drove the judge in the other direction.

    > MR. WADDEN: You have heard Mr. Stern asking questions in this trial. He testifies more than the witnesses.
    >
    > THE COURT: I don't accept that, Mr. Wadden. If he does, I am sure you will object to it when the proper time arises. No, I see no reason if we are going to have a voir dire on this question it should not be done in front of the jury. I don't see any reason. They are either going to be admissible as such or not. I don't see a reason to go through it twice, once out of the presence of the jury and once in their presence.

15. *See* pages 199–209 *supra.*
16. *See* page 196 *supra.*
17. That was D. Louis Tonti, executive director of the New Jersey Highway Authority. Just two years later, as United States attorney, I was to indict and convict him for extortion. But at the time his name meant nothing to me.
18. Since it is not reasonable to believe that the reader will plow through the entire hundreds of pages of Rigo's direct examination, which consumed nearly five days of testimony, a fair amount of editing is necessary. But the transcript use at this point is only for the purposes of illustrating, documenting, and putting flesh on the bones—so to speak—of the principles of advocacy and the techniques of direct examination that have earlier

been identified. In this regard the fear must be not that too much is deleted, but rather that the purposes not be suffocated by too much use of transcript.

19. If the reader cares to turn back to page 183, it may be seen that Rigo was going down the chart.
20. *See* page 212 *supra*.
21. The judge and I, both of us, had to stop him. We would have had a mistrial if he had continued his answer.
22. L. Packel and D. Spina, Trial Advocacy: A Systematic Approach 19 (1984).
23. *Id.* at 20.
24. T. Mauet, Fundamentals of Trial Techniques 94 (1980).
25. I. Goldstein, Trial Technique 260–262 (1935), quoting Harris, Hints on Advocacy.
26. It is odd to an American trial lawyer's ears, but our English colleagues believe that, absent unusual circumstances, it is "unethical" for a barrister to interview a witness—much less "prepare" him to testify—before presenting his testimony in court. The barrister relies on the solicitor's brief. The solicitor, presumably, has done all the preparing.

    The stated reason for the rule, as I understand it, is that it prevents tampering with witnesses, or even the appearance or possible accusation of such a thing. At the risk of infuriating the English Bar, I suggest that reason is nonsense. Why is it that the solicitor may be exposed and not the barrister? No, I believe that the Bar of England has imposed this rule on itself to make it possible for its members to try lawsuit after lawsuit, one right after the other, without the painful and laborious duty of preparing witnesses to testify.
27. To be sure, I knew nothing of these terms so long ago. Instinct rather than intellect led me to this.

28. For those who may be concerned about the ethical propriety of leading in such circumstances, *see* Federal Rule of Evidence 611(e), which provides that "Leading questions should not be used on direct examination except as may be necessary to develop his testimony." When a witness is frightened, or has exhausted his recollection, it is *necessary* to lead. The notes to the rule make that clear. And *no* rule requires an advisory opinion before a leading question is put. That is usually adjudicated *ex post facto.*

29. It must not be assumed that these exchanges betokened the slightest ill will between Joe Hayden and me. Far from it. I had tried the *Weber* case against him the year before, and I had the warmest admiration for him. And as for Joe, within a few months of the close of the *Addonizio* case, he wrote letters to President Nixon, Attorney General Mitchell, and Senator Case advocating my appointment as United States Attorney for the District of New Jersey when Mitchell and the President were holding up the nomination and I languished as United States Attorney by court appointment.

    But, friend or no, Joe Hayden would and did hit me as hard as he could in court—whenever he could. As well he should have.

30. In any event, I believe that the rule of thumb should be to leave nothing for redirect. But that is for later.

31. We started with seven, but Callaghan pleaded guilty during trial and Boiardo suffered a massive heart attack and was severed.

32. When the jury returned to the room shortly after 10:00 p.m., its foreman had to read the verdict. Sixty-four times he had said guilty as to each one of the five defendants. Finally, Judge Barlow stopped the elderly man standing in the jury box half way through. Taking pity on him, Judge Barlow told him he could deliver the rest of the verdict sitting down. What the judge said was, "You may sit down if you wish, Mr. Guilty."

33. T. Mauet, Fundamentals of Trial Techniques 88 (1980).
34. I believe this qualification is inserted for academic perfection. For the rest of the point makes abundantly clear that chronology is a virtue in and of itself.
35. J. Tanford, The Trial Process 346 (1983).
36. *Id.* at 347. Footnote 48 omitted. Footnote 49, however, is instructive.

> [49] *See generally* 1 L. Schwartz, Proof, Persuasion, and Cross-Examination: A Winning New Approach in the Courtroom § 5.04 (1973). A survey of jurors found that if they liked the victim, they tended to convict; if they liked the defendant, they tended to acquit. Sannito & Arnolds, Jury Study Results: The Factors at Work, Trial Diplomacy J. at 6, 9 (Spring 1982).

37. *See* page 31 *et seq. supra.*
38. For those interested in how to raise cash from political parties, the following is illustrative:

> Q: I show you Government Exhibits—may I have 793 in evidence.
>
> I show you this check or photocopy of a check already in evidence, 793 in evidence. It is an Allstate Associates check, one of Mr. Cestone's companies, made payable to Beame, O'Connor and Procaccino and I ask you whether or not you can identify this check.
>
> A: Yes, sir.
>
> Q: Have you seen it before?
>
> A: Yes, sir.
>
> Q: Do you recall when you saw it before?

A: Yes, sir. It is a check that Mr. Cestone obtained for me to pay for one of the ads in order to get cash.

Q: I show you these five checks, Government Exhibits 74, 75, 76, 243 and 244 and I ask you if you can identify them.

A: Yes, sir.

Q: What are those checks?

A: They are all checks to Beame, O'Connor and Procaccino.

Q: They all represent payments from Constrad?

MR. FEINBERG: I object to the question. It's leading.

THE COURT: That is leading, Mr. Stern. Reframe it, if you will.

Q: Where did the funds come from for those checks?

A: Constrad.

MR. STERN: I offer these five checks in evidence.

MR. NOONAN: I am going to have to take a moment, your Honor.

I renew my objection previously made to the Beame, O'Connor and Procaccino checks on the basis of relevancy, materiality, and, I add, prejudicial to the defendants in this case.

THE COURT: Objection overruled. They will be marked in evidence.

(Exhibits G-74, G-75, G-76, G-243 and G-244 received and marked in evidence.)

MR. NOONAN: I would also add so far the testimony with respect to the 20,000 dollar payment of those checks doesn't seem to be within the scope of the indictment. May I call for an offer of proof?

MR. STERN: It's within Count 1, the conspiracy count, to commit extortion, your Honor.

THE COURT: The objection is overruled.

Q: I show you these five checks in evidence, 244, 243, 74, 75, and 76, and the one in evidence, which is Government Exhibit 793, all payable to—well, two payable to the Journal Committee, to Beame, O'Connor and Procaccino, each check in the amount of $5,000, for a net of $30,000, and I ask you what if anything you did with those checks when you got them or when you made them on October the 14th, 1965.

A: I took them into the headquarters of the Beame-Procaccino organization in New York, and I gave them to them for three ads and $15,000 in cash.

Q: So you gave them checks, six checks for $30,000 and you got back $15,000 in cash?

A: Yes.

Q: And took three ads out of the book, is that correct?

A: Yes, sir.

Q: I show you this book, which is Government Exhibit 3 for identification, and I ask you if you can identify it.

A: Yes, sir, I can.

Q: What is that book?

MR. NOONAN: May we ask the number of that?

MR. STERN: G-3.

Q: Can you identify it?

A: Yes, sir.

Q: What is it?

A: The Journal of Independent Citizens Committee dinner in honor of Beame, O'Connor and Procaccino.

Q: And how many ads appear on behalf of either Constrad, Capen, Rigo or Mr. Cestone's corporation, Allstate, in that Journal?

A: Three, sir.

Q: You gave six checks?

A: Yes, sir.

Q: And $15,000 came back in cash, is that so?

A: Yes, sir.

MR. STERN: I offer it in evidence, if your Honor please.

39. Of course, Jules Feinberg could well have objected, "Asked and answered." But that objection would raise no different issues, and the determination of the objection would have been no less suggestive.
40. The reader will observe the principles of Rule I in operation. *See* Volume I, page 36.
41. *Id.*

42. E. Thomas, The Man to See 205 (1991).
43. *See Judgment In Berlin.*
44. The fact that the records were of an illegal enterprise, or that they were informal entries rather than formal books of account, is of no moment. *See* Rule 803(6) of the Federal Rules of Evidence.
45. Judge Barlow did this sort of thing more than once. He certainly did not regard it as strange or even unusual. See the following transcript several days later.

> Q: Count 52 charges that the defendant La Morte received his payment on December 23rd. Count 53 charges that the defendant Gordon received his payment on December the 23rd, and Count 54 charges that defendant Hugh Addonizio received his payment on December 23rd. If I understand your testimony, the dates alleged in those three counts are not accurate, is that so?
>
> A: That is correct, sir.
>
> Q: I also understand from your testimony that they are not off by more than 30 to 40 days.
>
> MR. FEINBERG: I object to what Mr. Stern understands.
>
> THE COURT: That is a little bit leading. Rephrase it, Mr. Stern.
>
> Q: By how much off are those counts?
>
> A: I would say approximately four weeks.
>
> MR. FEINBERG: I object to the answer as an approximation.
>
> THE COURT: If that is the best he can do, I will permit it.

MR. FEINBERG: If that is the best he can do, I will withdraw the objection.

MR. WALL: Without a side bar conference, may the record reflect that we object again on the same grounds as we did on similar occasions.

THE COURT: Yes.

MR. STERN: Would your Honor give the same instructions?

THE COURT: Yes.

Ladies and gentlemen, as I told you, I think on one previous occasion when in an indictment a criminal act is alleged to have occurred on a specific date the Government is not required to prove that exact date so long as the date that is established by the Government is within a reasonable time thereof.

MR. STERN: Thank you.

46. Lockjoint, or Interpace as it later came to be known, was the same company that had paid off the borough president of Queens—Connally—whom Buckner had prosecuted and Steuer had defended so many years before. The more things change, the more they stay the same.
47. For example, the previous day we could only do 129 pages of transcript.

Chapter Eleven

Conclusion

The work is still unfinished, of course. There are many subjects left to reach. And if there are days ahead enough, they will be.

But we have covered opening and direct. And these, I believe, are the most difficult—and the most important—of all the tasks of trial lawyering. Of late, the trial bar has come to appreciate the value and the power of the opening. But direct examination remains a largely uncharted continent in the world of the courtroom. Perhaps Professor Goldberg said it best when he wrote:

> *Conducting the Direct Examination*
>
> Direct examination is the easiest trial task to do in a minimally competent fashion, and the hardest to do well. It is the most important part of the case in most instances. The difference in effect between a minimally competent direct examination and a good direct examination is the difference between winning and losing the lawsuit. The difference in appearance between a minimally competent and a good direct examination is not so easily detected. Many trial lawyers never learn to distinguish one from the other, but most winners do.
>
> Direct examination competency usually falls into three categories (1) good enough to get the information out of the witness' mouth, (2) good enough to have the information from the witness understood by the jurors, and (3) good enough to have the testimony persuade the jurors. Every lawyer is capable of accomplishing the first level before entering law school. Unfortunately, many lawyers remain at the level long after they have been out of school and into court. Great cross examinations and exhilarating

addresses to the jury show off the lawyer as an advocate, become the stuff of which thrilling war stories are made, and are the skills that beginning lawyers are just aching to conquer. Direct examination success is not so alluring. It is not uncommon to hear the adage that "all a good direct needs is a good witness." Every time you hear that, you know that you are listening to a lawyer whose direct examinations depend entirely upon the skill of the witness. Since few of us are lucky enough to have great actors and actresses with the fine minds and powers of observation standing on the corner when the Ford runs the red, we must learn how to have a fine direct examination when we have an ordinary human being for a witness.[1]

ENDNOTES

1. S. Goldberg, The First Trial 225, 226 (1982).

Appendix A
The *Bank of the United States* Case— Excerpt of Direct Examination

The following excerpt of Emory Buckner's direct examination of Isidor Kresel is an object lesson in the possible consequences of inviting a narrative response. I have included enough of the questioning to demonstrate that Buckner was thoroughly capable of controlling the flow of information from his witness. But when Buckner chose to elicit a narrative response, he relinquished that control. If you are put off at having to read Kresel's incredibly long answer, just imagine the effect of that answer on the jurors who had to listen to it.

> Q: Have you a recollection as to who arranged the conferences at the Bar Association on September 14th and the 23rd?
>
> A: I have no distinct recollection, but I should state that it was I that arranged it.
>
> Q: Do you have a distinct recollection of the first meeting at the Bar Association?
>
> A: I have.
>
> Q: Who was present?
>
> A: Mr. Broderick, Mr. Egbert, Mr. Marcus, Mr. Singer, Mr. Mitchell, Mr. Kugel, the two McArdles, young Herbert Singer and I.
>
> Q: Have you any notation or any recollection as to how long the conference lasted on the 14th of September?
>
> A: I have no recollection, but my diary says all afternoon. Now, that may mean from three to five or half past five, something like that, I cannot tell exactly.

Q: I want you—did you say anything at the conference?

A: I did.

Q: Did you have any notes prepared from which you carried on your discussion?

A: I did.

Q: Have you still preserved your notes from which you made your statement to the Superintendent and Mr. Egbert?

A: I did.

Q: Now, I want you without any interruption from me at all, to start at the beginning and state everything which you can recall that took place at the Bar Association conference on September 24th—what the various people said? I mean September 14th; what the various people said, without any interruptions from me and today we are competing with the fans on account of the heat, so make a special effort to keep your voice up.

A: I can give you, of course, the substance only, not the exact words that I used.

Q: I do not want you to leave anything out, Mr. Kresel, no matter how long it takes. I want everything that you can recall that took place; everything that you said and everything that everybody else said.

A: I said to the Superintendent that we had had about two weeks in which time to prepare the answer to the report made by the examiner of the bank. That the bank examiner had had, I think, ninety-two assistants assisting him in the examination and had taken about seven weeks in which to make that examination, and that therefore the Superintendent must realize that there may be some matters contained in the report of the bank that we had not been able to be prepared to meet within the two weeks that we had the matter under consideration. I told him that I wanted the privilege of submitting a written memorandum in answer to the examiner's report on the bank. He stated that that privilege would be granted. I told him that I was not prepared to argue the matter of the report on Bankus Corporation. He stated we will see how far we will get along with the report on the bank and that he would make a decision as to the Bankus subsequently. I told him that the officers of the bank were very glad for the opportunity to make their views upon the subject audible before the Superintendent. I said that we were doubly glad of the opportunity because of what we considered to have been unjustified and unfounded criticisms contained in the bank report reflecting upon the management of the bank.

The Superintendent said that he had adopted a policy differing from that followed by his predecessors. He said that his predecessor's policy had been to get his Examiners to give him the facts without commenting and that he, the Superintendent, would then make his own comments; whereas Mr. Broderick said to us that his policy was not only to have the Examiners give him the facts but to give the Examiners every opportunity that they wanted to express their opinions and give their comments, and so he said, "Before I hear your argument, don't be so much disturbed by whatever comment there is in the Examiners' reports." He said, "After all, that is the Examiner's comment and not mine and I have not adopted it." He said, "That is the reason why I have given you people this report, so that you might have an opportunity to come here and tell me your side of the story."

With that introduction I then took up the various matters contained in the report and, as I recall it, the first matters that I took up were three certain surcharges or deductions from the capital and surplus of the bank that the Examiner had recommended should be made.

The first one, as I recall it, was that the Examiner recommended that a sum of approximately $60,000 should be deducted, stating that that was an amount of advances of salaries made by the bank to the employees, and the Examiner stated that in his opinion that should be deducted. I pointed out to the Superintendent that the facts really were that this $60,000 had been set aside by the various branch managers in readiness for payment of salaries to the employees on the 15th of July. This examination started on the 14th as at the close of business of the 13th of July, and I pointed out to the Superintendent that that money had not been advanced to any employees, that it was there set aside by these branch managers and that therefore there was no reason for any deduction of that amount.

The Superintendent said that he agreed with that contention.

The next item, as I recall it, was a recommendation by the Examiner that a sum of approximately $154,000 be deducted from the capital and surplus, stating that the books showed that that was a sum that had been expended in improvements to various offices. Our examination indicated that the sum had been expended, but it had not been expended simply for improvements, that part of it had been paid for getting leaseholds and that our suggestion to the Superintendent was that rather than deduct that amount from the capital and surplus of the bank, the amount should be charged to a new account to be called perhaps "Leasehold Account," and that the amount should be amortized over the period of the leases.

The Superintendent said that that was a matter of bookkeeping. I pointed out to him that the bank at that time had set aside over a million dollars in reserves to meet just such improvements, even if they were improvements and that, therefore, there was no occasion for deducting that amount from the capital and surplus. The Superintendent said he thought it was a matter of bookkeeping and, that while the Examiner might be right in his views, still if the bank felt that it ought to be set up and amortized over the period, he would raise no objection.

Then there was a large item of approximately $700,000, which the Examiner reported in his opinion was the amount of bad debts which ought to be deducted from the capital and surplus. I stated to the Superintendent that in preparation for this argument, I had asked Messrs. McArdle & McArdle to take up the classification of the loans as made by the Examiner with the credit department of the bank and with the executives of the bank and make a report for me as to what, in the opinion of the executives of the credit department and in the opinion of McArdle & McArdle, the classification of bad loans and slow loans and quick loans should be, and I presented to the Superintendent a written classification so made by McArdle & McArdle, set up in a way so as to have on one side the classification of those loans made by the examinations for the Department, the classification made by the executives and by the credit department, and by McArdle & McArdle; and I pointed out to the Superintendent from that exhibit that the classification by the credit department and McArdle & McArdle and the executives of the bank differed widely from the classification made by the Examiner for the Department: that as to bad loans, for example, our people said that the most that ought to be deducted is $500,000 and not $700,000, and I went on to point out to him that even if that were deducted it should not be deducted from the capital and surplus because the bank at that time had a reserve of over $4,000,000 for just such contingencies. And Mr. Broderick and Mr. Egbert both stated that they would come to no conclusion on that particular subject until after the Examiner who had made the report had had an opportunity to study the classification that we would present.

So that matter was left without any decision at that time.

Then, as I recall it, the Examiner in his report listed certain violations so-called. There is a section in the report, a printed form, which calls for entries of violations; and I then took up the violations with the Superintendent. The first one, as I recall it, or one of the violations pointed out by the Examiner, was that two certain mortgages made by the Astor Finance Company—as I recall the name—which came to our bank through the Trade Bank, introduced to our bank by Mr. Mitchell, one, I think, $30,000, and the other $150,000, that the violation there was that the bank had failed to record those mortgages in its name.

I said to the Superintendent that the Examiner was perfectly right about the criticism; the mortgages had not been recorded; that the mortgages would immediately be recorded. The Superintendent said, "We will pass that."

Among other violations the Examiner listed, I think, seven mortgages, second mortgages, which he said—claimed were in amounts larger than the statute permits. His argument in the report was—or his statement—that the appraised value of the property on which these second mortgages were placed after deducting the first mortgage ahead of the second would show that the second mortgage was more than 33 1/3 per cent. of the appraised value. The total amount of those seven mortgages, it is my recollection, was $62,000, and our inquiry had shown that of those seven mortgages four of them had come to our bank either from the Municipal or from the Colonial or from the Cosmopolitan, and I said to the Superintendent that inasmuch as the mergers had been made only within recent months he must realize that there are lots of things that come in from a strange bank into our bank, that perhaps we overlooked and could not be buttoned up, so to speak, readily. As to the other three second mortgages, I pointed out, as I was advised by our people, that appraisals that had been obtained upon those properties that are covered by these second mortgages—I mean recently obtained—showed a valuation far in excess which would make the second and the third mortgage such as not to have the second mortgage more than the third of the value.

The Superintendent said that he would want to look into that but he thought that that was not a very serious thing, and that he realized that there might be some things that, owing to these mergers, the bank had not been able to take care of properly in the meantime.

Another thing that I recall, which was a very serious matter for the bank, was the criticisms by the Examiner of what he called the quick position of the bank. The quick position, as he pointed it out in his report, was 31 per cent. That is, the quick assets of the bank were 31 per cent. as compared with the deposit liabilities of the bank; and the Examiner said that that was too low a ratio, but in his report the Examiner pointed out that in arriving at that 31 per cent. he had failed to give the bank credit for $24,000,000 of loans that had been made by the bank upon bank stocks, not units of Bank of United States and Bankus, bank stocks of other institutions and upon securities of finance companies, he claiming that in his opinion those were not quick assets and so that ought not to be included in the quick position. He also pointed out in the text of his report that he had failed to give us credit in arriving at that 31 per cent. for approximately $3,000,000 of loans that had been made by the bank upon units, that is, partly upon its own stock and partly upon Bankus Corporation.

I argued with the Superintendent that it was entirely unfair to the bank not to give it credit for the $24,000,000 of loans on banks and finance securities, and I pointed out to the Superintendent and presented to him a schedule showing the bank and finance companies securities that were held as collateral to that for $24,000,000, and pointed out to him that the maximum that we loaned on the bank stocks was 60 per cent. of their then market values, and argued that we ought to be given credit for that $24,000,000.

The Examiner also pointed out that he did not give us credit for $10,800,000 of paper that we had rediscounted with the Federal Reserve Bank, and I argued to the Superintendent that there was no justification whatsoever for not giving us credit for that $10,800,000; and the suggestion was made by Mr. Egbert, as I recall it, that it may be that the Examiner thought that that $10,800,000 was collateral loans and, if it were collateral, then he would be thoroughly justified in not including that in the quick position. But we satisfied the Superintendent that it was not collateral, that it was simply rediscountable paper that we had discounted with the Federal Reserve Bank.

And so I summed up with the Superintendent the argument of the quick position, by pointing out to him that if allowance was made to us for what we were rightly entitled, namely, those $24,000,000 of loans on bank stocks; of the $10,800,000 of rediscountable paper, that our quick position, instead of being 31 per cent., would be 45 per cent. The Superintendent said that it was another matter that he wanted to consider, but he said he thought that our quick position should be 55 per cent. and not 45 per cent.

Well, we told him that we would endeavor to make our quick position 55 per cent., but at least we ought to be given credit for the quick position that we then had.

Among other violations which the Examiner pointed out in his report was the fact that there were on our books loans approximating $3,000,000 on units, and he said that was improper; that the bank should not lend on its own stock. I pointed out to the Superintendent, in the first place, that the loans on units were not $3,000,000, but were $1,700,000 and some odd; that since the report made by the Examiner as of the 13th of July, such loans had been reduced from $3,000,000 to $1,700,000 some odd.

I pointed out to the Superintendent that as against that $1,700,000 odd of loans, the bank held approximately 20,000 units as collateral, and I said to the Superintendent that the theory upon which the bank officials were holding these loans was that they had a right to lend upon the value of the Bankus share in that unit, if they did not have the right to lend upon the bank share in that unit.

I pointed out to the Superintendent that the unit at that time was selling at approximately $200 a unit; that taking $1,700,000 as the amount of the loans, considering that we had approximately 20,000 units against that amount of loans, it would make the loan on the Bankus share approximately $85, and I said if it were necessary to justify that I would be willing to argue to him that the bank was thoroughly justified in lending $85 against a Bankus share; but I said to him "The bank is not making any loans now on units"; that most of those loans came to the bank through mergers. For example, I pointed out to him that when the Municipal Bank was merged into our bank, the Municipal Bank had a lot of Bank of United States Bank stocks as collateral and loans; naturally, when the Municipal Bank came into our bank that Bank of United States stock was converted into units and was continued to be held as collateral until the loan became due or was renewed, and that that was true not only as to the Municipal Bank; it was also true as to the Colonial Bank, as to the Bank of the Rockaways, as to the Cosmopolitan Bank and as to the Central Mercantile Bank & Trust Company, and that there was no way for the bank to take a man's loans just because he happened to have our own stock as collateral, though not with us originally, throw his loan out or call it or sell him out. And I said to the Superintendent that the bank was not then and would not in the future make any loans on units, whether on the bank shares or on the whole unit and would try to liquidate the balance of those loans as speedily as possible. He said that was all right.

The Examiner had pointed out in his report that there were loans of $7,000,000 and some odd, what he called subsidiaries of the bank.

I pointed out to the Superintendent that the Examiner made no comment about these loans; that he was satisfied simply to list them in the text so as to call attention to them.

I said to the Superintendent that I saw no reason why there should be any implied criticism, even of those loans to the subsidiaries. Of course, I pointed out that some of the items that he included as loans to the subsidiaries no longer were in the bank and never should have been included as such loans. For example, he listed among that $7,000,000 of loans to subsidiaries a loan of $175,000, which had been made to the B. K. Marcus and Saul Singer syndicate. I shall return to that Syndicate loan later, because it comes in in another relation; but I pointed out to the Superintendent that that was not a loan to any subsidiary of the bank and that the total amount of loans to the subsidiaries—real subsidiaries of the bank or affiliates of the bank—as of the 13th of July were only approximately $5,000,000. But I said to the Superintendent that, all the time I was arguing with him, the loans to the subsidiaries and the affiliates had increased and were approximately $10,000,000. And I said to the Superintendent that I saw no reason why there should be any criticism of those loans, and I called his attention to the fact that his own Examiner—I mean the Examiner who made the examination of the Bankus Corporation—reported to him that the loans were then $10,000,000, and that he said there wasn't any question of the safety of those loans, and so I said to the Superintendent that I saw no reason why any criticism should be levelled against those loans, whether there were $5,000,000, or as they were at that time, $10,000,000.

Another violation which the Examiner listed was this loan of $175,000 to the B. K. Marcus and Saul

Singer Syndicate. I had made an investigation of the facts surrounding that loan and I stated to the Superintendent that the facts were these: that Mr. White, who took charge of the daily operations of the Syndicate had himself, acting as agent for the Syndicate Managers, borrowed this money at the bank and himself signed the note as agent of such Syndicate Managers; that neither Mr. Marcus nor Mr. Singer knew at the time when the loan was made; that as soon as it was brought to their attention, which was within ten days after the loan was made, it was promptly paid and was no longer in the bank. And I said that if I were put to make an argument in support of that action, I should be willing to argue that when the statute provides that no officer shall borrow money from his bank, that means for his personal use and not in his representative capacity as a manager of such Syndicate. But I said there was no necessity for making any such contention, because it would never be repeated, and so that was passed.

Another violation that was noted was that one of our directors, a man named Revman, had overdrawn his account to the sum of $248; and I explained to the Superintendent that the facts were these: that Mr. Revman had obtained a letter of credit from his bank to our bank. He was about to take a trip abroad; that he did go abroad, and that he drew against that letter of credit, and that one of his drafts, amounting to $248, had come in to one of our branches and that the branch manager had failed to notify Mr. Revman's office to make the amount good, and it was overdrawn for 48 hours. And the Superintendent laughed and said that he did not think that that was very serious.

Another violation noted was that one of our directors, Mr. Rosenthal, did not have the requisite number of shares of bank stocks standing in his name to qualify him as a director, and called attention that the statute provides that a director must have at least $1,000 worth par value of stock of the bank to qualify as a director, and that there was no such amount of stock standing in the name of Mr. Rosenthal.

I looked into that and reported to the Superintendent that the Examiner was perfectly correct; that there was no stock standing in Mr. Rosenthal's name; that true, Mr. Rosenthal's corporation, called the I. Rose Corporation, had in its name thousands of shares of stock, but that was not meeting the provision of the statute, and I said to the Superintendent, "Now, what do you want me to do about Mr. Rosenthal,"—because, as I read the statute, it was rather strict on that point. And the Superintendent said, "Well, I will take that under consideration."

Of course, since the rendering of the report by the Examiner, Mr. Rosenthal had the sufficient number of shares transferred into his name and I so stated to the Superintendent, and he said he would give that matter consideration.

Then the Examiner pointed out that the bank had approximately $8,000,000 of real estate securities in its securities portfolio, which he thought were frozen. He said that for investment purposes they were worth 100 cents on the dollar, but he said in his opinion they were frozen assets. That is one reason why he did not include them in our quick position, so he said. And in the same connection, the Examiner reported that out of $305,000,000 of resources that our bank had at that time, approximately $70,000,000 was in real estate loans, securities, indirect real estate loans, and of that $70,000,000 he said $36,000,000 were in unsecured loans predicated on real estate. I am quoting his language: "predicated on real estate." And he concluded—that is, the Examiner concluded—that that was not a healthy condition; that 36 per cent. of our assets, or rather, $36,000,000 of our assets ought not to be in such real estate loans or loans predicated on real estate.

In answer to that, I said to the Superintendent, "The difficulty with the situation is that the Examiner does not give us any information so that we could meet it. He says there were $36,000,000 of real estate, or predicated on real estate. He gives us no detail." I said, "We have tried from our own investigation to determine just what he included in that $36,000,000, and that we have been unable to check back his figures."

I said to the Superintendent, "Of course, if he included any real estate or loans predicated on real estate, a loan to every man, every customer of the bank who, in his financial statement, showed that he has some real estate, it might well be that that amount would total $36,000,000." "But," I said to the Superintendent, "how can it be that a bank should be criticized, that it should be claimed that its assets were frozen in real estate just because it had made loans to persons that owned real estate? Does that mean that a man who owns real estate cannot borrow any money; that the mere fact that he has a piece of real estate and shows it in his financial statement, that that would bar him from any loans of the bank?"

The Superintendent said that he had in mind, after we got through, to take what information we were giving him, submit it to his Examiner; if necessary have his Examiner come back, re-examine in the light of what we were saying, and that therefore he could not pass upon this question at that time.

"But," he said, "I think that that is where your worst criticism lies. $70,000,000 of real estate loans or securities," he says, "if it is true, if it is anywhere near that, compared with your total resources, is too much; and," he said, "that is one point that I have got to give very serious consideration to."

And so we left that real estate point there with the idea that we would come back to it, or that he would come back to it for us.

Another criticism that I recall concerned what the Examiner was pleased to call "window dressing." He pointed out that in July of 1929 the bank had made a loan of $1,000,000 to the National American Bank—I think that is the name—and that it was paid within two or three days; and the Examiner's conclusion was that that was window dressing, not only for the National American, but also for the bank. Window dressing for the National American, in that they could show $1,000,000 ready cash; window dressing for the bank in that they could show $1,000,000 additional deposits.

He also pointed out that this loan had not been reported to our Board of Directors, and so he criticized it for both reasons.

I looked into that and I found this to be the situation, and so reported to the Superintendent; that this loan was made by Mr. Mitchell to the National American Bank on the 28th of June, 1929, and that it was paid on the 2nd or 3rd of July of that same year. In other words, it was outstanding four or five days. That in between those two dates there was no meeting of the Board of Directors of the bank. I said to the Superintendent, "That is no reason why it should not have been reported the following meeting held, I think, on July 11th, and," I said, "as was pointed out to me this morning." I said, "I am not offering this as an excuse for not reporting it eventually. There was no reason why it should not have been reported, but I am pointing out the facts, showing the reason why somebody slipped up in not reporting it, that the loan was made and paid in between meetings of the Board of Directors."

The Superintendent said that I need pay no further attention to that.

Another criticism was that the bank was abusing its borrowing privilege at the Federal Reserve Bank. I am almost quoting the language of the criticism and the grounds upon which that criticism was based were these, as stated by the Examiner: that the bank had borrowed $10,800,000 from the Federal Reserve Bank and that, at the same time, it was lending moneys to its subsidiaries and lending moneys on units, and lending money on an unsecured basis to its customers who, at the same time, had money out on call.

And so he said that was a terrible thing, that we were abusing our privilege of borrowing at the Federal Reserve Bank. Now, he gave two examples of loans made by our bank to its customers on an unsecured basis. When those customers had money out in the street on call. I haven't the exact figures. I can, by looking at my notes, give you the exact figures; but I recall them substantially.

There was a man named Leviton, L-e-v-i-t-o-n I think it was spelled, to whom the bank had made three loans totalling $20,000 on an unsecured basis. One loan of $5,000 was made in March of 1929; another $5,000 in April of 1929, and I think a third of $10,000 in May of 1929. We looked to see about this idea of Mr. Leviton having money out on call, and we found that it was perfectly true that Mr. Leviton did have $100,000 out on call; that he had put it out on call through our bank, so that we knew about it, but that it was put out on call in November of 1928—months before any of these three loans were made to Mr. Leviton.

Another man—customer—whose name I cannot just now recall, had also a substantially small loan from the bank. He also borrowed it on an unsecured basis. He had $200,000 out on call that likewise was put out in November of 1928; and I said to the Superintendent, "Now, assuming that it was a justified criticism of our bank, borrowing at the Federal Reserve Bank, lending to a man who then put his money out on call," I said, "assuming we knew that he was going to do it when we made him the loan, the fact is that the loan was made to him long after he put his money out on call." The Superintendent said I need not pay much attention to that.

Another criticism was that the bank was making loans to its customers, in order to enable them to buy units.

Now, that was a very serious criticism, and the Examiner gave two instances of what he construed to have been such loans. And I said to the Superintendent that I was entitled to assume that the Examiner in his report gave the Superintendent the strongest possible proof for his criticism, and so I took those two examples that he gave. Perhaps I had better look at my notes to give you the exact language. (Examining notes.)

There were two loans, one to a man named Sol Raphael, and another to a man named Finn. Now, Sol Raphael had had a loan at the bank—I want to get this entirely correct—our bank has got to be taken over by somebody else?" I said to him, "If this report goes to the Federal Reserve Bank what do you think they are going to say about our institution?"

He said, "Don't worry, it is not going to the Federal Reserve Bank until I pass on it."

Substantially, Mr. Buckner, that is what I said to this man. Of course, we were there two and a half hours, I think; there may be things that I have not examined on my notes.

THE COURT: Five minutes recess. Don't talk about the case or permit anybody to talk to you about it.

MR. BUCKNER: About ten minutes recess?

THE COURT: All right, ten minutes.

(A short recess was here taken.)

Appendix B

The *Bank of the United States* Case—Excerpt of Cross-Examination

I have included this excerpt of Max Steuer's cross-examination of Isidor Kresel for those who wish to make their own judgment concerning Kresel. The excerpt also provides a marvelous example of how truly relentless Steuer could be on cross.

After Recess.

ISIDOR J. KRESEL, resumed the stand.

Cross examination (continued) by Mr. Steuer:

Q: Mr. Kresel, before the grand jury, can you recall having been asked this question:
"Q: You know now, Mr. Kresel, do you not, as to the form that this transaction of the 13th of January took?" And answering to it: "Yes."

A: I don't remember it, Mr. Steuer, but if that is the record, I won't deny it.

Q: (Handing transcript to witness.) Will you just look at the last question on page 1012, Mr. Kresel?

A: I have seen it.

Q: How?

A: I have read it.

Q: Does it refresh your recollection?

A: It does not. But as I say I don't deny that I made that statement.

. . . .

Q: Now, the next question.

"Q: And do you say that you did know about the Premier and the Bolivar Corporation?"—You know the form of the question: "And do you say that you did not know about the Premier and the Bolivar Corporation?"

If you had been held to any yes or no answers, that was a question that called for a yes or no, did it not?

A: Yes.

Q: Your answer—you recall that your answer was as follows:

"A: Mr. Steuer, *I hope you believe me* when I tell you that I knew absolutely nothing about it. *It may be difficult to understand why—why my employee carried through a transaction like that and I shouldn't know about it.* But if you gentlemen understood the workings and the relationships I have, you would believe me. In the first place, I was down at 15 Broad Street, attending to—at least trying to attend to—a law practice down there, and the matters up there were incidental, and I put that young man up there with the idea of taking care of details, and he became extremely proficient; and why this Bolivar and this Premier—I understand now that those are two corporations that he got through Mr. Pollock's office."

Do you remember saying that, Mr. Kresel?

A: I did.

Q: Unfortunately or fortunately—it doesn't matter, you were then interrupted by some question by the foreman. But I want to go back over what you said thus far.

"Mr. Steuer, I hope you believe me when I tell you that I knew absolutely nothing about it."

That means the form that the transaction took on the 13th of January, does it not?

A: I should say that that refers to your question which was as to whether I knew it was the Premier and the Bolivar.

Q: Well, look at it. Let's read the question again: "You know now, Mr. Kresel, do you not"—

A: That is not the question you asked me, to which that is an answer. The question to which that is an answer is on the following page, page 1013.

Q: Naturally.

A: That's the question I was answering I say, not the other one.

Q: But let us understand this thing, Mr. Kresel, and get it right. Please follow and see whether I read correctly from the minutes. I have read the question from the middle of the page on page 1012, which you said that you recognized. I then read the answer, which was "Not another solitary thing."

"Q: You known now, Mr. Kresel, do you not, as to the form that this transaction of the 13th of January took?

"A: I do.

"Q: And do you say that you did not know about the Premier and the Bolivar Corporation:

"A: Mr. Steuer, I hope you believe me when I tell you that I knew absolutely nothing about it."

If you had been answering whether you knew about the Premier and Bolivar Corporation, wouldn't you have said, or very likely have said, "Mr. Steuer, I hope you believe me when I tell you that I knew absolutely nothing about them?"

A: It might have been better English, yes. But I still think that that is what I was referring to.

Q: Then you still think now that what you meant to convey at that time was that you hope that you will be believed when you say that you knew absolutely nothing about the Bolivar and the Premier. That is correct, isn't it?

A: Yes.

Q: "It may be difficult to understand why, why my employe carried through a transaction like that."
Weren't you then referring to the whole transaction?

A: I was.

Q: And weren't you then meaning to convey that you didn't know about the transaction?

A: I did.

Q: And weren't you giving your reasons why you didn't know about the transaction? Just listen and see if this helps you—

A: You don't have to give me any help. I answered the question: "I was."

Q: I didn't hear it.

A: I said that.

Q: Pardon me. My mistake. And did you mean to convey that the transaction was carried through, as it was, without your knowledge, by your employe?

A: What I meant to convey was this: that the details of the transaction as—

Q: Now, Mr. Kresel, let me suggest this: if you will be good enough to answer that question, you may then add to it anything that you want. But first I want an answer to the question that I put. Now, will you read the question?

A: What I started to say was an answer to your question. Have it read again. Go ahead.

(The Stenographer read the question as follows: "Q: And did you mean to convey that the transaction was carried through, as it was, without your knowledge, by your employe?")

A: I did not mean to convey that at all. What I meant to convey was that the details of the transaction were carried through by Herbert Singer, without my knowledge and that is the fact. I knew nothing about what he did on the 13th of January, and nobody claims that I did.

MR. STEUER: At least, I move to strike out that "nobody claims that I did."

THE COURT: Strike that out.

MR. TUTTLE: Exception.

By Mr. Steuer:

Q: "It may be difficult to understand why, why my employe carried through a transaction like that and I shouldn't know about it. But if you gentlemen understood the workings and the relationships I have you would believe me. In the first place, I was down at 15 Broad Street, and the matters up there were incidental. And I put that young man up there with the idea of taking care of details."
Where was "up there"?

A: 475 Fifth Avenue.

Q: How often did you go to 475 Fifth Avenue?

A: Quite frequently. I tried to get there every other day.

Q: Did you see Herbert Singer when you got there?

A: I did.

Q: When you made use of these words, Mr. Kresel, "and why this Bolivar and this Premier," didn't you mean by that to convey that you knew nothing about it, and didn't know that they had been used?

A: I did not.

Q: You are sure about that?

A: I have answered.

Q: Now, these are the foreman's questions and answers. After you said, "I understand now that those are two corporations that he got through Mr. Pollock's office"—

"By the Foreman:

—all of these questions, until I call attention to it, are by the foreman:

"Q: Where was Mr. Pollock's office?

"A: At the bank.

"Q: Not at 475 Fifth Avenue?

"A: Oh, no, no. You see, Mr. Pollock had a separate legal organization, an inside legal organization for the bank.

"Q: What was the address of that organization?

"A: At 575 Fifth Avenue.

"Q: Two blocks away?

"A: Yes. He employed—I don't know—three or four, perhaps half a dozen lawyers under him. He had a regular legal business that he did there for the bank. I did not do all the legal business for the bank by any means. I took care of some of its litigation. I took care of preparing the minutes, or rather Herbert Singer did, under my direction. I attended the meetings. I advised them on such matters as they asked advice on. But they had Pollock and his staff. They did all the mortgage business. They had Jacobson, Pollock's former partner, who took care of all the small litigation, like suing people on promissory notes and all that. I have been termed the general counsel of the bank. I do not know whether that is a title or not. I do not know—I was counsel, as I described it to you, of the bank. *Now I come back to it. I had nothing to do, and did not know of the course that this transaction took. I do not understand why it should have been necessary to have this devious way of having these two corporations."*

When you made that statement, did you mean to convey to the grand jury that you knew nothing of the course that the transaction took?

A: I did not.

Q: Even by the use of the words, "now I come back to it. I had nothing to do, and did not know of the course that this transaction took." Even by that language, you did not mean to convey to the grand jury that you did not know the course of the transaction?

A: I did not mean to convey any such thing, and they didn't understand me, and you didn't understand me.

THE COURT: Strike that out.

Q: To get the continuity, I hope you will pardon me, if I read it again.

"Now, I come back to it. I have nothing to do, and did not know of the course that this transaction took. *I do not understand why it should have been necessary to have this devious way of having these two corporations.* I have talked about that. One explanation given to me is that there was a tax problem involved. That if one of these corporations for $4,800,000 of property, which it then sold for $8,000,000, realized the difference as a profit, it would be subject to a tax; and they, up there, were advised by outside tax people, so I understood—I am not vouching for this—that it was wiser to pass it through another corporation. *But the very fact that it was passed through that way indicates that there was something suspiciously wrong about it. I would have nothing to do with that sort of a transaction. It is unfortunate that the man who was in my employ was the man who had charge of it.*"

Did you make that statement to the grand jury?

A: I did not.

Q: You did not make that statement?

A: I did not.

Q: Will you be good enough to look at the transcript before you, and begin at the top of page 1013 with the question:

"Q: Do you say that you didn't know about the Premier and the Bolivar Corporation?"

Read it to yourself, and tell this jury whether I read it just as you there find it.

A: I have read it, and as far as I can recall your reading it as you read it. And yet I say that I didn't make that statement—that last statement—

Q: Which last statement? Just read to the jury what it was that you did not say:

A: The statement that the very fact that it was passed through that way indicates that there was something suspiciously wrong about it and that I would have nothing to do with that sort of a transaction.

Q: In other words, you say that that is interpolated by somebody, although you did not say it?

A: I have no explanation to make of how it gets there.

Q: You find—let me ask you to go back. Did you say this: "Now I come back to it. I have nothing to do, and did not know of the course that this transaction took. I do not understand why it should have been necessary to have this devious way of having these two corporations."

A: I did not use that language. I am certain.

Q: Did you use this language: "I have talked about that. One explanation given to me is that there was a tax problem involved. That if one of these corporations for $4,800,000 of property, which it then sold for $8,000,000, realized the difference as a profit, it would be subject to a tax; and they, up there, were advised by outside tax people, so I understood—I am not vouching for this—that it was wiser to pass it through another corporation."
Did you use that language?

A: I do not recall that exact language, but in substance I have no doubt that I said I had heard there was a tax problem involved in it.

Q: Well, after the word "corporation," there is a comma and then follows: "But the very fact that it was passed through that way indicates that there was something suspiciously wrong about it. I would have nothing to do with that sort of a transaction. It is unfortunate that the man who was in my employ was the man who had charge of it."

A: I made no such statement at any time, anywhere.

[Emphasis added.]

Index

Z